THE SPHERE

HISTO
BRITAIN

c55BC — 1485

Derived from The Oxford Illustrated History of Britain

Edited by Kenneth O. Morgan

Sphere Reference

Sphere Books Ltd
30–32 Gray's Inn Road
London WC1X 8JL

© Oxford University Press

First published as part of
The Oxford Illustrated History of Britain in 1984

First published in this paperback edition
in 1985

Printed and bound in Great Britain by
Collins, Glasgow

CONTENTS

EDITOR'S FOREWORD
TO THE OXFORD EDITION

THE distinctiveness, even uniqueness, of the British as a people has long been taken for granted by foreign observers and native commentators alike. Visitors from overseas, from those omnipresent Venetian ambassadors in the late fifteenth century, through intellectuals like Voltaire or Tocqueville, to American journalists in the twentieth century, have all been convinced of the special quality of British society. This has equally been assumed by modern native chroniclers of the British scene, as opposed in their ideological outlooks as Sir Winston Churchill and George Orwell, patriots both. But the nature or essence of the Britishness of the British is far easier to proclaim than to define, let alone to explain. Very few attempts to encapsulate its quality have been more than marginally successful. One of the most celebrated, addressing itself to the English people alone and first published in 1926, came in G. M. Trevelyan's remarkable synoptic *History of England*. Trevelyan here focused on a number of themes which he believed to have marked out the separate experience of the English through the centuries—geographical severance from the European continent, with the consequent centrality of sea-power; a broad social fluidity in which the early demise of feudalism helped generate a new industrial and commercial enterprise; a flowing cultural continuity from the time of Chaucer and Wycliffe onwards; and above all—a theme especially dear to the heart of an old late-Victorian Liberal like Trevelyan—a long political and legal evolution expressed in the durability of parliamentary institutions and the rule of law. Secure in itself, a vibrant, outward-looking island had proceeded to colonize and civilize the world. None of Trevelyan's themes can be dismissed. Equally, none can be accepted uncritically in the more tormented, doubt-ridden age of the late twentieth century, with its well-founded suspicion of national and racial stereotypes. The problem of trying to come to grips with the essential reality of the British experience remains as pressing and as fascinating as ever.

The purpose of this book is to isolate and uncover the main elements in that experience throughout British history, from the earliest Roman period down to the later twentieth century. It is not concerned with the protean concept of 'national character', a difficult and perhaps unrewarding enterprise even when considering the English alone—and almost impossible when the distinct traditions of the Welsh, Scots, and Irish are included. It is rather intended to disentangle the main political, social, economic, religious, intellectual, and cultural features of these islands as they have revealed themselves to successive generations, and as trained scholars have tried to examine them. The illustrations provided in this book are offered not merely as physical embellishments, important though that may be, but as vital explanatory tools in demonstrating key points in the narrative. The question of a British 'national character', or the lack of it, will, therefore, be implicit rather than explicit. Readers will be left to draw their own conclusions, and to form their own personal visions. This is, inevitably, a multi-author volume, written by ten professional historians in close collaboration with one another. Such a collective approach is inescapable, since the days when one compendious mind such as Trevelyan's could have the capacity and the confidence to treat all aspects of British history with equal ease probably died with the Liberal intelligentsia some time after 1914. It is certainly neither practicable nor desirable, now that Renaissance men have vanished from the earth. Rather, each major phase in the history of Britain is examined here in depth by a specialist working in that field, but always directing his findings to the general reader. A basic premiss of this book is that it deals with the history of Great Britain, two partitioned, poly-cultural islands, and not merely with England alone. Indeed, the fact that the ten authors include three Welshmen and two Scots may help towards that end! Again, while the geographic and other distinctiveness of Britain from the European continent and the world beyond may constantly emerge, so too will the economic, intellectual, cultural, and religious links by which Britain and overseas nations helped shape each other's experience. The dynamic urge for exploration, colonization, and conquest from the Tudor period onwards, which led in time to the creation of the greatest empire the world had ever seen, also lent an outward-looking aspect to British historical development. Britain in this book remains the geographical island familiar to schoolchildren. But it is an island whose physical insularity was always qualified by a wider process of transmission from continental Europe, and later from North America, Africa, Asia, and Australasia, from the first arrival of the Roman legions onwards.

These chapters help to show how old clichés have dissolved in the searching light of modern research and scholarship. The 'anarchy' of the mid-twelfth century, the chaos of the Wars of the Roses, the inevitability of the Civil Wars, the serenity of Victorian England, familiar to readers of *1066 and All That*, tend to disappear like the autumn leaves at Vallombrosa. Again, the notion that British history, unlike that of less fortunate nations elsewhere, is uniquely marked by a kind of seamless, peaceful continuity emerges here as needing the most severe qualification. The history of the British people is a complex, sometimes violent or revolutionary one, full of disjunctions and abrupt changes of pace or of course. The idea of a tranquil, undisturbed evolutionary progress even for England, let alone the turbulent, fractured, schizophrenic history of the Celtic nations, comes out here as little more than a myth, fit for the refuse-heap of history, like romances of 'golden ages' over the centuries from Arthurian times onwards.

  Roman Britain, as Peter Salway shows, was marked by constant, alternating phases of social upheaval and re-adjustment, long before the final retreat of the Romans in the early fifth century. John Blair describes the dynastic turbulence and the dramatic growth of urban life in the Anglo-Saxon period, until the final, violent end at Hastings. In the early Middle Ages, John Gillingham depicts a saga of conquest punctuated by frequent defeats on French and British soil, with an exploding society under such strain by the late thirteenth century that it is described here as being possibly on the verge of class war. Although that was avoided, in the later Middle Ages, as Ralph Griffiths writes, long wars in France were followed by aristocratic turmoil in Britain in the fifteenth century, accompanied by domestic recovery from plague and social revolt. The Tudor Age, as John Guy demonstrates, suffused in a golden glow in the patriotic effusions of later generations, was marked in fact by extreme pressure of population upon economic resources, by religious conflict, and the threat of foreign invasion. The resultant political and religious tensions inherited by the house of Stuart are analysed by John Morrill for a century in which—despite a marked decline in internal lawlessness—two civil wars, regicide, a republic, a restoration, and a revolution, followed each other in bewildering, breathless profusion. The apparent surface stability, prosperity, and cultural expansiveness of the Georgian age, as Paul Langford shows, gave way to an explosive tumult of industry, trade, and technology unprecedented in the history of the world, and also to the new revolutionary impulses surging in from the American colonies and from republican France. Somehow, the picture of Edward Gibbon, the urbane chronicler of the Rome of the Antonines and their successors, fleeing across Europe in the face of the Jacobin hordes in his beloved France, is symbolic. The early nineteenth century, as Christopher Harvie explains, did indeed manage to avoid the revolutionary malaria raging through other European states. But instead it brought massive dislocations in the social fabric and the notion of the legal community, and a seemingly unbridgeable class division that led Marx, fancifully, to see Britain as being in the forefront of the revolutionary apocalypse. The later nineteenth and early twentieth centuries, as outlined by H. C. G. Matthew, moved on rapidly from the bland self-assurance of the Great Exhibition, to the anxieties of the *fin de siècle* period, with its social tensions, imperialist neuroses, and sense of national vulnerability. The years since 1914, described by the present writer, saw two world wars, pulverizing economic pressures in the thirties and the seventies, and a forcible wrenching of Britain out of its place in the sun. The history of Britain, then, is not one of harmonious continuity, broadening from precedent to precedent, or from status to contract, as Victorian intellectuals would have it. It is a dramatic, colourful, often violent story of an ancient society and culture torn apart by the political, economic, and intellectual turmoil of human experience. Britain in many ways has been the cockpit of mankind.

And yet, a reading of these chapters may also leave the clear impression that, however elusive in definition, the sense of Britishness always survived in the post-Roman and post-Norman periods. Some elements of that consciousness, not necessarily closely related, can be clearly traced through the centuries. There were, variously, that Celtic Christian identity that survived the invasion of the Romans; the artistic flowering seen in the miniatures and sculpture of the late Anglo-Saxon era; the centralized governmental and ecclesiastical system created by the Normans and Angevins; the vivid sense of an English nationality emerging in the poetry, and perhaps even the architecture, of the fourteenth century. Even in the Tudor twilight, Shakespeare's plays testify to a growing sense of national cohesion—while the presence of that ubiquitous Elizabethan Welshman, John Dee, who invented the ambiguous term 'British Empire', indicates some wider horizons, too. Equally, the intellectual values embodied in the revolution of 1688, Macaulay's famous 'preserving revolution', suggests a social and cultural continuity beneath the surface turbulence of high politics in the seventeenth century. The communal stability of much of the eighteenth and nineteenth centuries, together with their integrative developments in industry, transport, and communication, and perhaps even the democratic advances, political and social, of the present century, have reinforced this perceptible current of national awareness. At key moments in British history, society coalesced rather than divided. Class war, however defined, did not in fact take place in the later Middle Ages; while Marx's prophecies of violent revolutionary upheaval in the modern industrial period were, fortunately, not fulfilled. That Britain was able to assimilate the strains of its political revolution as early as the seventeenth century and of its industrial revolution as early as the eighteenth, in each case long before other European nations did so, testified to the rooted strength of its institutions and its culture. Consensus, no less than conflict, is a central part of our story.

In its many forms, this rooted patriotism, embracing the Welsh, Scots, and Ulstermen over the centuries—though, significantly, never the southern Irish—endured and remained unquenchable. The visible, recognized symbols of that patriotic sense still survive—Crown, Parliament, the processes of law, the legacy of empire, the urge for individuality and domestic privacy, the collective enthusiasm for recreation and mass sport. But what is equally striking, perhaps, is the patriotism of the dissenting critics also, with their alternative scenarios. The Levellers, Daniel Defoe, William Cobbett, William Morris, R. H. Tawney, George Orwell, all in their time emerged as passionate, libertarian opponents of the social inequalities and political imbalance of their day. Yet each of them emerged, also, as deeply committed to an almost religious sense of the civilized essence of their country and its people, their history and destiny. By setting this sense of national continuity against the recurrence of disruption and crisis through the centuries, the historian derives perhaps his ultimate justification in thrusting the British people face to face with their past and with the image of themselves. We hope that general readers will understand themselves, their society, neighbours, and an encompassing world with more clarity, subtlety, enthusiasm, and even affection, after reading this book.

KENNETH O. MORGAN

INTRODUCTION TO VOLUME 1

THE history (as opposed to the prehistory) of Britain began with a crisis of empire. It grew out of political tensions in Rome which led to the invasion of 43 AD and the subsequent conquest. Over the next four centuries, the pattern of Roman occupation was to leave a permanent mark on the landscape and on the culture of the British people. There followed a new structure of military command; the founding of new towns as administrative and commercial centres; a growing prosperity for agriculture which led to the early fourth century being seen as something of a golden age. The roads, temples, villas and colourful mosaics of that period partly survive today as physical memorials to the achievement of Roman Britain. And yet, in the late-fourth and early-fifth centuries, in one of those great disjunctures which mark the turbulent history of Britain, Roman rule collapsed, partly through internal decay, partly through external barbarian attacks. The withdrawal of the Roman legions brought this first phase of our recorded history to an abrupt end.

It was succeeded by waves of settlement by Germanic peoples, introducing a new form of tribal society. Yet, by the start of the seventh century, the kingdoms of these Anglo-Saxon invaders testified to a remarkably sophisticated fabric of government and social organization. They were reinforced by the arrival of Roman Christianity to which the Celtic monasteries of the north and west eventually had to bend the knee. By the mid-eighth century, the heyday of the Mercian kingdom, the unmistakable material evidence of the first English towns, often developing around important churches, can be discerned. These newly settled Anglo-Saxon invaders were themselves now invaded in turn by Vikings and Danes from Scandinavia. But this crisis threw up its own national saviour in Alfred, King of Wessex. His military victories, planning of towns, fostering of the coinage, and encouragement of literacy, gave an English nation new foundations for expansion. The tenth and eleventh centuries seem to have been a time of advance in population and in the agrarian economy. Villages, manor houses and parish churches increased and multiplied. In the eleventh century, however, there was again repeated external challenge. The Danes under Cnut established temporary hegemony over the land. More decisively, at Hastings in 1066, the most familiar of all historical landmarks, William, Duke of Normandy, finally overthrew the house of Wessex and the remnant of the Anglo-Saxon kingdom.

The effect of the Norman conquest was terrible and shattering: its impact endured for centuries to come, even to the reign of Queen Victoria. It marked an upheaval in land-ownership, in the feudalized social order and even in the arts. It also meant a continuing involvement of the insular English with the continental complexities of Norman France. Not until the end of the civil wars of Stephen's reign did Henry II establish a new firm basis for royal authority, with bureaucratic and judicial direction permeating outwards from the centre of government. The earlier middle ages were marked by ceaseless crisis on many fronts. There were constant frontier engagements with the Welsh (conquered by Edward I, finally, in 1282), the Scots (who were never subdued), and the Irish across the sea. The British were also repeatedly sucked into the territorial conflicts of the Angevin empire, a process not ended even by the loss of Anjou and Normandy by King John in 1203–4. Within Britain itself, the limits of royal authority were repeatedly challenged, unsuccessfully by the Church under such prelates as Anselm or Becket, more effectively by the barons at Runnymede, and in the disputes over royal taxation that led to Edward I's so-called 'parliament' of 1290. Perhaps the most critical problems of all were economic—the pressure of a rapidly rising population upon resources, with advancing rents for rich landowners and the steady impoverishment of poor villagers. By 1300 England appeared to be almost on the verge of class war.

Edward I and his successors responded partly by strengthening the levers of royal power, partly by renewed foreign adventure. Claims to the crown of France led to over a hundred years of intermittent warfare overseas, often successful, but culminating in the ignominious retreat from Gascony in 1452. England's insular role was confirmed, while Wales, Scotland and Ireland remained proud, insurgent nations. Again, foreign war produced economic strains (reinforced by the human catastrophe of the Black Death which killed off a third of the English population), and social revolt by the peasantry resulted. This was suppressed; but tension between successive kings and great territorial magnates in the fifteenth century led to the wearisome conflicts of Yorkists and Lancastrians which disrupted political life for thirty years. And yet the legacy of medieval Britain was far from being wholly dismal. The land was becoming more orderly and better governed; living standards again seemed to be rising. Further, Britain—or at least England—was showing some awareness of its national characteristics as in popular assemblies like the 'parliaments', in the strongly English tone of the late-medieval Church, in the distinctly native perpendicular architecture, and above all in the spread of the English language and the writing of creative works of English literature. The fourteen hundred years between the coming of the Romans and Henry Tudor's victory at Bosworth Field in 1485 were violent, disruptive, often appalling. But out of the maelstrom was emerging the outline of a nation.

KENNETH O. MORGAN

PETER SALWAY

1. *Roman Britain*
(c.55 BC–c. AD 440)

The Beginnings of British History

IN Roman times Britain had as many people as at its peak in the
Middle Ages. For four centuries it was an integral part of a single
political system that stretched from Turkey to Portugal and from
the Red Sea to the Tyne and beyond. Its involvement with Rome
started before the Conquest launched by Claudius in AD 43, and
it continued to be a part of the Roman world for some time after
the final break with Roman rule. We are dealing with a full
half-millennium of the history of Britain.

The origins of later Britain go back beyond the Roman period.
Aspects of the society the Romans found in Britain were
beginning to emerge in the Neolithic and Early Bronze Ages. At
the time of the Roman Conquest, the culture of Britain had
something like fifteen hundred to two thousand years of
development behind it—although the prehistorians are greatly
divided on the details. By the end of the pre-Roman Iron Age,
society had evolved forms of organization closely similar to those
encountered by the Romans elsewhere in north-western Europe,
and had adopted versions of the culture and language we call
loosely 'Celtic'. Outside the imperial frontiers in Britain these
continued largely unchanged; inside, the Celtic substratum
persisted, assimilated and adapted by Rome in ways not in
general closely paralleled by modern colonial empires.

Why, then, are we not either starting this *History of Britain*
before the Romans, or consigning Roman Britain, as some
modern writers would have us do, to 'prehistory'? The answer
lies in the real distinction between the Roman period and what
went before. There is some truth in the assertion that the study of
Roman Britain is prehistory, in the sense that we have to lean
very heavily on archaeology—and this is also true of the early
Anglo-Saxon period. However, our sources for Britain are by no
means solely archaeological, and the interpretation of the mater-

ial remains themselves cannot be divorced from the study of the written sources. It is true that the quantity of contemporary or near-contemporary literary evidence is not great in comparison with later periods but there is enough to be significant. Moreover, we have the very considerable remains of the once huge routine output of a literate society—and in a form not subject to the inevitable corruptions of the Greek and Latin literary texts, which have largely survived only by being copied and re-copied by hand down the centuries. Actual examples of writing found in Britain, mostly as inscriptions on stone but some in other forms, constitute a major primary source for the Romano-British period. They include trade marks on manufactured goods; a small but growing number of personal letters and other documents in a variety of materials, discovered in excavations; even graffiti— the everyday writing and reading matter of ordinary people. Nor can we ignore the specialized and difficult but rewarding study of Roman coinage, which had a peculiarly important part in the politics and economics of the Roman world. Not only was the currency itself manipulated by government as money but also the wording and images upon the coins were consistently exploited as a powerful medium for mass propaganda which possessed the insistence of a television commercial repeated over and over again. The ability to read was, admittedly, very much commoner in the towns than in the Romano-British countryside but it was compulsory in the army and essential in many other walks of life. It was certainly not, as in other ages, restricted to a small or specialized class.

The critical difference between Roman Britain and what went before is that its society was literate, perhaps more literate than at any other time till the end of the Middle Ages. Alongside and allied to this is the fact that it was a world dominated by the rule of law, which closely regulated the relations between the individual and the State and between one man and another, however corruptly or inefficiently it might often have been administered. As a society that became more and more dominated by regulations and procedures contained in official documents, the contrast between Roman Britain and the country as it was at the end of the Iron Age is startling. Then, even at the top of the social scale, where the import of Roman luxury goods was a notable feature, writing was totally absent except on the splendid but limited coinage—and even on that the language employed was almost universally Latin and the moneyers themselves often Roman.

Once Julius Caesar's expeditions of 55 and 54 BC had pointed the way, it was more or less inevitable that Rome would try her hand at conquest. Romans did not acknowledge any limit on their right to expand their rule: indeed they saw it as a divine mission. From Caesar onwards, Britain occupied a particular and significant place in the Roman consciousness. The Roman period is a turning-point, not so much in the underlying story of man's settlement of the land of Britain but in the country's emergence from prehistory into history.

The character of the physical geography of a country has a great effect on how people live, and Britain is no exception. Its outstanding permanent characteristic is the broad division between 'highland' and 'lowland'—in rough terms, between the north and west of mainland Britain and the south and east—but it is a distinction which can be overdone in historical analysis. Moreover, in Britain man has shown a considerable capacity to adapt the landscape, sometimes intentionally, often in pursuit of some other end, such as fuel. There have also been important fluctuations in the physical conditions, especially in the relative level of land and sea, with considerable effects on the coastline and inland on the pattern and level of rivers. To what extent the causes were climatic or a matter of movements in the geology is uncertain. In general, such evidence as we have for the Roman period suggests that the climate was broadly similar to present-day Britain. A period of relatively high sea-level was succeeded in the first century AD by a 'marine regression', opening up new lands for exploitation. In the third century the onset of rather wetter climatic conditions seems to be revealed by evidence of flooding in many parts of Europe, with serious problems for low-lying land, rivers, and harbours. So it would seem that climatic conditions were by no means constant throughout the period.

The once popular belief that Britain was largely covered with forest until cleared by the Anglo-Saxons is now discredited. By the Roman Conquest, although there was still a great deal of natural forest, the population had already grown to something of the order it was under the Romans, two or three times greater than during the reign of William the Conqueror (1066–87). The proportion of forest to open, settled landscape had dropped to the level of the later Middle Ages. From about 1300 BC what was to become the classic Iron Age pattern had started to take shape: hill-forts, isolated farms or groups of farms sometimes amounting to villages (often surrounded by small enclosures), larger expanses of permanent fields, woodland, and great open stretches of pasture. In the last 600 years before Caesar, Britain adopted many of the characteristics of the successive phases of

The agricultural wealth of Britain. Roman model of a ploughman at work.

the Continental Iron Age, though often with insular variations. This has led to unresolved debate among the prehistorians as to whether the changes that succeeded one another primarily reflect actual invasions on a substantial scale, the arrival of relatively small numbers of influential or conquering newcomers (such as the Normans), or the exchange of ideas through travel and trade. But whatever the mechanism, Britain had reached the point by Caesar's time where, as he himself says, the tribes he met in the parts he penetrated—the south and east—were very similar to those he encountered in Gaul. Beyond these, archaeology reveals that there were some less-advanced peoples, but all of them seem to have shared the same British version of the Celtic language and a broadly similar culture.

There is some reason to think that the tribal system we find in Britain in Claudian times was not fully developed in Caesar's, and there are other important changes in the period between the Roman invasions which we shall examine later. In southern Gaul, the native tribes had largely passed from rule by kings to elective magistracies and tribal councils, but in northern Gaul kingship was still common when Caesar arrived. In Britain it was to remain so down to Claudius, though there are some signs of joint or divided rule by pairs of kings. Society divided broadly into a warrior aristocracy and a largely agricultural commons. The priests, the druids, were a third group whose position and function is debated, though for Britain at least the evidence is against the popular notion of their having a prominent political role. The Celts were characterized by quarrelsomeness, both within the tribe and in their indulgence in inter-tribal warfare. Only on rare occasions, in the face of great danger, would Celtic tribes combine to choose a single leader; though in Gaul at least there was some tradition of periodic gatherings of prominent men from various tribes. There was little or no 'national' sentiment.

By Caesar's day, close relationships had been established between southern Britain and northern Gaul. The pattern of archaeological finds reveals two main groups of routes by which goods and people travelled between the countries. The most important at this time was between Brittany and Lower Normandy (in ancient times known collectively as Armorica) and south-west Britain, particularly through a port at Hengistbury Head in Dorset. The other routes were from Upper Normandy and the Low Countries, the lands between the mouths of the Seine and Rhine, to southern and eastern England. Caesar moreover reports that 'within living memory' a Gallic ruler had exercised power in Britain as well as his own homeland, and he was not only to find British contingents fighting alongside his Gallic enemies but to be thwarted by fugitives seeking refuge from Rome with friends or kin across the Channel.

To understand why Caesar was in Gaul and what may have prompted his campaigns in Britain we need to look briefly at the condition of Rome at this time. Rome's expansion in the third and second centuries BC from being an Italian city state to the greatest power in the Mediterranean had been under her traditional form of government. This was theoretically democratic, with assemblies of the people and annually elected magistrates, but in practice public office was held century after century by a relatively small number of aristocratic families. The senate, notionally an advisory body, came to have a dominant role, being composed of magistrates and all those who had previously been elected to the qualifying magistracies. The highest offices, the two annual consulships, were almost exclusively held by an even smaller group within the senatorial class, and its families possessed special prestige. Religious and social attitudes, closely intertwined, placed a very high value on veneration of the family ancestors and the preservation of family honour. It was a characteristic of the classical world that a man's reputation—what his peers thought of him—was of the highest importance. At Rome, the individual aristocrat was under constant pressure, both of family duty and personal ambition, to emulate his forebears by pursuing a public career and by striving for the highest office.

Reputation was won by success primarily in two fields—the law and the army. A senatorial career normally included posts in each area. Of the two, proven military prowess won the greater prestige. Holding certain senior offices, even below the consulship, brought with it eligibility to command armies and govern provinces abroad. Caesar's contemporary, the orator, politician, and moralist Cicero, states categorically what conferred the greatest personal status: there was more glory to be won by extending the empire than by administering it.

In the ancient world, wars of conquest usually showed a handsome profit for the victor. The immense wealth brought into Rome by her conquests and the opportunities and temptations offered by her Mediterranean empire put intolerable strains on the political and social system that had been adequate for a small Italian state. By the middle of the first century BC, the Roman Republic was falling apart. The old conventions within the governing class could not cope. Ambition to join the select few at the top had been replaced by an inability to tolerate even equals in power and fame.

Part of the visible prestige of a great Roman aristocrat had long been the number of people dependent upon him. Indeed whole communities could regard themselves as among his 'clients'. Such 'patronage' was a feature of society that was to be of great importance to provinces such as Britain, otherwise far from the centre of power. By the first century BC, the old citizen armies, raised for a specific war, had been replaced by professionals. The senate made the fatal mistake of allowing these new soldiers to become dependent upon their own generals rather than the State for the rewards of service, particularly the all-important provision on retirement. The conditions for recurrent civil war were now all present and the Republic effectively doomed. Attitudes, practices, and social relationships had been set up that were to haunt Rome for the rest of her history. For Britain, it was not only the great events of the subsequent history of the empire that directly affected her destiny, but also the extraordinary success the Romans had in transmitting their values to the populations they absorbed—particularly to the native ruling classes. Indeed, the creation of a common upper-class culture, critical to the successful working of the empire itself, was in many ways also central in its downfall. The story of Britain in Roman times reflects this fundamental pattern.

The British aristocracy before the Roman conquest.
A nobleman's shield of the period from Caesar to Claudius.
Bronze, elaborately decorated in characteristic Celtic style (the small
circles contain patterns of applied red glass, and the whole was given
a golden finish). From the river Thames at Battersea.

Julius Caesar's conquest of Gaul must be looked at in the context of the struggle for power in the closing years of the Republic. We shall probably never know exactly why he launched his two expeditions to Britain in 55 and 54 BC nor whether he intended conquest—though there is a possible parallel in his punitive foray across the Rhine into Germany. More important were the consequences for the future. In immediate military terms the results were modest, though we do not hear of Britons fighting in Gaul again. Because of the explosive state of Gaul, Caesar was prevented from following up his victories and from taking advantage of the surrender of the temporary confederation of the British tribes. Indeed, a Roman historian writing in the next century even represented a British leader as claiming the 'repulse' of Caesar by the ancestors of his hearers.

Caesar's British enterprise made a lasting impression on Rome, however. Britain was a remote, almost fabled island across the 'Ocean', a fearsome sea to Romans as yet unaccustomed to the tidal conditions outside the Mediterranean. Britain was beyond the known world. In two brief campaigns Caesar had put Britain on the Roman map. Retaining its aura of mystery, it would henceforth always occupy an alluring place in the minds of those eager for military ambition—and Caesar had set a goal and a precedent for subsequent members of the Julian family. Moreover his experiences—he had a number of close shaves at the hands not only of the British but also of the elements—provided practical lessons for a future expeditionary commander.

Caesar had also set important precedents for intervention in Britain. He had received the surrender of powerful kings and accepted the friendship of others. A tribute—or annual tax—to be paid to Rome had been imposed. He had also installed as king of the Trinovantes of Essex a young prince who had fled to him in Gaul. The father of this prince had been killed by Cassivellaunus, the same Briton who was elected by the British confederation to lead them against Caesar—and who was now forbidden to interfere with the Trinovantes. Rome could, therefore, claim some sort of overlordship, the right to exact payments and an obligation to protect her friends, if she chose to move. (Rome rarely did so in fact, unless it was in her own interest: many small countries under her nominal protection failed to appreciate this basic fact of ancient life, with unfortunate consequences.) But precedent, we may remember, was important to the Romans, and after Caesar they had ample.

For two decades after Caesar, the attention of the Roman world

Roman silver cup, decorated with vine leaves and olives, one of a group of silver vessels of Italian workmanship of the Augustan period, probably imported before the Claudian invasion, found at Hockwold, Norfolk.

was monopolized by the series of civil wars that brought the Republic to an end and put Caesar's adopted heir Octavian (later to assume the name Augustus) into power. Caesar had himself taken no action when his erstwhile Gallic friend Commius, whom he had installed as king of the Atrebates in Gaul, joined the great revolt. The crushing of that revolt saw Commius in flight to Britain—where he had earlier been used as Caesar's agent—to found a dynasty among the British Atrebates. The lack of Roman interest in Britain at this time is understandable. More interesting for us is that we are now beginning to identify tribes and plot the history of dynasties. Commius' own case is particularly intriguing. His rule over a Roman-devised 'client' kingdom of Gallic Atrebates and the Morini of the Channel coast north of the Seine had put him in control of much of the area through which the routes from the main concentration of 'Belgae', straddling the Meuse, ran towards Britain. Somewhat earlier than Caesar, there seems to have been the beginning of a movement from the Belgic part of Gaul into Britain which probably accelerated as Caesar's conquests progressed, estab- lishing, at the least, related royal houses in Britain.

In the course of the first century BC, Belgic culture became dominant in southern Britain, even among tribes themselves not

The pattern of life was changing. The division of labour
ᴇty became more pronounced, with more and more
ᴀᴄᴜᴠᴜᴇs, such as pottery-making, becoming the preserve of
craftsmen rather than domestic. British art reached a magnificent
peak, especially in metalwork, all swirling motifs and fine
enamelling, but it concentrated on the equipping of warrior
chiefs and possibly the adornment of shrines. In the most
Belgicized areas, hill-forts tended to give way to large
settlements on lower ground, sometimes with their approaches
defended by great running earthworks. These have been seen as
the forerunners of Roman towns, though some were more in the
nature of royal residences than urban in the contemporary
Mediterranean sense. But for the future of the British landscape
the most interesting change is the widespread emergence,
particularly in the period between Caesar and Claudius (54
BC–AD 43), of a more permanent pattern of rural land settlement,
with regular boundaries that suggest regular tenure. There is a
growing feeling among archaeologists that this period may mark
the beginning of a framework of land-division that has persisted
to the present day. Those who worked and owned the land have
certainly changed many times. The skeleton of the landscape, in
this credible hypothesis, has survived into modern times.

In the year before his first expedition Caesar had fought and
destroyed at sea the fleet of the Veneti of Brittany, whose ships
had controlled the carrying trade between Armorica and south-
west Britain. About this time, archaeology shows a dramatic
switch in emphasis to the routes between Belgic Gaul and the
south and east of Britain. Henceforth, the sea passages from the
Seine to the Southampton area, the short crossings from Boulogne to Kent, and the route from the Rhine and the Low
Countries to the estuaries of Essex were paramount. It is not,
perhaps, surprising to find that the greatest wealth and sophistication were now in these areas of Britain. From 12 BC, indeed
when Augustus launched his armies on the conquest of Holland
and Germany, the new importance of the northern links with
Britain must have further sharply increased. Although in the
long run Augustus' attempt to extend the empire to the Elbe
failed, from this time large Roman armies were permanently on
the Rhine. Britain was exporting corn, hides, cattle, and iron to
the empire, all items of vital importance to the Roman military
effort. Recent research has indicated that the technologically
efficient British agriculture was producing, at least in grain, a
large surplus over the subsistence needs of its people. We may
reasonably surmise that the increasing wealth, the changes in

Chain intended for a chain-gang, possibly in the course of the slave-trade.
Found among an Iron Age votive deposit, Llyn Cerrig, Anglesey, but thought to
originate in East Anglia.

society, and even the new pattern of British agriculture were
stimulated, perhaps even caused, by the opportunities offered by
the needs of the army of the Rhine and the emerging civil
markets of the new Roman provinces across the Channel.

In his early days Augustus was acutely conscious of the legacy
of Caesar's memory and the urgent need to establish a military
reputation for himself. Even before his final defeat of Mark
Antony he seems to have planned an invasion of Britain; and at
least two more attempts were made to put it into effect. All were
frustrated by more pressing demands. After 26 BC, however, he
was content to let the imminent conquest of Britain remain an
uncorrected impression that served as useful propaganda at
Rome, while developing diplomatic relations that may have
sprung out of negotiations we know were already in progress,
perhaps to re-establish Caesar's taxation. Strabo, an author
writing late in Augustus' reign or under his successor Tiberius,
confirms that the Britons were paying heavy customs dues to
Rome on their import and export trade. He seems to reflect a

party line that sought to justify the shift in policy away from invasion when he claims that Rome forbore to make the easy conquest of Britain because taxation without occupation was more profitable. The Britons, he adds significantly, posed no military threat.

Commius was succeeded on his British throne by a son, Tincommius, and around 15 BC there seems to have been a reversal of attitude which put this important kingdom at the British end of the Seine–Southampton route into friendship with Rome. The reason may have been the growing power of one British tribe, the Catuvellauni, centred in Hertfordshire. Whether they had recently coalesced from smaller clans or had already been the force behind Cassivellaunus is uncertain; but the history of Britain up to the Claudian conquest is now dominated by Catuvellaunian expansion. For the time being, however, Rome chose to turn a blind eye. Even the expulsion of Tincommius and another British king, and their seeking refuge with Augustus, were only treated by Rome as support for the Augustan claim to exercise virtual sway over Britain, propaganda for internal consumption. Indeed, there is every sign the Catuvellauni were careful not to display open hostility. The balance was mutually profitable to the governing classes on both sides. British aristocrats were enjoying the imports from the empire, while the list of exports that the Roman author thinks worthy of mention shows that the Britons were not only paying for these luxuries with supplies important to the army; by sending gold, silver, slaves, and hunting dogs they had also become a source of commodities of direct interest to the emperor himself and to the rich at Rome. After disaster in Germany in AD 9, Augustus and his successor Tiberius erected non-intervention outside the empire into a principle—the absolute opposite of previous Augustan practice. It must, however, be a measure of the satisfactory nature of the working relationship that Cunobelinus, Shakespeare's Cymbeline, now king of the Catuvellauni, managed to avoid Roman retribution even when he took over the territory of Caesar's old protégés, the Trinovantes, and transferred the centre of his kingdom to Colchester. He now had command of the lucrative route to the Rhine. Within Britain he could cut the supply of their status symbols to other British princes at will; and whether by conquest or other means the power and influence of his kingdom continued to expand.

The Roman Conquest

The state of mutual toleration, satisfactory as it doubtless was for Rome and the Catuvellauni—but perhaps not so welcome to other Britons—started to crumble when the unstable Gaius (Caligula) succeeded Tiberius. At some point in this period, Cunobelinus expelled one of his sons, who eventually fled to the emperor, to whom he made a formal act of submission. Gaius not only claimed the surrender of Britain; he also gave orders for an invasion. These he subsequently countermanded, but only at the last minute, and it is this that is important. The staff work had been done, the whole massive process of build-up to an invasion had been gone through, not as manoeuvres but as a real operation, and the Roman public had been reminded of unfinished business. Everything lay ready for a more determined hand.

The murder of Gaius hoisted unceremoniously to the throne his uncle Claudius, previously ignored by the rest of the imperial family under the mistaken notion that he was of defective intelligence. In fact, he combined common sense, an original mind bordering on the eccentric, a professional interest in

The auxiliary troops: bronze parade helmet with decorative face-mask, used in formal cavalry exercises. From Ribchester, Lancashire.

history, and a profound veneration for Roman tradition. Faced soon after his elevation by a serious military revolt, the need to establish his reputation with the troops and gain respect at Rome must have been obvious to him. Such a man could hardly miss the chance of military glory offered by Britain and the opportunity not only to carry out the invasion cancelled by Augustus and Gaius before him but even to outdo Julius Caesar himself. Personal and family reputation could not be better served.

There was a pretext, too—and one which could be referred back to sound precedent and provided a strategic reason for intervention. Cunobelinus was now dead, and his realm had fallen into the hands of two other aggressive sons—Caratacus and Togodumnus. The eastern entrance to Britain was, therefore, unreliable. In the south, pressure on Tincommius' old kingdom had reduced it to a rump on the coast: now that entrance, too, closed when an internal coup expelled Tincommius' brother, Verica. The latter, in the time-honoured fashion, also fled to the emperor. All Britain seemed to be turning hostile, and the valuable traffic between it and the empire was threatened. Like Caesar, Claudius could respond to an appeal from a British prince.

Caesar had relied upon inspired generalship and the devotion of the troops who had served long under him. The new standing regular army that Augustus and his successors had created still depended on generalship, but was more firmly based on meticulous organization and training and the permanence of its institutions. At this period, the legions, the backbone of the army, recruited only from Roman citizens, still drew most of their men from Italy. Gradually, the citizen colonies founded in the older provinces outside Italy were to provide men for the military career. Each legion had an establishment of something over five thousand men, mostly heavy infantry, backed by small cavalry contingents, catapults, and other engines of war. The legions also provided a wide range of skilled craftsmen and administrators; and individual soldiers, all of whom were required to read and write, could be used on a vast range of government tasks. The 'auxiliary' units were, in the first half of the first century AD, evolving from native irregulars under their own chieftains into regular regiments of provincials, mostly non-citizen, but with Roman commanders. These regiments were normally five hundred strong, cavalry, infantry, or mixed, with status and pay inferior to those of the legions. Both legionaries and auxiliaries, however, enjoyed those extreme rarities in the ancient world, a regular money wage, an assured career, and provision for

The army under the early Empire. The legions: tombstone of Marcus Favonius a centurion of the Twentieth, buried at Colchester. The stone was overturned during the Boudican revolt and consequently preserved intact.

retirement. Education, training, and opportunities for self-advancement—not to mention self-enrichment—made the army a major force in social mobility. Both serving and retired soldiers were persons of consequence in their communities. Auxiliaries automatically received Roman citizenship on retirement and their sons were eligible to join the legions. These units thus provided a continuous process of turning unlettered barbarians into literate Roman citizens and were a major element in the assimilation of new peoples into the empire.

The force assembled to sail to Britain in AD 43 comprised four legions and about the same number of auxiliary troops, around 40,000 men in all. Facing this disciplined machine, the British forces retained their old character. The permanent warriors were the aristocracy; their favourite weapon was the chariot, which they used for rapid transport in and out of battle and in the handling of which their drivers were extremely skilled. The exact status of the cavalry is uncertain: they were probably men who could provide their own horses, but it is not clear that their prime occupation in life was fighting. The mass of the British armies was the levies, summoned from the farms. Unlike the armoured Romans, the Britons wore little or no body protection and depended on speed, impetus, and the long slashing sword. Before they could get near to Romans in battle order they were liable to lose many men to the clouds of Roman javelins; and in hand-to-hand combat their long blades were at a disadvantage faced with the closed ranks and short stabbing swords of the enemy infantry. Successes by these Celtic troops against the Romans were usually gained in surprise attacks, in ambushes, and when overwhelming detached units by sheer numbers. They could rarely match the legions in pitched battle, and Roman commanders aimed to force them out into the open or to pen them behind ramparts where Roman siegecraft and artillery could beat them down or starve them out. But perhaps their greatest disadvantage in the face of the Romans was that as farmer-soldiers they could only stay in the field for a short part of the year. If they were not sent home, the population starved. The supply system of the Roman army, on the contrary, permitted it to campaign so long as the weather permitted, and to build fortified, well-stocked camps in which to sit out each winter. Such a system permitted a war to be carried on for year after year, and provided the basis for the garrisoning required for permanent occupation. Faced with such an opponent, it is remarkable that the British resisted so long and so hard.

The invasion met with fierce resistance from some of the British tribes. Others, no doubt not sorry to see the Catuvellaunian hegemony in southern Britain destroyed, surrendered easily or joined the Romans. The campaign was crowned by the submission of eleven British kings to the emperor and his triumphant entry into Colchester, for which he had joined his

The Roman Conquest. Roman fort planted in the corner of a British hill-fort, seen from the air at Hod Hill, Dorset, in the region where the future Emperor Vespasian overran thirty native strongholds in AD 43.

advancing forces, complete with elephants. His delight was marked by the revival of ancient rituals once performed by Republican victors and the proud proclamation of the extension of empire, in which the Conquest of Ocean once more figured large (it was no hollow boast: the army had at first refused to sail).

By AD 47 the Claudian armies occupied Britain as far as the Severn and the Trent. The work of organizing Britain as a regular province was now in progress. Its governorship enjoyed high status. It was reserved for ex-consuls and carried with it the command of an exceptionally large group of legions. In its first century and a half as a province, men of particular distinction were regularly chosen. It was not only a military challenge where reputations could be won, but—though we shall never have the figures to compare income from Britain with expenditure on its defence and administration—it was regarded as a land of natural abundance as late as the fourth century. By AD 47, indeed, the exploitation of Britain's mineral resources—one of the chief objectives of victory—had begun (the silver-bearing lead of the Mendips was being mined under state control by this date). It might have saved Rome much trouble and expense if she had limited her conquest to the area she already controlled; but it is very doubtful whether Roman ambition could long have been restrained, even if the warlike and unstable tribes of the north and Wales had not been a threat to the peaceful development of the south. As it was, the events of the next two or three years committed Rome to a different course.

Roman practice in the provinces was always to shift as much of the burden of administration on to loyal locals as soon as might be. The Claudian intention seems to have been to employ 'client' kings as far as possible—the most economical method, where they were reliable. A substantial part of the south, including Verica's old kingdom, was put in the hands of one Cogidubnus, who may not have been a native Briton. The Iceni of Norfolk were kept as 'allies'; and an understanding was reached beyond the border of Roman rule with Cartimandua, queen of the Brigantes (a vast grouping of clans that encompassed most of northern England), with the object of securing the province from attack from the north. One success of this policy was when Cartimandua handed over the fugitive Caratacus to Claudius; another was the enduring loyalty of Cogidubnus, which was almost certainly of critical importance during later crises in Britain.

The rest of the province the governor would expect to administer chiefly through the tribes, reorganized as Roman local government units (*civitates*) with their nobles formed into councils and holding local magistracies—scaled-down versions of the Roman constitution, in fact, but often adapting existing institutions. In addition, throughout the province ran the writ of the chief financial secretary of Britain, the *procurator provinciae*. These provincial procurators reported direct to the emperor. This was natural enough, since they had particular responsibilities for crown land (the emperors automatically acquired the royal estates of defeated enemies, besides much else by inheritance or confiscation) and crown monopolies; but they also acted as a check on the governor, the emperor's military and judicial representative. Friction was not uncommon and not wholly unintentional.

The train of events that made it certain the province would not remain confined to the south started in AD 47 with the Roman

The client kingdoms. Gedding trenches from the formal Italianate gardens of the palatial villa at Fishbourne, near Chichester, probably the property of King Cogidubnus.

response to raids from outside. Measures taken included not only counter-attacks but also the disarming of Britons within the province. This was bound to have come eventually, since civilians were forbidden to carry arms within the empire except in certain very limited circumstances—something that says much about everyday security in Roman times—but those who had voluntarily submitted to Rome had not expected it to apply to them. The Iceni revolted and were put down by force: the true status of the client kingdoms had now been made plain. The next step was the moving forward of the legion that had been stationed at Colchester and its replacement in AD 49 by a colony of Roman legionary veterans. This was intended as the seat of the Imperial Cult—the formal worship of Rome and the Imperial Family which focused the loyalty of the province—and the veterans were to act as a bulwark, against possible revolt. In

The client kingdoms. Crop marks, revealing from the air at Thetford, Norfolk, a rectilinear multiple-ditched enclosure.

practice, Colchester was now an ungarrisoned civil city. Perhaps at the same moment, London was founded as a supply port. It is possible that from its beginning it was intended in due course to become the administrative centre of Britain as well. It was in all probability created as a deliberate act, rather than emerging out of a casual settlement of traders, as was formerly thought. The pre-eminence of the Essex coast was now challenged by the Thames, and London's position at the hub of the radiating system of main roads now being built, designed for official purposes, very soon made it also the business centre of the province.

The 50s were a decade of urban development. Only the agricultural hinterland remained largely unchanged, at least on the surface, and progress towards the universal adoption of the money economy was slow. By AD 60, however, with the governor, Suetonius Paullinus, about to subdue the troublesome tribes of North Wales, the province looked set to progress steadily. What went wrong? Why did the provincials, led by Rome's old friends the Iceni and Trinovantes, turn into a raging horde, set on destroying every trace of Rome?

We have only the Roman account, but it is enough to reveal maladministration ranging from the callously negligent to the undeniably criminal. Tacitus makes a general comment on the British character: 'The Britons bear conscription, the tribute and their other obligations to the empire without complaint, provided there is no injustice. That they take extremely ill; for they can bear to be ruled by others but not to be their slaves.' The responsibility for AD 61 cannot be confined to the procurator alone, the traditional villain of the piece. The governor has to take a share, and it cannot stop there. The young Nero, now on the throne, can hardly be blamed directly, for he was under the influence of his 'good' advisers, Burrus, the praetorian prefect, and the philosopher and dramatist Seneca. Of these two, it seems very likely that Seneca, at least, knew what was going on in Britain because he suddenly recalled, in a ruthless manner, large sums of money he had been lending to leading Britons at a high rate of interest. Reports coming out of Britain may well have indicated unrest that might put his investment at risk. In the event, the action fuelled the flames. There are two main threads to the grievances, represented respectively by the Iceni and the Trinovantes. At his death, Boudica's husband, Prasutagus, the client king of the Iceni, had left half his possessions to the emperor, expecting that this would protect his kingdom and family. Agents of the procurator and of the governor, however, had treated this as if it were the unconditional surrender of an enemy. The king's property was confiscated, nobles were expelled from their estates, and taxation and conscription

Bronze head from a public statue of the Emperor Claudius, found in the River Alde, Suffolk, and probably looted from Colchester during the revolt of Boudica.

enforced. The Trinovantes were suffering other insults. The main burden of the Imperial Cult, designed to promote loyalty to the emperor, had fallen on their nobles, while the Roman colonists—significantly with the encouragement of serving soldiers—seized their lands and treated them with contempt. They (and probably the aristocracies of other *civitates*) were facing financial ruin, the last straw being the reclaiming of grants made by Claudius and the recall of Seneca's loans. The Imperial Cult, as represented by the Temple of the Deified Claudius at Colchester, was, ironically, the focus of British hatred.

In answer to Boudica's protests, she was flogged and her daughters raped. Rousing her own tribe and her Trinovantian neighbours and carrying other *civitates* with her (but clearly not Cogidubnus) she swept through southern Britain, burning Colchester, London, and Verulamium (near St. Albans), torturing every Roman or Roman sympathizer she could catch, and inflicting devastating defeats on the few Roman units that had been left in that part of the country. The governor only just avoided the total loss of the province. After the eventual victory when he had brought her to battle his retribution was all the more extreme. For a while it looked as if the ruin of the province of Britain would now ironically be achieved at Roman hands. Nero, indeed, at one stage in his reign—possibly earlier, perhaps now—had been inclined to abandon Britain altogether. In the end two factors saved the province: the intervention of a remarkable new provincial procurator, Classicianus, himself of Gallic origin, and the recall to Rome of the governor.

The recovery that occupied Britain for the decade after Boudica was genuine but unspectacular. There is some evidence that under the last governor appointed by Nero it was beginning to accelerate. But the outbreak of civil war across the empire in AD 69 ('The Year of the Four Emperors') revived the spectre of generals fighting for supremacy. However, the outcome of the wars brought in a vigorous new administration in the persons of the Flavian emperors. For Britain, this spelled provincial renewal and the expansion of Roman power. As Tacitus says, 'Now come great generals and magnificent armies, and with them the hopes of our enemies fall into ruin.'

While the Roman world had been distracted by the civil wars, a fresh outbreak of strife among the Brigantes had lost Cartimandua her kingdom and embroiled the Roman army. The north of Britain was no longer secure. The old policy of client kingship, already shaken by Boudica and previous Brigantian disturbances, was finally discredited. Within a few years even Cogidubnus was probably pensioned off to live in the splendid villa of Fishbourne. By AD 83 or 84 a succession of first-rate governors had carried Roman arms to the far north of Scotland and garrisons to the edge of the Highlands—and were pressing ahead with Romanization. Tacitus, in describing the work of his father-in-law Agricola, uses words that can characterize the Flavian period as a whole:

In order to encourage a truculent population that dwelled in scattered settlements (and was thus only too ready to fall to fighting) to live in a peaceful and inactive manner by offering it the pleasures that would follow on such a way of living, Agricola urged these people privately, and helped them officially, to build temples, public squares with public buildings (*fora*), and private houses (*domus*). He praised those who responded quickly, and severely criticized laggards. In this way, competition for public recognition took the place of compulsion. Moreover he had the children of the leading Britons educated in the civilized arts and openly placed the natural ability of the Britons above that of the Gauls, however well trained. The result was that those who had once shunned the Latin language now sought fluency and eloquence in it. Roman dress, too, became popular and the toga was frequently seen. Little by little there was a slide toward the allurements of degeneracy: assembly-rooms (*porticus*), bathing establishments and smart dinner parties. In their inexperience the Britons called it civilization when it was really all part of their servitude.

To a certain extent this urbanization under the Flavians was less than completely successful. The core of its more securely-based development can reasonably be associated with the visit of the Emperor Hadrian to Britain in person in 122, when existing schemes were revived or replaced and vast new works put in hand. But, looked at in longer perspective, the period from AD 70 to the 160s is the age when Britain truly became Roman and its lasting features as part of the empire emerged. Central to this absorption into the Roman system was the more or less universal devolution of the burden of routine administration to the local aristocracies that replaced the client kingdoms. It was crucially important to this policy to win over the native aristocracy whose confidence had been so disastrously lost in the reign of Nero, and it is in this context that Tacitus must be read.

Archaeologically, we can observe in the late first century and the beginning and middle of the second century the development of the cities and towns of Roman Britain to their full extent. The administrative centres of the *civitates* were provided with civic centres: the forum and basilica that provided market, law courts, civic offices, and council chambers; the public baths which in the Roman world provided the urban centre for relaxation and social life; engineered water supplies; public monuments honouring imperial figures and local worthies; and, in a number of cases, theatres or amphitheatres. This archaeolo-

The mixing of cultures. Tombstone of Regina, a Catuvellaunian Briton, wife and former slave of Barates of Palmyra, shown seated in a wickerwork chair with her workbasket and jewel box.
The inscription is in Latin and Palmyrene. From the civil settlement outside the fort at South Shields, at the mouth of the Tyne.

gical evidence is all the more significant in that in the empire it was normally the local notables themselves (in council or as individuals) who paid for such amenities, not State or emperor. Occasionally, a great private patron with local connections might favour the town with a benefaction or by acting as friend at court. Only in rare and well-publicized instances did emperors take a part, directly or through their representatives.

The urban expansion could not, of course, have rested solely on the basis of a relatively small native aristocracy taught to accept Roman ways. Indeed, the fact that this spread of town life was followed by the appearance of many 'villas' in the country-side—at this stage mainly modest but comfortable Roman houses, often replacing native homesteads—indicates that the British gentry retained their connections with the land. Most probably they were still chiefly resident on their estates, and many ordinary farmers shared their prosperity. In this period, too, veterans discharged from the legions were principally concentrated in the small number of cities deliberately founded to take them: Colchester, Lincoln, and Gloucester. The flourishing of the towns as a whole, therefore, depended equally on the emergence, well attested, of a lively urban population made up of officials, the professions, traders, and skilled artisans.

Some of these people, particularly among the craftsmen and traders, were immigrants or visitors from other parts of the empire, and many officials were on short-term postings to the province. Nevertheless, the population of Roman Britain remained overwhelmingly Celtic. The ranks of the Roman army, too, were increasingly recruited from the provinces in which units were stationed; gradually Britons who had been, like the mass of their fellows, without the distinctive Roman citizenship when they joined the army, must, as discharged veterans with their grants of citizenship and substantial gratuities, have formed an important part of the solid centre of the Romanized society now emerging. In the towns, slaves were set up in business by their masters; and the frequent use in the Roman world of the power to set slaves free or allow them to purchase their liberty expanded the skilled labour force and added to the body of businessmen. Whatever the condition of the agricultural labourer, social mobility was high in the skilled and educated portion of society. Whilst the vast bulk of the ordinary people of Britain undoubtedly remained on the land—and we have to recall that industry too, was largely concentrated in the country-side—the towns of the Early Empire came to provide centres of public life, exchange and services for the rural hinterland, and wide opportunities of advancement at different levels of society.

Hadrian's revival of flagging Flavian initiatives was thus of major importance. But his impact on the province was great in

Hadrian's Wall and Housesteads fort. The Wall joins the front of the fort at the right-hand corners. In the centre is the headquarters building, with commanding officer's house (*left*) and a pair of granaries (*right*). *Behind* lies the military hospital. In the bottom right corner are three barracks and bottom left a latrine block. Outside the fort are visible a few of the many houses, shops, and temples of the dependent civil settlement.

other ways. A man of restless and extraordinary character and energy, much of his reign was taken up with tours of the provinces. One of the few emperors deliberately to set himself against the tradition of expansion of the empire, he was personally unpopular with the Roman aristocracy and many of his vast enterprises were only partially successful, though whether due to internal opposition or to flaws in planning is not always clear. In Britain there are at least three major examples. Hadrian's Wall was constructed on the line to which Roman forces had been withdrawn in stages over the thirty years since the extreme point of expansion, partly because of demands for troops elsewhere, partly due to fairly serious local reverses in the field. Such a policy suited Hadrian's general inclination to limit the empire, and the design of the Wall was brilliantly original. Partly because of this, however, detailed study of its early history has revealed a remarkable series of changes of plan within Hadrian's reign; and it must have cost many times the original estimates of the expenditure and time required for completion. Similarly, the agricultural colonization of the Fenlands of East Anglia involved water engineering on a grand scale, yet many of the farms failed after only a few years. Hadrianic London, too, saw the demolition of the substantial Flavian forum and basilica and their replacement with a complex twice the normal size. In Gaul and elsewhere Hadrian intervened to help cities erect public buildings. In London this was probably related to the presence of the emperor himself during his visit to Britain in AD 122, which is supported by the erection of a permanent fort in the city at about this time—something almost unparalleled in the cities of the empire outside Rome. But when a great fire had swept through London later in Hadrian's reign the effort to reconstruct areas that had been devastated was relatively short-lived, and in the later years of the second century London shows signs of advanced urban decay.

Hadrian's frontier line from Tyne to Solway Firth represents broadly the limit within which the province settled for most of its history. Yet there were at least three major wars of conquest northwards subsequent to Hadrian, two of them commanded in person by emperors; and for long periods garrisons were maintained at points beyond the Hadrianic line and a degree of control exercised. Indeed, within months of his death in 138 plans were in hand to launch a new invasion of Scotland; and by AD 142 the armies of his generally unmilitary successor, Antoninus Pius, had, like those of Claudius, provided him with a conquest in the prestigious field of Britain. Scotland as far as the Firth of Tay was in Roman hands, and work commenced on a new, shorter, and more simply-built linear barrier to run from the Forth to the Clyde. Elaborate commemorative stone relief sculptures, set at positions along what we know as the Antonine Wall, record the confident mood of what was to be the last period of unconstrained expansion of Roman rule.

In this early Antonine period, the developments we have seen in town and country reached their first peak. Elsewhere, the empire is generally considered to have been enjoying a golden age of tranquillity and prosperity. In Britain the economic system of the Early Empire had been fully accepted, based on a money

Second-century Britain

economy and large-scale, long-distance trade. Culturally, Roman fashions were dominant, and classical art and decoration widely adopted. Perhaps, historically, the most important artistic impact on the Britons of Roman conquest was the introduction of figurative styles, particularly in sculpture, wall-painting, and mosaic but also in a vast range of minor arts and crafts—jewellery, pottery, furniture, and household goods of every description. First-rate works of art from Roman Britain are relatively few compared with, say, southern Gaul, but they do exist. The middle range of material is, however, quite plentiful and it is abundantly clear that mass-produced articles were freely available. It is these, rather than the few works of high art that have survived, that reveal an everyday revolution in the way of life since the pre-Roman Iron Age. Roman pottery alone reveals the existence of a 'throw-away society' that is quite different from what went before or came after.

Because it affected the deepest levels of consciousness, the most telling evidence for the assimilation of Roman and native comes from religion. Roman Britain was a religious kaleidoscope, ranging from the formal rites of the Roman State—Jupiter, Juno, and Minerva, in particular—and the Imperial Cult that had more recently been grafted on to it, through a wide range of religions imported both from the neighbouring West and from the East, to the local Celtic cults. People from overseas often retained their own favourite practices: Diodora, a Greek priestess, dedicated an altar at Corbridge in her own language to the demi-god Heracles of Tyre; soldiers from the Netherlands set up others at Housesteads on Hadrian's Wall to their native goddesses the Alaisiagae, Baudihillia and Friagabis, Beda and

The Antonine Wall in Scotland. Second-century cavalry trooper riding down barbarian enemies, depicted on a 'distance slab' recording a sector constructed by a named unit, the Second Legion *Augusta*. From Bridgeness, on the Firth of Forth.

Fimmilena. But for our purpose the most significant are the 'conflations' or amalgamations of classical and Celtic deities. This was a difficult and uncertain process, since Celtic religion identified its deities much less clearly than Roman, but it was very widespread. That its acceptance was more than superficial is clear, for example, from an altar in the great complex of temple and baths at Bath erected to Sulis Minerva—the native healing spirit of the hot springs conflated with the Roman goddess of wisdom—by Lucius Marcius Memor, *haruspex*. The function of the *haruspices* was divination of the future from the entrails of sacrificial animals. This ancient practice, held in the highest honour, went back to very early Etruscan strands in Italian religion, yet it is here related to a half-Celtic deity. Again, on Hayling Island, a major shrine of the pre-Roman Iron Age—more than likely associated with the kingship of Verica—was rebuilt subsequently in Roman materials, probably by an architect from Roman Gaul commissioned by Cogidubnus. It is a particularly fine example of a very large class of distinctive shrines known to archaeologists as 'Romano-Celtic temples', found right across Britain, Gaul, and Roman Germany, and quite clearly the expression in Roman architectural terms of a pre-existing type peculiar to the Celtic peoples. They are instantly recognizable, being square, circular, or polygonal structures, usually box-like with a concentric 'ambulatory', and often set within enclosed precincts which may sometimes have preserved sacred groves from pre-Roman times.

At a much less formal level we find in Weardale a cavalry officer giving thanks to Silvanus (a Celtic rural god in Roman guise) for 'a remarkably fine boar no one had previously been able to catch' or at Greta Bridge two ladies setting up an altar to the local nymph. These are typical of the deep belief of both Celts and Romans that every place had its own deity. Romans found no difficulty in accepting these deities of place in the lands they conquered. Indeed, they showed real anxiety to find out their names and honour them, as a precaution if nothing else. The darker side was a belief in ghosts and the need to placate them. Here we are at the heart of Roman religion, very congenial to the Britons, the animistic belief in the localized spirits of hearth, home, family, and ancestors, and of places and objects outside, which long pre-dated the public adoption of the classical gods of Olympus. The black element is represented archaeologically by written curses, some still sickening to read. From Clothall near Baldock comes a lead plate bearing a message written backwards (a practice common in magic), declaring that 'Tacita is hereby

The Emperor's property. An administrative centre on an imperial estate. Artist's impression of the Hadrianic tower building, with reception hall added later in the second century, at Stonea in the Cambridgeshire Fens. Probably used for collecting rents and taxes, and issuing leases.

cursed, and this curse shall reveal her to be putrefying like rotting blood'. It is surely not just chance that excavation of a temple at Uley in Gloucestershire has approximately doubled the total of curse-bearing tablets known from the entire Roman world. The Britons, we are told by a classical source, were obsessed with ritual. The specifically Roman contributions were to provide new artistic and architectural forms to express religious feelings, and written language in which to make those sentiments clear and permanent. Roman religious practice, with that same sense that informed Roman law, depended on the exact performance of every act and word. The care with which the Romano-Briton phrased his dedications and curses demonstrates how well the new capacity to set wording down indelibly accorded with his own ritual inclinations.

After the invasion of Scotland, Antoninus Pius waged no more aggressive wars anywhere in the Roman world, and in the 160s the mood began to change. In Britain something had gone seriously wrong around 158. There is some evidence that the Brigantes had to be suppressed, a situation perhaps made possible by premature thinning out of troops on the ground in the Pennines under the demands of the occupation of southern Scotland; and it seems the Antonine Wall itself was temporarily lost. A brief reoccupation of Scotland, perhaps after a punitive campaign (though the chronology of this period in the north is exceptionally obscure), was followed by a definitive return to the Hadrianic line. In the reign of the next emperor. Marcus Aurelius, barbarian pressure on the frontiers of the empire generally became serious. The initiative, though Rome did not recognize it for centuries, had passed from her.

For a traveller arriving from the Continent, there was one particularly striking fashion in which Britain would have seemed different from northern Gaul, whose development it had in so many ways paralleled, allowing for the century less of time it had been under Roman rule. The permanent military presence will have made him aware that a primary concern of governors in Britain was always one of defence: there were three legions, two in the west in fortresses at Chester and at Caerleon in South Wales, and one in the north at York, together with a very large number of auxiliary units, many occupied in containing the nominally pacified tribesmen of the hills inside the province by means of a network of forts and patrolled roads. But the most visible difference in the south was the presence of *town walls*. The building of these walls was not (other than at one period) a general response to a particular crisis. It was a leisurely process, starting in the first century with towns such as Winchester and Verulamium and still in progress in the 270s. By the early second century the three prestigious colonies had walls; and an element of civic rivalry may have stirred elsewhere. The main reason for their walls, however, had to be something sufficiently important to overcome the reluctance of Roman emperors to allow the construction of fortifications that might be held by an enemy or insurgents (locals paid for the walls, but the emperor's express permission was required); and permanent enough for the process to continue even though Britain was several times implicated in major challenges to authority. Lack of defences to the villas rules out a disorderly countryside or fear of peasant revolt. The reason must be the same factor that kept the legions in the province and the auxiliary units stationed where they were—apprehension of barbarian incursions from outside and risings in the hills within the province. The cities and towns, lying on the main roads, were the obvious targets for tribes or war parties on the move. In the ancient world city walls were more or less impregnable, except to armies with sophisticated siege machinery and the logistic support necessary to sustain a prolonged siege, or where the attackers had friends within the town. Against tribesmen, therefore, walls were a first-rate form of civic defence; and their prevalence in Britain must indicate a much greater awareness of threat than was abroad in Gaul.

The walls, however, took a long time to build, and a speedier remedy was sometimes needed. An indication of impending crisis is the appearance on a large number of urban sites in

Roman road crossing Blackstone Edge, Yorkshire. The official network of communication served the needs of external and internal security and of administration, and incidentally promoted the spread of trade and ideas.

Britain of *earthwork* defences, apparently in the second half of the second century. At Cirencester, for example, an earth rampart was thrown up to link monumental stone city gates and interval towers already built, as if an urgent decision had been taken to interrupt the leisurely construction programme and put the defences into immediate commission. Of the various candidates that have been proposed for this period of crisis, the most likely seems the outbreak in the north around 180 which included barbarian penetration of the frontier, reported widespread damage, and the death of a Roman general. A much less likely context is the candidacy of a governor of Britain, Clodius Albinus, for the imperial throne in the years 193–7.

The events surrounding his attempt, however, herald a new age in the history of the empire, in the course of which Britain's fortunes diverged much more sharply from that of neighbouring Gaul. Marcus Aurelius' great wars on the Danube, which in the event marked the beginning of the unrelenting barbarian pressure in the West, might, had not his death intervened, have led to his achieving his aim of conquering Central Europe north of the Danube. Instead, the year 180 saw the breakdown of the system of nominating successors to the imperial throne that had produced a century of moderate and extremely able emperors. The accession of Marcus' dreadful son, Commodus, coincided in Britain with the outbreak of the serious warfare in the north mentioned above. In Britain and elsewhere, attempts to tighten up discipline in the Roman army had ironic consequences. A short period that saw a return to a rapid succession of murdered emperors and fresh outbreaks of civil war ended not only with the army in a much stronger position in society but with other profound changes in the system. The final victor, after the defeat of Clodius Albinus in Gaul, was the immensely tough Septimius Severus. But, far from being brought back to the disciplined loyalty of the previous hundred years, Severus' strategy for the survival of his own dynasty was to subordinate everything to the interests of the troops.

The third-century emperors abandoned the pretence of rule by consent. The senatorial class, which the second-century emperors had, with varying degrees of sincerity, tried to keep involved in the responsibilities of government, both civil and military, lost ground to the career soldiers who were providing the professional officers whom the army increasingly required. The old distinction between Roman citizens and provincials without the citizenship, already fading as more and more of the latter won Roman status, was now swept away and replaced by a new class structure before the law—an upper division (*honestiores*) and a lower (*humiliores*). Significantly, soldiers fell into the former category. By the middle of the century, rampant inflation had severely damaged confidence in the currency; and the old economic pattern of major centres of production serving very large areas of the Roman world by means of long-distance trade based on a money economy was tending to be replaced by more localized industries.

For the first quarter of the third century, Septimius Severus and his dynasty seemed to offer a renewed stability, even if one based on military autocracy. But that in itself was an insecure foundation. In the middle of the century, one assassinated emperor followed another in rapid succession as army officers changed their allegiances. The old, fatal weaknesses of personal ambition and the readiness of the Roman soldier to follow his commander were unchecked. At this point almost total disaster struck as barbarians attacked in both East and West. In the East a newly-invigorated Persian Empire captured the Emperor Valerian, while successive Germanic invasions wrecked the unwalled cities of Gaul and prevented Rome from any more shielding her towns and territories across the Rhine with a permanent military presence. By 260 much of the empire was in a sorry state.

It was formerly believed that Britain had been similarly devastated when Clodius Albinus' unsuccessful campaign on

Roman London: early second–century

the Continent against Severus was supposed to have stripped
Britain of troops and opened the way for a major barbarian
invasion. The archaeology will no longer support such a
hypothesis. Problems with the tribes beyond the northern
frontier towards the end of Severus' life did, however, give him a
reason to choose Britain to launch a new war of conquest. There
was no slackening of Roman ambition. Here the intention was
the total subjugation of Scotland, to complete the conquest of the
island. There is, indeed, cause to think that the interest of the
Severan House in Britain revived a province that had become
somewhat run down. Perhaps in connection with the imperial
visit itself, London was tidied up, given new public buildings,
provided with the longest circuit of walls in Britain and, at some
time in the Severan period, its waterfront magnificently re-
equipped with continuous quays running for more than half a
mile. While the war was being planned, the imperial household
itself probably settled at York. Much work had already been
undertaken on the forts of the north behind the Wall, many of
which seem to have been neglected, since the defeat of the
barbarian intruders in the early 180s. There is some reason to
think that York itself had assumed some of the governmental
functions formerly located at London, perhaps when the Antonine reoccupation of Scotland extended the lines of communication. Sometime early in the third century the city that had grown
up alongside the legionary fortress was dignified with the
honorary rank of Roman colony. It is not, therefore, surprising to

The provinces of Roman Britain

find London and York being chosen as twin capitals when, at some not entirely certain point in the Severan period, Britain was divided into two provinces. This was in line with a new policy to reduce the number of legions under the command of any one provincial governor and thus the temptation to revolt.

The planned conquest of Scotland was called off—but only after substantial successes—owing to the death of the emperor and the pressures on his successor. Security of the frontier was, however, accomplished. Britain as a whole shows every sign of having escaped the disasters of the age elsewhere. There was a slowing of new development, but the towns remained active and the villas were, if not expanded, kept up. Industry, if pottery is an indication, benefited from the problems of its rivals on the Continent. Some public work that might have been expected was not undertaken: restoration in the Fenlands after severe flooding, for example. But the defences of Britain continued to be refurbished, and new forts built on the south and east coast, at Brancaster and Reculver, probably for purposes of political control of the routes to the Continent and not yet indicative of an acute threat from sea-borne barbarians. In Gaul, AD 260 saw yet more trouble from the Germans—not yet by any means the worst—and the central government in Rome lost control. Germany, Gaul, Spain, and Britain adhered to an independent emperor, comprising together the 'Empire of the Gallic Provinces' (*Imperium Galliarum*). This grouping had been foreshadowed under Clodius Albinus and re-emerged later as a structural part of the restored empire. For the time being, however, possession of peaceful, prosperous Britain with its powerful and undamaged forces and its almost legendary propaganda value must have been a considerable comfort to the Gallic emperors.

Britain under the Late Empire

In the 270s the imminent collapse of the empire—imminent, that is, with hindsight—was averted. Romans did not behave then or later as if Rome could ever fall. Emperors and would-be emperors or emperor-makers did not cease murdering one another, but a series of great soldier-emperors nevertheless restored the military balance against the barbarians, put down rival administrations, and began to repair the physical and institutional fabric of the State. This was done to such an effect that the imperial system was enabled to survive another two centuries in the West (and might have lasted much longer) and twelve in the East. In 274 Britain was brought back under the central government when the Emperor Aurelian eliminated the Gallic Empire. Britain's immediate fate, however, was very different from that of the Gallic part of the former independent north-western state. In 276 the towns of Gaul were still unwalled when, as a literary source tells us, the worst of the barbarian invasions yet saw the capture of fifty or sixty towns and their retaking by the Romans. In north-eastern France archaeology has revealed the abandonment in the late third century of villa after villa in what had been a region outstanding for its extraordinarily dense pattern of really large country houses and their estates. These houses were not to be reoccupied.

In Britain the contrast is acute. In the period 250–70 there are signs of a modest amount of building and none of universal neglect, while archaeologists are tending to date an increasing amount of new construction, particularly of villas or of enlargements and improvements to villas, to around 270–5—for example in the villas of Witcombe and Frocester Court, on the western edge of the Cotswolds. An interesting hypothesis has been advanced that there was a 'flight of capital' from Gaul to Britain. There is no positive evidence for this theory yet, but if modified a little it is attractive. It is certainly true that the great age of the Romano-British villa, long recognized as being at its peak in the fourth century, must have had its beginnings in the 270s. It seems unlikely, however, that landowners could have 'extracted their capital' from their ruined Gallic estates (in other words, sold them at a good price). When these estates were reoccupied at the end of the century it was as abandoned land given over to settlers imported by government. Behind the argument, however, lies too parochial a view of land ownership,

Naive art. Late Roman bone decorative plaque, perhaps showing a city-goddess symbolizing Rome or Constantinople. From Great Casterton, Leicestershire.

an unspoken assumption that the typical provincial landowner possessed a single estate and lived in its villa most of the time. Possession of more than one estate was common among the upper classes of the Roman world, where wealth and status were quintessentially marked by landed property, sometimes in many parts of the empire simultaneously. For the pattern of Britain and Gaul at this period it is thus much more likely that owners with land on both sides of the Channel decided to transfer their personal residences from their Gallic villas to their properties in what must have seemed an exceptionally secure haven in an age of extreme danger; and the movement may already have started among the more cautious under the Gallic Empire. Perhaps a small piece of circumstantial evidence is that when the cities of Gaul finally were walled after 276, the circuits, though very strong, were in general short (quite unlike Britain), sometimes more like those of very powerful fortresses than walled towns. This is just what one would expect if there were no longer enough magnates with active local interests who could be tapped for the funds to defend the whole urban area.

Architecturally, the walls of these Gallic fortress cities do have close relations in Britain which are more or less contemporary, but they are not the towns. A number of new coastal fortresses were built in southern Britain—with the same pattern of very high stone walls and massive projecting towers—and older forts such as Brancaster and Reculver were modernized after the same fashion. At a much later date—in the fifth century—they are listed under a commander 'of the Saxon Shore', which has persistently suggested that they originated as a planned system of defence against Saxon sea-pirates. This is probably an anachronism. There is some reason to think that Aurelian's successor, Probus, created a tighter control of both sides of the Channel by establishing in Britain and Gaul similar strings of coastal forts; but the prime purpose has not been proven. The fact that Probus had more than once to quell serious moves against his authority in Britain may suggest that the 'Saxon Shore' had more at this stage to do with political security within the empire than frontier defence. Britain was an important asset—even more so in these straitened times—but control of the Channel was essential to its retention.

This fact was demonstrated in a remarkable fashion. In 287 a senior Roman officer named Carausius, who had been put in charge of a campaign to clear an infestation of pirates out of the Channel, came under strong suspicion of allowing the raids to happen and misappropriating the loot when it was subsequently seized by his fleet. Anticipating execution, Carausius rebelled and took control of Britain. Once again Britain was under the rule of a local emperor. This episode has attracted much romanticizing, but the fact is that neither Carausius nor other Romans before or after him who claimed the imperial title regarded Britain as something separate. Carausius is typical in blandly claiming on his coinage equality and fraternity with imperial colleagues, who, in fact, held the rest of the empire but with whom his fiction implied shared rule of the whole. The Carausian regime proved remarkably hard to dislodge, protected as it was by the sea. Carausius himself was unseated and murdered by Allectus, one of his own men, when he had lost a foothold on the Continent with the end of the siege of Boulogne in 293; but it was another three years before the central Roman government could launch a successful invasion. The Channel had proved formidable again.

Despite the fact that an element of inspired seamanship and a good deal of luck contributed greatly to the defeat of Allectus—not to mention what looks very much like lack of enthusiasm for his cause on the part of the regular garrison of Britain—in fact by 296 the rebel administration in Britain had faced a much more formidable central power. Major changes had taken place in the Roman State in those few years which move us into the period known as the 'Late Roman Empire'. The driving force was the Emperor Diocletian. Rooting himself in Roman precedent like Augustus, he initiated through his reforms a period of change that transformed the Roman State over half a century. He attempted to deal with the chronic political instability by creating a system of two senior emperors (*Augusti*) and two

AD 296. Gold medallion found at Arras, N. France, depicting Constantius I and his fleet, greeted by a personification of London, kneeling in front of the city in gratitude for rescue from the retreating Frankish troops of the defeated Allectus, successor of Carausius. Mint mark of Trier, at bottom.

juniors as 'Caesars', with automatic succession. The individual provinces were once again reduced in size, and now grouped in 'dioceses', under a new tier of civilian officers known as *vicarii* to whom the governors (no longer commanding armies) were now made responsible. The frontiers were strengthened by approximately doubling the units of the army, under new commanders. Against domestic conspiracy or military revolt a deliberate attempt was made to create a greater aura around the persons of the emperors. The overall increases in the civil service were noted as phenomenal. The effects on art, fashion, and manners were hardly less pronounced.

The economic ravages of the century had been acute. Manpower shortages were now tackled by imposing rigid controls on the movement of labour, making many occupations hereditary. The problem was exceptionally severe on the land. There, the estate system which under the Late Republic had relied on a ready supply of cheap slaves from foreign wars had, in the course of the Early Empire, moved extensively to letting-out to large numbers of free tenant farmers on short leases. The disastrous economic conditions of the third century over large parts of the empire encouraged drift from the land. In reply, Diocletian virtually created a tied peasantry (the *coloni*) by law. Inflation was—ineffectually—tackled by detailed price legislation (on British duffel coats, rugs, and beer, for example). Persons in the public service were increasingly protected by being paid partially or wholly in kind. Troops, who had formerly had to buy their personal equipment out of their pay, were henceforth supplied from state factories, while officials' allowances came to be valued as much as their salaries. Taxation soared to meet the cost of reform; and the new rigidity of society had to be further tightened against attempted avoidance of the specific tax liabilities imposed on certain classes in the social hierarchy.

The new order must have arrived in full force in Britain soon after the reconquest in 296 by the Caesar in the West, Constantius I, the father of Constantine the Great. His timely rescue of London from a retreating force of Frankish mercenaries who had been in the pay of Allectus was a huge propaganda victory. It will be seen to be prophetic in more ways than one.

Most of the disorder seems to have been in the south, confined to the short campaign when Allectus was defeated. In the north, archaeological evidence for vigorous rebuilding of military installations initiated by Constantius seems more to indicate an intention for the future than repair of damage caused by enemies. The evidence suggests that a lengthy period of peace had allowed maintenance and manning to have low priority. Constantius had different ideas. Indeed, an unconvincing contemporary denial strengthens the impression that he had every intention, when opportunity offered, of launching another of those prestigious campaigns in Scotland that seem to have appealed so much to ambitious Roman emperors. Certainly, he lost no time after he became Augustus in preparing for such a war, and in 306 he was in the field. The sources claim a victory over the Picts (the first time the enemy in Scotland appears under this name); and pottery of the period found at Cramond at the eastern end of the Antonine Wall and from the old Severan fortress on the Tay suggest another sweep up the eastern side of the Highlands as his plan. Like Severus, Constantius returned to York and there died. Like Severus he had had his successor with him.

In the elevation of Constantine the Great by the army, York can fairly be said to have witnessed one of the turning-points in history. It was a curiously haphazard affair, strongly influenced by a German king named Crocus in command of a unit of regular troops that had Germanic origins—and was completely contrary to the spirit of Diocletian's settlement. It set off a chain of events that ended with Constantine as sole emperor, putting into supreme power a man quite unlike Diocletian in having little adherence to the traditional past but like him capable of thinking and acting on the grandest scale. Constantine's innovations on the basis of Diocletian's conservative but immense reforms set patterns for centuries to come.

It has long been recognized that the first half of the fourth century was something of a 'golden age' for Roman Britain. We can now see that this was based on sound foundations from the previous century and continued trends already emerging in the 270s. This period of great prosperity certainly continued till the 340s, possibly till just after the middle of the century. It can legitimately be suspected that the most brilliant phase owed something to the favour of Constantine. There is some reason to suppose that, like his father, he too returned to Britain and celebrated military success here. We certainly know that for part of his reign he promoted to major status the mint at London that had been set up by Carausius. It is not impossible, too, that it was he who was responsible for changing London's name to 'Augusta'; and we may strongly suspect that the superb new river face of the walls of the fortress of York was a deliberate expression of the power of the man who had been proclaimed there, and who shared Hadrian's pleasure in vast architectural gestures.

The spirit of the age is typified by the great villas of fourth-century Britain. Socially and economically, the Late Empire in the West was marked by a polarization of wealth and to some extent power between the greater landed aristocracy on the one hand and emperor, court, and army on the other. These forces were often in conflict, but gradually tended to merge. Between them they left relatively little for the old urban middle class and the lesser gentry. Generally in the empire it was on the members of the local councils, the *curiales*, that the burden of paying for the new order fell most heavily. What had once been an honour now became a hereditary burden, and ways out were gradually sealed off by legislation.

Who, then, can have been the obviously wealthy inhabitants of the larger Romano-British villas? Some may have been rich citizens who had transferred themselves from elsewhere. If senators, or imperial officials of appropriate standing, they will have been exempt from the duties of *curiales*. Yet the curious persistence in Britain of forms of Latin indicative of educated speech but tending to be peculiar to the island does suggest that the native aristocracy remained a significant element in society. It is highly probable that they had, exceptionally, not been too badly hit in the previous century. It is tempting to wonder too, whether Constantine may not have shown them special favour.

Like the eighteenth-century English country house, to which they may in many respects reasonably be compared, these villas vary in plan, complexity, and size. Certain features are generally present—notably, construction in permanent materials, central heating (in the form of wood-, sometimes coal-fired hot air systems), glazing, tessellated floors, and very often one or more complete bath suites. Agricultural buildings normally adjoin, and like their Georgian counterparts it is probable that most had land attached. It is clear from Roman literature that the degree and importance to the individual occupier of any particular villa of its 'economic' activity could vary enormously, from being a major source of income to little more than an amusement. Significantly, the great houses such as Woodchester, Chedworth, or North Leigh did not stand alone, but formed the top of a very broad pyramid of villas. The modest villas that had developed in earlier times out of Iron Age farms survived, improved, or were replaced by new middle-range and small villas. This is the best evidence for the survival of a solid gentry in Britain. Some villas, it is true, disappear; but this is in the natural order of things even in a completely settled age. It is more important that in this age the villa is becoming a more prominent feature of the landscape, not less.

Grand mosaic from a villa of the early fourth century AD with a central roundel bearing a portrait of Christ. From Hinton St. Mary, Dorset.

It has been observed that villas often display duplication in their main facilities. This has led to a somewhat complicated hypothesis to suggest that surviving Celtic custom led to a widespread shared (or divided) use of one complex by two families or two owners. An infinitely simpler explanation is that in the Roman world a gentleman of any consequence travelled with a considerable retinue of servants and friends, and that visiting one another's country houses was part of the regular social round. For journeys, the reputation of inns was so evil that anyone with the right connections preferred to travel by moving from one acquaintance's villa to another. Most Romano-British villas seem to have been connected by a drive or lane to a public road and the majority were within ten miles or so of a town. Their social relationships to the towns, and perhaps even more to one another, are therefore likely to have been as important as their economic effects.

How much the development of the large villas changed the agricultural scene we do not know. As early as the second century an occasional pattern of villa and village has been observed which seems not unlike that of manor house and village in later ages. It may be that in fourth-century Britain there were comparatively few Diocletianic *coloni*—or that changes in the law made little difference to a situation that had long existed in this relatively undisturbed region of the empire. Small, native-style farms are still much in the majority, though there are some signs of consolidation into larger units. A greater change was the encouragement given to the various trades that served the decoration of the great houses. The best known of these are the regional 'schools' of mosaicists—firms or groups of firms with workshops centred respectively on Cirencester, Chesterton (Water Newton), Dorchester (Dorset), Brough-on-Humber, and somewhere centrally in the south. Other trades, working in more perishable materials, perhaps operated in similar fashion—for example fresco-painters (of whose work just enough survives to demonstrate its importance and the quality it could reach); furniture-makers; and other suppliers of major items for the well-to-do household.

The ancient countryside was not exclusively agricultural—nor only for the pleasure of the rich. The falling-off of long-distance trade in the third century had given encouragement to more than one British industry, for example the vast potteries of the Nene Valley. In the fourth century we can observe how a similarly huge ceramic industry in Hampshire which had also expanded in the third century—mostly within the area of the later royal forest of Alice Holt—now captured the London market and flourished greatly.

In these early years of the Late Roman period the principal features of the administrative system had emerged into which the new-style provincial governors fitted. Ultimate decisions might emanate from Milan (which emperors had for some time found more convenient than Rome) or, after 324, Constantinople. But from the time of Constantius I, the central government was for routine purposes situated at Trier, on the Moselle. The head of the civil administration as far as Britain was concerned was the praetorian prefect of the Gauls, based in Trier, to whom the *vicarius* of the British diocese was responsible. The prefecture grouped together Britain, Spain, and northern and southern Gaul. The headquarters of the British *vicarius* was almost certainly in London. Under him were four provincial governors—of Maxima Caesariensis (also probably based in London), Britannia Prima (Cirencester), Flavia Caesariensis (Lincoln?), and Britannia Secunda (York?), each with his own staff. As well as normal civil duties, this structure had a vital military role in being in charge of supply, including the new state factories (a weaving-mill of the sort that supplied the Late Roman army with material for uniforms is, for example, recorded in Britain). A fifth-century document, showing unusual insignia for the *vicarius* of the Britons, may denote that by that time at least he had, exceptionally, some troops under his command. More important is the fact that with supply in civilian hands there was some potential check on the army. Socially the senior members of this new administration were drawn from the educated middle and upper part of Roman society. The British vicariate could be an important stage in a fully professional career, and the men in the post of whom we know were not mediocrities. Into the beginning of the fifth century it remained policy not to employ men in their own provinces in senior posts, and most would expect to serve at some stage at the imperial court.

The financial administration of the provinces was very different from that in the Early Empire. Though the financial headquarters was again in London, the old provincial procurators had disappeared. The governors of the individual British provinces were responsible to the *vicarius* for the taxation in kind which the municipal councils were expected to raise from the individual taxpayer. Independent of the *vicarius*, however, were two other separate financial departments each with a diocesan chief officer, eventually responsible directly to the imperial secretariat. One handled taxation in cash, controlled the issue of coinage, and administered mines and certain other operations. The other was responsible for crown property throughout Britain, and to it reported the local procurators who acted as agents in charge. These two branches, however, often worked closely together and could call on the assistance of provincial governors to carry out their functions in the field.

The command structure for the army no longer had to correspond with provinces. At the same time the old distinction between legions and auxiliaries was replaced by a new one categorizing units into garrison, or frontier, troops (*limitanei*) and new, mobile field forces (*comitatenses*), the latter having higher status and remuneration. Many of the old units retained their identity, especially in Britain, where much of the old frontier remained substantially unchanged even if the internal character of units altered. At this time, the units stationed in Britain were classified as *limitanei*, emphasizing its character as a region to be defended rather than a place from which a field army might rapidly be deployed. The commander of a garrison army was entitled *dux*—the *dux Britanniarum* being one such. Mobile forces, on the other hand, tended to be led by a *comes rei militaris*, of superior rank. Under Constantine himself there was only one central field army. But under his warring sons several major field armies emerged, under generals of even higher rank. Certain of these army groups achieved permanence; and smaller task forces

Gold buckle, from the Thetford Hoard, depicting a satyr, the hoop in the form of opposed horses' heads. Probably intended as a presentation piece, to be worn in the insignia of a senior officer or official.

drawn from them became operative under such *comites rei militaris*.

The field armies contained both old units that had been retained or reformed and many new ones. Among the latter, an important proportion was raised from peoples of Germanic origin; and in the fourth century there were also many individual German recruits. Something like half the regular army in the West was German, and half Roman, including the officer corps. In 367 the *dux Britanniarum* defeated by barbarians, for example, was named Fullofaudes. By the end of the century, German generals were occupying the very highest commands. Though it was no longer fashionable for such men to adopt Roman names, they fully absorbed the attitudes and ambitions of their native-born Roman equals. However, as a group the fourth-century army officers tended to be noticeably different, culturally, from their counterparts of equivalent rank in the civil service. Important cultural prejudices, not to say dislike and contempt, appeared between certain emperors and their officers on the one hand and leading civilians on the other; and stresses between emperors, their courts, and their new capitals, and the old aristocracy that still looked towards Rome, became socially and politically important.

The final element in the Constantinian equation was the Church. The traditional public religion of the Roman State had sufficed for public purposes, but offered little to the individual. The breakdown of the Antonine peace and the crises of the third century coincided with a widespread desire for a more personal religion that offered consolation and meaning in this world and a better life in the next. Concomitantly, close contact with the East brought about the spread of various Eastern 'mystery religions', religions offering mystic revelation and personal contact with a deity. Hadrian himself had worshipped at the ancient shrine of the Eleusinian mysteries in Greece and a variety of mystery religions became respectable and accepted. The Persian cult of Mithras gained a powerful hold in military and commercial circles, where its insistence on high standards of probity and discipline and its tightly-bound brotherhood matched the ideals and interests of businessmen and officers. Unlike Christianity it was not politically suspect, and therefore not persecuted. In Britain, its chapels appear exclusively where the army or trading community were strong—at Rudchester, Carrawburgh, or Housesteads on Hadrian's Wall, and in London. Its weakness was its very exclusivity, closed to women and largely restricted to one social class. Its rites were sufficiently close to those of Christianity to make them appear blasphemous, and there are possible signs in London and at Carrawburgh, for example, of Christian attack during the Christian ascendancy, and it largely faded away during the fourth century.

Recent work on the survival of Roman Christianity in Britain after the end of Roman rule has suggested that it was more widespread and deeply-rooted than was formerly thought. It is important, however, not to read too much back from the fifth and sixth centuries into the third and fourth. It is generally agreed that Christianity had little hold in Britain before the fourth century. Third-century Britain had, indeed, its martyrs—St. Alban at Verulamium, SS Julius and Aaron probably at Caerleon. The fact that Britain fell in the part of the empire ruled by Constantius I, whose former wife was St. Helena, mother of Constantine, and who permitted the last great persecution to go no further in his area than the demolition of churches, may have had the negative effect of preventing a substantial early martyr cult in Britain. On the other hand, it may also have attracted well-to-do Christians to transfer their residences from more dangerous parts of the empire, unobtrusively increasing the villa-dwelling population.

Britain has produced the earliest set of church plate yet known from the Roman Empire (from Water Newton), almost certainly very early fourth century in date, while British bishops appear only a year after the 'Edict of Milan' legalized the Church, bearing titles indicating as their sees the capitals of the four British provinces. These facts draw our attention to the fundamental change that came with Constantine the Great. The growth of absolutism in the third century had been accompanied by sporadic imperial attempts to introduce a monotheistic state religion. From the time of Constantine the central new factor in Roman politics (and increasingly in the private sphere as well) was ideology. It was no longer sufficient to observe the customary formalities of the state religion to demonstrate loyalty: Christianity, as the new state religion, required belief. Toleration of pagan practices lasted for long. But it was gradually withdrawn, despite intense opposition during the whole of the fourth century from a powerful section of the Roman aristocracy, who both saw the old religion as central to Rome herself, and identified with it in opposition to the court. There were even to be short periods when there were pagan emperors again, sympathetic to them. Within the Church itself, however, there was a further development of immense significance for its future when the Emperor Constantius II decided that it was an imperial duty to ensure unity on doctrine. From the middle of the fourth century the hunting of heresy by the State added a new dimension to the politics of loyalty.

What must, therefore, surprise us in Britain is not that recent research has indicated a considerable amount of Christianization in the fourth century, but that there is not more. This will lead us to examine the apparent nature of the British church. The old notion of urban Christianity and rural paganism certainly cannot be sustained. Urban communities under Constantine are suggested by the bishops mentioned. A very small and unusual church excavated inside the walls at Silchester, and probable examples of the much more common cemetery churches over the graves of martyrs and other prominent Christians at Verulamium, Canterbury, and elsewhere, all point in the same direction. But the grand monuments of fourth-century Romano-British Christianity are associated with the villas: mosaics at Frampton and Hinton St. Mary, for example, or the wall-paintings of Lullingstone. The distribution of archaeological evidence suggests that the incidence of Christianity was very patchy. A cemetery at Dorchester in Dorset indicates a large and wealthy Christian community, supported by the surrounding villas; elsewhere similar cemeteries have nothing. A remarkable series of lead baptismal fonts has not come from cities but rural locations or small settlements, likely to have been under the eye of the landowning gentry, and a very substantial proportion of them has been found in East Anglia, where there is evidence of real personal wealth in the Late Roman period.

Constantine had dealt a massive blow both to the pagan cults and to the municipalities by distributing the endowments and treasures of the temples to the Church and by diverting funds from the civic treasuries. Wealth in the fourth century increasingly fell into the hands of the greater landowners, on the one hand, and of the State and its institutions, on the other. In Britain, where the villas are such an outstanding feature of the period, it is not surprising to find them in the forefront of the development of Christianity. Nor, under these circumstances, is it surprising to find the evidence so patchy. If the strength of Christianity in a district depended on whether the local landowner was an enthusiastic Christian (or politically ambitious) or not, then this is exactly what we might predict. If the erection of churches and other Christian monuments had depended on an energetic town council, as had the provision of public temples and other civic amenities in earlier periods, then the provision might have been relatively more even. It is clear that substantially more bishops from Britain were present at the Council of Rimini in 359, but no titles survive and it is therefore not known whether they were city-based. It is perhaps significant that some, at least, were known to have had difficulty in raising the money to pay their travelling expenses. If, then, the urban Christian communities were weak—or declined over the century after an initial Constantinian boost—what does this imply for the survival of Christianity after the end of Roman rule? The clue is perhaps the eventual reconciliation to Christianity of the landowning class as a whole elsewhere in the West, if it was paralleled in fifth-century Britain. In that period, quite unlike the fourth century, we ought to see a fairly uniform spread of Christianity among the rural population. Since most of the population had, anyhow, always lived on the land, that ought to lead us to expect the general persistence of Christianity, at least as a subculture. Indeed, the fact that in Late Roman times the rural clergy, unlike their urban counterparts, were relatively poorly educated and socially obscure (in the country, even bishops could be little more than dependants of landowners), may have assisted their identification with the agricultural multitude and ensured the survival of a Church as well as a faith, whatever eventually happened to the landed proprietors themselves.

How long did the villa-based society of the fourth century retain its brilliant early prosperity, so different from so many other parts of the empire? Describing a series of raids by barbarians on places near the frontiers of Britain in AD 360, the well-informed contemporary historian, Ammianus, tells us that at that time 'a pall of fear lay over the provinces' and adds, significantly, that they 'were already exhausted by the accumulation of disaster over the years'. The opinion, moreover, has been advanced, based on the archaeology of the towns, that the latter were 'finished' by about 350 (an opinion which we shall have to interpret later). Details apart, however, the picture is startlingly different from the earlier years of the century.

There is good reason to think that the 'golden age' did not long outlive Constantine himself. His death in 337 left the empire uneasily divided between three sons, Constantius II, Constans, and Constantine II. Britain came within the dominions of the younger Constantine. Dissatisfied with his share, he attacked Constans in 340 and suffered total defeat. It was a long time since the army of Britain had been involved in a military disaster. Subsequent weakness—and possibly disaffection—are probably reflected in a most unusual and unexpected journey across the winter Channel by Constans in person in 343, the brief surviving references to which hint at pressures on the northern frontier. Border problems were certainly acute by 360, the moment to which our quotation from Ammianus refers, when Scots from Ireland and Picts from Scotland had broken an agreement with Rome, implying that there had been earlier threats settled by diplomacy (and probably, in the usual style, with gold). In 364 they were back time and time again, now accompanied by 'Attacotti', probably also from Ireland, and by Saxons. The great barbarian invasion of 367, to which we shall come, was therefore the culmination of a long period of trouble from outside. But events at least as bad had occurred inside the territory under Roman rule.

In 350 a palace conspiracy ended in the murder of Constans and the elevation of an officer of Germanic descent named Magnentius. The Western part of the empire was now at war with the East, under the surviving son Constantius II. The three-and-a-half-year rule of Magnentius, Christian but tolerant

Late Roman defence. Town wall of Caerwent, Gwent, built in the second half of the fourth century AD.

of pagans, proved disastrous in its consequences. Constantius II, whom we have already seen assuming the duty of suppressing Christian heresies, also hated paganism—indeed he reintroduced the death penalty for its observance and scandalized the senate by removing the ancient Altar of Victory from the Senate House in Rome. With his final victory, Britain came under special scrutiny. The appointment of the head of the imperial establishment records office, one Paulus, was made with the aim of hunting down dissidents in the island. Black humour aptly nicknamed him 'The Chain'. His brief was to arrest certain military men who had supported Magnentius, but he soon extended this, unchecked, into a reign of terror in which false evidence played a dominant part, horrifying even the most loyal officers. Constantius' own *vicarius* of Britain, Martinus, sacrificed himself in a brave but unsuccessful attempt to put an end to Paulus. One cannot but suspect that many leading families which had been implicated in incidents in the past half-century were drawn into this whirlpool, in addition to those involved in current politics. Confiscations, exile, imprisonment, torture, and executions were approved by the emperor without any questioning of the evidence. The confiscations of property alone must have had a profound effect on the landed prosperity of Britain, while the devastation of morale among both civilians and army can only have left them in a weaker state to resist the barbarian troubles now pressing in on them.

The nadir came in 367. Picts, Scots, and Attacotti invaded Britain; Franks and Saxons attacked the coast of Gaul. Both the central imperial command—the Emperor Valentinian himself was in northern Gaul—and the senior officers responsible for Britain were taken by surprise. The *dux* in command of the static garrison of Britain was put out of action and the *comes* in charge of coastal defence killed. The most remarkable event was the concerted action of such disparate barbarians. Treachery by native frontier scouts in the north is one attested part of the situation, but to account for the total operation we have to suppose an unknown barbarian with extraordinary military and diplomatic ability. Detailed knowledge of Roman dispositions and understanding of Roman military methods were not hard to come by, with so many Germans in the Roman army (though conscious disloyalty to Rome is very rarely indeed to be suspected). What convinces one of inspired barbarian leadership is the fact of simultaneous attacks by peoples with very different cultures, from homelands relatively distant from one another, with a very clever division of targets—and, perhaps most of all, with the maintenance of complete secrecy. The Romans certainly called it a conspiracy, and it is difficult not to agree with them.

Once in Britain, the barbarians ranged unchecked in small bands, looting, destroying, taking prisoners, or killing at will. The countryside near to roads must have been particularly vulnerable and not all walled towns seem to have resisted. Both civil authority and military discipline broke down. Troops deserted, some claiming—unconvincingly—to be on leave. Political opportunists seized their chances. Britain was being used as a place of dignified exile for high-ranking offenders, and one well-documented conspiracy among them was nipped in the bud just after the Roman recovery of Britain. But there is also some evidence that one of the provinces of the British diocese (which had now been divided into five, rather than four) fell temporarily into the hands of rebels.

The response of Valentinian to the calamity was the dispatch of a small but powerful task force of élite troops under a *comes rei militaris*, Theodosius, who was the father of the later Emperor Gratian and grandfather of Theodosius the Great, and whose own father had himself served as a *comes* in Britain, under Constans. Such task forces became a frequent method of dealing with emergencies under the Late Empire: Britain had at least once already been the scene of such an expedition (in 360), possibly more than once. At this time these forces were usually made up of *comitatenses*. From the end of the fourth century, barbarian war bands under their own kings, even whole tribes, became more and more often accepted into Roman armies. Task forces thereafter tended to be made up of a mixture of whatever regular troops could be found and barbarian allies, or sometimes barbarians alone on contract for a specific campaign or operation. Looking forward, it is important to realize that in the fifth century, as military practice evolved out of that of the fourth century, 'the barbarians' were not like some hostile aliens from outer space but were a familiar fact of life. Barbarian warriors were frequently employed against other barbarians in the suppression of internal disorder, and for the prosecution of Roman civil wars.

Theodosius' conduct of the campaign and subsequent reconstruction of Britain seems to have been both brilliant and thorough. London was spectacularly relieved. Garrison troops were reassembled, deserters pardoned, and an effective army recreated. The barbarian war parties on land were picked off one by one and the Saxons defeated at sea. Goods stolen from the provincials were recovered and returned. Civil authority was restored under a new *vicarius*; the province that had been lost to rebels was regained and named Valentia in honour of Valentinian, and his eastern colleague and brother, Valens. Forts were rebuilt and damaged cities restored.

The extensive remodelling of town defences in Britain by the addition of prominent external towers, dated archaeologically to somewhere in the middle of the fourth century, is more convincingly to be attributed to Theodosius' initiative than to any other, although the variety in design and arrangement does suggest that, once again, the cost and responsibility fell on the local councillors. However, the fact that it is always the full circuit that was retained in use has very important implications for the state of the towns in the middle and late fourth century. Such wide circuits cannot have been kept solely to provide military strong points or even as refuges in time of danger for a dispersed rural population. There was something worth while defending with permanent works. What, then, are we to make of the notion that the towns of Britain were 'finished' by about 350? The unspoken assumption that fourth-century towns were of the same sort as those of the second is clearly mistaken. We have, of course, to be careful not to assume that all towns changed in the same ways. Yet the decay or disuse of civic public buildings is hardly surprising in the context of municipal treasuries raided by central government and councils made up of now unwilling members. Fourth-century legislation repeatedly tried to prevent members of the class that now had the hereditary obligation to serve from moving their main residences away from the towns, while those in higher social classes were exempt from municipal obligations. The new element in society was the vastly-expanded bureaucracy, and it is in their direction that we should probably be looking. Five governors, their staffs, households, companies of guards, and the many others connected with them needed housing; and there were numerous other officials with inflated establishments and life-styles supported by substantial allowances. At each level in the hierarchies, expectations existed which in the end filtered down from the lavish grandeur of the Late Roman court. Large areas of fourth-century capitals such as Trier or Arles, once normal municipalities, were given over to palaces and other associated official buildings. On a smaller scale, we ought to expect such a pattern in many towns in Britain. In fact, archaeology has demonstrated the building of large town houses in places as different as London and Carmarthen, and urban development into the middle of the fifth century at Verulamium and, of a distinctive sort, at Wroxeter. In the cultivated open spaces of this period observed within the city walls in excavations we should perhaps see the gardens and grounds of the new-style establishment rather than a decay represented by abandoned building sites. Indeed, in London and York at least we may reasonably expect the presence of emperors themselves from time to time to have made a mark on the archaeological record.

There is no reason to think that the Theodosian restoration was other than outstandingly successful. Archaeologically, it is clear that many villas continued in occupation; some were enlarged and others built from scratch. Hadrian's Wall was occupied to the end of Roman rule, even if individual garrisons were smaller than before. A new system of signal stations was established on the north-east coast. Much industry had been interrupted by the war of 367, but the many changes in pattern after it indicate vigour and new initiatives. Not surprisingly, some pagan religious sites disappear, but others continue in cult use, while still others show signs of conversion to new uses, some perhaps Christian, towards the end of the century. The forty years from 369 do not have the brilliance of the early fourth century, but the island does not provide any evidence for the sort of despair that the historians report for the 50s and 60s. In order to understand what happened in 409 it is important to realize that in the last part of the fourth century Roman Britain had not been running rapidly downhill.

This period is, in fact, marked by two more occasions on which major attempts on the imperial throne were launched from a base in Britain. In 382 a victory over the Picts by a general named Magnus Maximus (Macsen Wledig in Welsh legend) created for him a reputation that led to proclamation as emperor and the rule, for five years, of the part of the empire represented by the Gallic prefecture—Britain, Gaul, and Spain. In Britain, some forts, notably in the Pennines and Wales, were abandoned at this time and the Twentieth legion was withdrawn from Chester, but it remains still entirely uncertain whether Maximus' campaigns and eventual defeat at the hands of the Emperor Theodosius the Great had any significant overall effect on the defensive capability of the army in Britain. Between 392 and 394 Britain was peripherally involved in another palace revolt for the duration of which Theodosius lost control of the Western empire, but the significance of this incident lies more in the appearance of a general, a Frank in this case, overshadowing a compliant emperor in the West. The death of Theodosius in 395 made this new balance of power in the Western imperial government the rule, rather than the exception, for the rest of its history. The joint accession of Theodosius' sons, Honorius in the West, and Arcadius in the East, inaugurated a period in which the pattern of government in the two halves of the empire diverged fundamentally. In the East, it remained firmly in the hands of the emperor, or his chief civilian minister. In the West a powerful landed aristocracy, rooted in its estates, vied for influence with the professional soldiers who commanded the armies. After three-quarters of a century, both these parties were to come to the conclusion that they could manage without an emperor in the West.

The End of Roman Rule

The effective control of the West by the late Emperor Theodosius' chief lieutenant, Flavius Stilicho, Vandal by birth, was accompanied by a claim to the East as well. Plot, counterplot, and civil war between Stilicho, Honorius, the Western senate, and the Goths under Alaric did much to ensure in the long term the collapse of Roman rule throughout the West. In Britain, initial successes against Picts, Scots, and Saxons, and restoration of defences under Stilicho's direction were probably followed at the very beginning of the fifth century by some posting elsewhere of troops. We do not know the extent of the postings, but the cessation of bulk import of new coinage in 402 must mean that neither remaining regular troops nor civil officials were henceforth paid from central sources. It is not surprising that we find a mood of extreme discontent. In 406 the army in Britain elevated the first in a rapid succession of three emperors. On the last day of that year, large numbers of barbarians crossed the Rhine. The central government withdrew the administration of the prefecture of the Gauls to Arles, and had no time to deal with usurpers in Britain.

The third usurper ran true to form, seizing Gaul and Spain, and for some while was recognized as a legitimate colleague by the unwilling Honorius. Once again, we do not know if there was an overall reduction in the garrison of Britain, but some further withdrawal of regular units seems likely. The north-western empire of Constantine III, however, was to be the last of its kind, and before it was finally extinguished Britain had ceased for ever to be under any sort of imperial rule.

We know tantalizingly little about the process by which this happened, but something can be pieced together. In 408 the absence of the bulk of Constantine's army in Spain left him unable to deal with heavy barbarian attacks on Britain. In 409 the mutiny of that army under its British-born commander (and his deliberate incitement of the barbarians in Gaul) coincided with renewed assaults on Britain by enemies who included Saxons. At this point, Britain, too—along with parts of Gaul—rebelled, expelling Constantine's administration. Britain successfully took on the barbarian invaders, and henceforth broke decisively with Roman rule.

How Britain expelled the invaders and what was then the state of the country can only be the subject of informed speculation. There are slight hints that Stilicho and Honorius had taken some steps to encourage local organization of, or payment for, defence. It is most unlikely that the regular army was retained when Constantine's officers were deposed, or that the elaborate administrative structure which supported it was manned and paid. Under the Late Empire, the landed class strongly resisted both the conscription of the agricultural labour force into the regular army and the payment of taxes. Elsewhere in the fifth century units whose pay stopped disbanded and dispersed or settled on the land. Indeed, from AD 455 the final running-down of the Western regular army seems to have been in progress. In Britain, with no central government, it is all the more likely that in the years from 409 groups of barbarians were paid to undertake the fighting, and some of these may already have been brought in under Constantine III or even Stilicho.

There is no sound reason for thinking that the Britons elevated any more emperors, or recreated any of the mechanisms of central government. Not only had very few of them had experience of senior office (unlike recent Gallo-Romans), but if they shared the sentiments of the landed class elsewhere in the fifth-century West, they are most unlikely to have wanted to reassume the burdens of supporting the system of imperial administration once they had been rid of it. The critical success of the Flavian governors of Britain in the first century had been to convince the native aristocracy that its advantage lay with Rome. There is no good reason to think that the events of 409 had destroyed the position of the landowning class. They are, however, very likely indeed by now to have lost confidence in the system of emperor, bureaucracy, and army as the best way of securing their still prosperous way of life. They will not have been encouraged by the ruthless political persecution in Gaul by Honorius' officers after the fall of Constantine III.

The presence of a full paper establishment of military and civil posts for Britain in the *Notitia Dignitatum* suggests that into the fifth century it was assumed centrally in the imperial ministries that Britain would be recovered—as it had so often been in the past. There was, in fact, only one short period, from 425 to 429, when a Roman military intervention in Britain was again a serious possibility. But by that time other groups of well-to-do Roman provincials, particularly in a large area of Gaul, were starting to settle down tolerably comfortably, employing, in alliance with, or under the rule of, barbarians.

Provided that the barbarians remained amenable, any of these arrangements might suit the gentry better than direct imperial rule. But for the weakened middle and artisan classes, who in the fourth century had depended more and more on the army, civil service, and urban church for jobs, patronage, or markets, the change must have been disastrous. In Britain, the Roman archaeology supports such a picture. Early in the fifth century, the massive pottery industry comes to an apparently abrupt end; by 420–30 coinage ceases to be in regular use. These facts, incidentally, make the dating of the end of the occupation of Roman sites in the fifth century much more difficult than in earlier periods. There is, however, certainly no evidence for villas having come generally to a violent end. Signs of how late towns might be active vary a good deal. At Lincoln we find a main street being resurfaced well into the fifth century; in London imported Mediterranean pottery in the ash of the heating system of one house combines with other evidence to suggest normal occupation in the early fifth century; the forum at Cirencester was being kept up after the cessation of general circulation of coins; and at Verulamium a sequence of important buildings succeeding one another on the same site is closed, strikingly, by the laying of a new water-main at a time that cannot be far short of the middle of the century.

After the break with Rome the Britons, we are told, lived under *tyranni*, or 'usurpers', best interpreted as local potentates who had filled the vacuum left by the removal of legitimate authority. Their background was probably very varied, some perhaps landowners, others military men, Roman or barbarian, who had been invited to take control or seized power. At Gloucester, a rich warrior burial is British in character rather than Saxon, and may represent a *tyrannus*, or a *condottiere* in local pay. At Wroxeter, ambitious fifth-century timber buildings may well represent the headquarters of such a leader.

In 429 St. Germanus, a prominent Gallo-Roman bishop who moved in high Roman circles, visited Britain to combat heresy, debating publicly with British magnates at Verulamium 'conspicuous for their riches, brilliant in dress, and surrounded by a fawning multitude'. This visit to Britain he repeated around 446/7, though apparently in deteriorating circumstances. At least until the 440s, therefore, something survived in Britain that was very like 'post-Roman' or 'post-imperial' life elsewhere in the West.

JOHN BLAIR

2. *The Anglo-Saxon Period*

(*c*.440–1066)

The Age of the Settlements

THE sources for the fifth and sixth centuries are so few that they
can all be listed here, and so unsatisfactory that their faults must
be clearly stated. On the one hand is the archaeological evidence,
mainly objects from graves in pagan cemeteries. This evidence
cannot lie, but the questions which it answers are strictly limited.
On the other hand is a small group of texts, annals, and
fragments. Of these the only substantial contemporary work is
The Ruin of Britain, a tract written in the 540s by a British monk
named Gildas whose purpose was to denounce the evils of his
day in the most violent possible language. The Venerable Bede, a
monk in the Northumbrian monastery of Jarrow, completed his
great *Ecclesiastical History of the English People* in 731. This
overshadows all other sources for the seventh and early eighth
centuries, and although the invasion period was remote from
Bede's own day he provides some surprisingly well-founded
scraps of tradition. The only other narrative sources are fragments of chronicles preserved in later compilations, a few
poems, and passing references by Continental writers. Of a very
different kind are the late Saxon annals known collectively as *The
Anglo-Saxon Chronicle*, which give a year-by-year summary of
events in the southern English kingdoms. The early annals are
much less reliable than those for later centuries, and their
chronological framework is suspect before the late sixth century.

Thus there is no near-contemporary source of Anglo-Saxon
origin. The reason is obvious enough: the Germanic peoples
were illiterate during their first two centuries in Britain. So their
early fortunes can only be glimpsed through the hostile eyes of
Britons, through the ill-informed eyes of foreigners, and by
means of their own half-remembered traditions. Until the late
sixth century, informed guesswork must make do for history.

Archaeology provides the first clue, for it shows that there were Germanic warriors in Britain some years before 410. Late Roman cemeteries, especially along the Lower Thames Valley from Oxfordshire to the Essex coast, have produced burials with belt-fittings of a type worn by Frankish and Saxon mercenaries in the Roman army. If such troops were settled in Britain, as they certainly were in Gaul, the mid-fifth-century invaders may have joined relatives who had come two or three generations back. Sunken huts with gable-posts are characteristic of English settlement in the fifth and sixth centuries, and over two hundred of these have been found at a huge site near Mucking on the Thames estuary. It has been suggested that this complex housed mercenaries who were settled in *c*.400 to guard the approach to London. If so, the continuous history of Anglo-Saxon settlement begins under Roman rule.

The English of later centuries dated their ancestors' arrival some decades after this, and it does seem to have been from the 430s onwards that Germanic settlers arrived in large numbers. Before considering this remarkable process, it must be asked who the invaders were and what they were like. The first question is answered, almost as well as any modern scholar can answer it, in a startlingly well-informed passage quoted by Bede from an unknown source:

They came from three very powerful Germanic tribes, the Saxons, Angles and Jutes. The people of Kent and the inhabitants of the Isle of Wight are of Jutish origin, and also those opposite the Isle of Wight, that part of the kingdom of Wessex which is still today called the nation of the Jutes. From the Saxon country, that is, the district now known as Old Saxony, came the East Saxons, the South Saxons and the West Saxons. Besides this, from the country of the Angles, that is, the land between the kingdoms of the Jutes and the Saxons, which is called *Angulus*, came the East Angles, the Middle Angles, the Mercians, and all the Northumbrian race (that is those people who dwell north of the River Humber) as well as the other Anglian tribes. *Angulus* is said to have remained deserted from that day to this.

Archaeology confirms Bede's analysis: objects found in English graves are comparable to those from North Germany and the southern half of the Danish peninsula. Some urns from the fifth-century cremation cemeteries in East Anglia may even be work of the same potters as urns found in Saxony, and Kentish pottery and jewellery resembles material from Jutland. A district north-east of Schleswig is called to this day Angeln. To Bede's list we can probably add Frisians, mixed with Saxons who seem to have been infiltrating the coastal settlements of Frisia in the early fifth century. Even Bede's statement that some of the homeland settlements were deserted is confirmed by excavations at Feddersen Wierde, near the mouth of the Weser. Here a village of large

timber buildings was abandoned in *c*.450, apparently in consequence of rising sea-levels. With the natural fertility of lowland
Britain, and the evidence that its inhabitants deliberately
imported mercenaries, this flooding of coastal settlements helps
to provide an explanation for the Migrations.

Bede's racial division of the kingdoms of his own day is
probably over-neat. The men of Kent may well have been mainly
Jutish, and the other major peoples certainly thought themselves
either 'Angles' or 'Saxons'. But archaeology does not suggest a
very firm distinction, and by the late sixth century, when the
kingdoms emerge into the light of day, there is much blurring at
the edges. Thus, the finest metalwork of the East Angles
resembles that of Kent, and their royal dynasty seems to have
been Swedish. Sea-passage must have weakened ethnic ties, and
new types of settlement and social organization apparently
developed to suit the needs of pioneer colonists. It is worth
noting, for instance, the contrast between the large rectangular

*Belt-set of c.*AD 410–20 from a
grave at Mucking, Essex.
Such fittings were worn by
late Roman auxiliary troops,
but the decoration is
Germanic. This object must
have belonged to one of the
very first Anglo–Saxon
settlers, perhaps employed as
a mercenary immediately
after Roman troops were
withdrawn.

halls at Feddersen Wierde and the formless clusters of little sunken huts which are found on English sites. What mattered was not so much that the settlers were Angles, Saxons, or Jutes, as that they belonged to the same broad culture as southern Scandinavia, Germany, and northern France. Their earliest known poems include hero-legends set in Denmark and Frisia; an early seventh-century East Anglian king possessed Swedish and Gaulish treasures; and Christianity reached England through a Kentish king's marriage with a Frankish princess. Britain exchanged the Roman Empire for another, if very different, international community.

What were these people like? Obviously they were far less civilized than the Romans, yet they had their own institutions which proved astonishingly tough. Much that the first-century historian Tacitus wrote of the *Germani* applies to their distant descendants in England. As with the *Germani*, so throughout Anglo-Saxon history, the strongest social bonds were the claims of kinship and the claims of lordship.

Kin-groups were close-knit in the homeland, and they remained so in England. The families and dependants of one man may sometimes have formed their own settlement units, with shared resources and systems of land-allotment. The influence of such extended 'affinities' on the character of the settlements is shown by the numerous place-names ending *-ing*, *-ingham*, and *-ington*. Hastings means 'the people of Haesta', Reading 'the people of Reada', Wokingham 'the farm of Wocca's people', and so on. Although it is now thought that not all of these names belong to the first settlement phase, many are early and important and refer to large tracts of land. They show that when territories came to be defined, it was often in terms of the tribal groups which had settled them. Society developed, but family loyalties remained vital. Safety lay in knowing that relatives would avenge one's death, and to neglect such vengeance meant undying shame. Already in Tacitus' day, however, honour might be satisfied by a *wergild*, a payment by the slayer to his victim's kin. Anglo-Saxon law codes list scales of *wergilds* in accordance with the victim's rank, and kings increasingly encouraged this non-violent type of retribution.

Tacitus also stresses the loyalty of the *Germani* to their lords. Sometimes they had hereditary kings, but in battle they were usually led by elected chiefs: 'It is a lifelong infamy and reproach to survive the chief and withdraw from the battle. To defend him, to protect him . . . is the essence of their sworn allegiance.' Nine centuries later, in 991, an Anglo-Saxon army was defeated by Vikings at Maldon on the Essex coast. By then England was a civilized state, long since Christianized; yet the words which a contemporary poet ascribes to one of the defenders after his leader's death are a clear echo of Tacitus:

> 'I swear that from this spot not one foot's space
> Of ground shall I give up. I shall go onwards,
> In the fight avenge my friend and lord.
> My deeds shall give no warrant for words of blame
> To steadfast men on Stour, now he is stretched lifeless,
> —That I left the battlefield a lordless man,
> Turned from home. The irons shall take me,
> Point or edge.'

Clearly, loyalty to lord might sometimes conflict with loyalty to kin. In the interests of good order and their own authority, later kings tended to promote lordship: thus King Alfred's laws allow any man to 'fight on behalf of his born kinsman, if he is being wrongfully attacked, except against his lord, for that we do not allow'. But on both counts, Anglo-Saxon society always set great store by faithfulness and the keeping of oaths.

Their principal gods were those of later Norse mythology, Tiw, Woden, and Thor. They are remembered in the day-names Tuesday, Wednesday, and Thursday, as well as in a few place-names (Tuesley (Surrey), Wednesday (Staffs.), Thursley (Surrey), etc.) which presumably indicate cult centres. Even when converted, the English named one of the main Church festivals after their old goddess Eostre. Shrines, like those of the *Germani*, were in remote places, in woods or on hills: a few place-names include the element *hearg* (shrine), as at Peperharrow (Surrey) and Harrow-on-the-Hill. Since later Church councils forbade the veneration of 'stones, wood, trees and wells', it can be presumed that such activities featured in pagan English cults. At least in its outward forms, this religion does not look so very different from that of the pagan Britons under Roman rule.

The narrative of events before *c*.600 does not amount to much. Plagued by the Picts and Scots, says Gildas, the British under the 'proud tyrant', Vortigern, imported the first Saxons to defend the east coast. Bede and other sources add that the Saxons were led by brothers named Hengist and Horsa, who founded the kingdom of Kent, and date their landing to about 450. Although this is rather too late, the tale is very consistent with the archaeological evidence: if Germanic mercenaries were settled under Roman rule, it is entirely likely that the successor states continued the same policy. Then, according to Gildas, the mercenaries rebelled and attacked their hosts; many years of inconclusive warfare followed, culminating in a major British victory, perhaps in c.500, at an unidentified place called *Mons Badonicus*. Meanwhile, the *Chronicle* notes the arrival of other chieftains on the south coast, the semi-legendary ancestors of later kings: Aelle in Sussex in 477, and Cerdic and Cynric in Wessex in 495.

One figure from these years who is familiar to everyone is, of course, Arthur. Unfortunately he has only the most shadowy claims to historical reality. The two or three possible fragments of genuine tradition were written down centuries later, and the legends which have gathered around his name are romantic inventions from the twelfth century onwards. We can only say that there seem to have been memories of a British war-leader called Arthur, who was associated with the battle of *Mons Badonicus* and subsequent campaigns. Possibly there was such a chieftain or over-king, the last man to unite the former Roman province before it collapsed finally into a patchwork of British and Anglo-Saxon states. So general is our ignorance of major political events that there seems little point in speculating further.

Gildas says that the peace won at *Mons Badonicus* lasted until his own time, fifty years later, when there were five British kingdoms ruled by wicked 'tyrants'. How far their power still extended into the future English lands is a matter for conjecture, but the re-fortification of hilltop sites in the south-west suggests many years of inconclusive skirmishing. Through all this time, as excavated cemeteries prove, the invaders were pushing steadily further inland, up the Thames Valley, westwards from East Anglia, and northwards from Wessex. The *Chronicle* shows the Wessex Saxons advancing into Wiltshire in the 550s; capturing a large block of the South Midlands in 571; and winning a decisive battle at Dyrham (Glos.) which gave them Gloucester, Ciren-cester, and Bath in 577. Meanwhile, other English kingdoms were emerging from the shadows: the East Angles, the East Saxons, the Mercians, and the Northumbrian kingdoms of Bernicia and Deira. By the end of the century we are again on the firm ground of some reliable facts, and find the invaders in permanent control of half the island.

What had happened to the native peoples? Sixth-century Scotland was still mainly Pictish, though the settlements of Irish (the future 'Scots') on the west coast had created a settled kingdom, Dalriada. Centuries later, a king of Dalriada was to initiate the formation of a united Scotland. There were also three northern British kingdoms: Strathclyde, centred on Dumbarton,

England in c.600

Rheged on the Solway Firth, and Elmet in the region of Leeds.
Northumbrian designs on the Picts were ended by a major defeat
in 685, and expansion here was mainly at the expense of the
Britons. Strathclyde survived, but Rheged and Elmet were
swallowed up by Northumbria during the late sixth and seventh
centuries.

The main British enclave was, of course, Wales. Refugees from
the east had doubtless swelled its population. Christianity
survived, and with it some distinct traces of Roman culture.
Scores if not hundreds of little monasteries were probably
founded there during the sixth century, and charters from
south-east Wales suggest the continuance of functioning Roman
estate units. The kingdoms of Gwynedd, Dyfed, Powys, and
Gwent existed by c.550, and some minor kingdoms by the end of
the century. At least two of Gildas's tyrants ruled in Wales:
Maglocunus (Maelgwn) of Gwynedd, 'first in evil, mightier than

many both in power and malice', and Vortipor (Gwrthefyr) of
Dyfed. Vortipor's monument still remains in a Dyfed
churchyard—a reassurance that some substance underlies the
rantings of Gildas:

Your head is already whitening, as you sit upon a throne that is full of guiles and
stained from top to bottom with diverse murders and adulteries, bad son of a
good king . . . Vortipor, tyrant of the Demetae. The end of your life is gradually
drawing near; why can you not be satisfied by such violent surges of sin, which
you suck down like vintage wine—or rather allow yourself to be engulfed by
them? Why, to crown your crimes, do you weigh down your wretched soul with a
burden you cannot shrug off, the rape of a shameless daughter after the removal
and honourable death of your own wife?

Cornwall, Devon, and Somerset formed the British kingdom
of Dumnonia. Its king, according to Gildas, was as bad as the
others: 'Constantine, tyrant whelp of the filthy lioness of
Dumnonia.' The inhabitants were pushed back by the Anglo-
Saxons during the seventh and eighth centuries, though Cornwall held out until 838. Thanks to this relatively late conquest,
much survived. Excavation suggests that in some of the old
cities, especially Exeter, Dorchester (Dorset), and Ilchester, life of
a sort trickled on through the fifth and sixth centuries. Many
major churches in these counties have Celtic origins: excavations at Wells in 1978–80 revealed a sequence of religious
buildings from a late Roman mausoleum to the Anglo-Saxon
cathedral. Here, as in Wales, smaller churches can often be traced
back to a Celtic monastic enclosure (*llan*) or a cemetery around a
martyr's grave (*merthyr*).

The hardest task is to estimate British survival in the regions
which were firmly Anglo-Saxon by 600. From the facts that
England in 1086 probably contained less than half its late Roman
population, and that even this was after growth during the tenth
and eleventh centuries, it is clear that depopulation in the fifth
and sixth centuries was indeed drastic. Many fled westwards, or
else to Brittany, and epidemic disease may have played its part.
More generally, the Romano-Britons simply suffered a common
fate of shattered societies; the decline in numbers is perhaps the
clearest sign that their society *was* shattered. This is not to say
that none remained: there are hints that the population contained substantial British elements, especially in the north and
west. Sometimes (in the early Kentish laws, for instance) they
appear as peasants or perhaps semi-servile estate labourers—
which helps to explain how elements of Roman land organization may have passed into English society. Significantly, the
English word *Wealh* ('Welshman', i.e. Briton) came to mean

'slave', making it hard to know whether the place-name Walton means 'the Britons' settlement' or 'the slaves' settlement'. However numerous, they were subservient: little of their culture passed to the Anglo-Saxons, and almost none of their language.

The early Anglo-Saxons were a non-urban people: their important places were important for hierarchical rather than economic reasons. But the view that they looked on the crumbling Roman towns with nothing but superstitious fear goes too far. The English knew what a *ceaster* was (the word is used with remarkable consistency), and often they knew its Roman name: *Mamucion* becomes *Mame-ceaster* (Manchester), *Venta* becomes *Ventan-ceaster* (Winchester), and so on. Towns occupied focal points in the road system, and their walls were strong. They were good places for chieftains to make their headquarters, and some towns may never quite have lost their local administrative functions. This does not, of course, amount to urban life: the Roman towns were not toally abandoned, but *as towns* they died.

Why was Roman Britain obliterated so much more completely than Roman Gaul? One reason is that the settlers were different: the Franks and Visigoths had come to know far more about Roman ways than the Angles and Saxons ever did. But it may also be true that the Britons themselves had changed greatly between the early fifth and mid-sixth centuries. The earliest Welsh poems show a society remarkably like that of the Saxons, dominated by the same loyalties and with the same emphasis on treasure, gift-giving, and the fellowship of warriors in their chieftain's hall. Even if no Saxon had ever set foot in Britain, it may be that its Roman civilization would have proved too fragile to last.

The Seventh Century

The first impression of early seventh-century England is that it was divided into large kingdoms: Kent, Sussex (the South Saxons), Wessex (the West Saxons), East Anglia, Essex (the East Saxons), Mercia (including the Middle Angles), and Northumbria (comprising Bernicia and Deira and, a little later, Lindsey). Reality was not quite so neat. Kingdoms were only gradually emerging from a state of flux: Middlesex, for instance, is probably the remains of a much larger Mid-Saxon territory dismembered before any surviving records could note it. There were also an unknown number of smaller peoples, lying between the big kingdoms or absorbed within them. Some, like the Hwicce of Worcestershire and the Magonsaete of the Welsh border, had their own kings who were gradually subordinated as the 'sub-kings' or 'aldermen' of greater rulers. There may have been many others: Surrey had a 'sub-king' named Frithuwold in the 670s, and it is quite possible that his ancestors had been rulers of an independent kingdom. There are also occasional hints of local separatism, and resentment against the bigger powers. Bede says that in 643 a monastery in Lindsey refused to receive the Northumbrian King Oswald's corpse, since although they knew he was a holy man 'he had come from another province and had taken authority over them'. It is possible that in 600 English kings could be counted in dozens.

Even the big states experienced a shifting power balance. Bede and other sources mention a series of over-kings (*Bretwaldas* or *Brytenwaldas*), from various kingdoms but successively wielding authority over all or most of the Anglo-Saxon peoples. Whether or not the *Bretwalda*-ship was a formal office (which seems doubtful), it was certainly possible for an individual king to establish an extensive, if short-term, political dominance. The first four in Bede's list, Aelle of Sussex, Ceawlin of Wessex, Æthelberht of Kent, and Raedwald of East Anglia, bring us to the 620s. We cannot say what their authority may have meant outside their own kingdoms, though we know that in 616 Raedwald took an army through Mercia, and defeated the Northumbrians on their own frontier. The fifth and sixth were both Northumbrian rulers, Edwin (616–32) and Oswald (633–42). These are Bede's heroes, his models of victorious Christian kingship. It is with them that we first get a clear idea of relations between the English kingdoms.

Northumbrian expansion westwards led Mercia to make common cause with the Welsh. In 632 Cadwallon, Christian British king of Gwynedd, and Penda, pagan Anglo-Saxon king of Mercia, won a short-lived victory over Northumbria, but the following year Oswald recovered power and Cadwallon was killed. The Welsh continued to support Penda, and in 642 Oswald was slain at Oswestry, campaigning far from home. This fact, and an incidental reference to his relations with the king of Wessex, show that Oswald's lordship and military activities extended far outside Northumbria. A group of early Welsh poems give the other side of the story from Bede's: his heroes are their aggressors. In the lament for Cynddylan, a nobleman from Powys who seems to have died in Penda's service, we glimpse the Northumbrians through British eyes:

My brothers were slain at one stroke,
Cynan, Cynddylan, Cynwraith,
Defending Tren, ravaged town
  . . . . . .
More common was blood on the field's face
Than ploughing of fallow
  . . . . . .
The hall of Cynddylan, dark is the roof,
Since the Saxon cut down
Powys's Cynddylan and Elfan . . .

In 655, Penda was defeated and killed by the Northumbrian Oswy, Bede's seventh over-king, who thereafter enjoyed great influence over the other kingdoms. None the less, the rising star was Mercia. The Mercian nobility soon expelled Oswy and chose Penda's son Wulfhere as their king. By the early 670s Wulfhere seems to have dominated the southern English kingdoms, and in 679 his successor won a victory at the Trent which finally ended Northumbrian expansionism. In the south, however, Mercian power was abruptly checked by Caedwalla of Wessex, who annexed Kent, Surrey, and Sussex during his short reign of 685–8. Caedwalla and his successor Ine built up resilience of power in Wessex which was to determine the fate of England two centuries later.

In the world of seventh-century politics, then, it was possible to gain great power but hard to keep it for long. Why did kings rise and fall so quickly? One reason is that power and conquest depended on military forces; forces were attracted by gift-giving; gift-giving depended on wealth; and wealth in its turn was gained by power and conquest. Society was riddled with feuds, and the succession to kingdoms was fluid and uncertain; hence there were many royal and noble exiles from their own kin in search of generous and congenial lords. King Oswin of Deira, says Bede, 'was tall and handsome, pleasant of speech, courteous in manner, and bountiful to nobles and commons alike; so it came about that . . . noblemen from almost every kingdom flocked to serve him as retainers'. Such a system could hardly be stable: when a king grew sick, poor, or mean his retinue would collapse, and his heirs, if they survived at all, would become sub-kings or followers of a new lord.

What kingly magnificence could mean was brought to life, in 1939, by the discovery of a great royal burial at Sutton Hoo on the East Anglian coast. Since it seems to date from the 620s it was probably the tomb of King Raedwald, the fourth in Bede's list of over-kings. He was buried in a ship under a great mound, with his armour, weapons, and a mass of incomparable treasures. The gold and jewelled ornaments are perhaps the finest of their kind surviving in northern Europe, and no less remarkable is the range of countries from which items in the barrow came. An extraordinary ceremonial whetstone can scarcely be anything other than a sceptre. To judge from Sutton Hoo, poetic accounts of royal wealth contain no exaggeration: kingdoms were won and lost for treasures such as these.

From its beginnings, English society included a military aristocracy, probably with some kind of territorial base. But in the early centuries the king's followers or 'thegns' were tied less to their estates than to the king himself. They were expected to accompany him, to witness his public actions, to live in his hall, and if necessary to fight and die for him. Aristocratic life was strongly communal: the great hall as a place of good cheer, a haven in a dangerous world, is a powerful image in Anglo-Saxon writing. Nobody puts it better than Bede, in the famous words which he gives to a Northumbrian nobleman who is urging King Edwin to accept Christianity:

'This is how the present life of man on earth, King, appears to me in comparison with that time which is unknown to us. You are sitting feasting with your

King David surrounded by court musicians, from a Canterbury manuscript of c.720 (British Library MS Cotton Vespasian A i). Recitation of poetry accompanied by strokes of the lyre was prominent in courtly life, and the Sutton Hoo burial contained a lyre such as this.

ealdormen and thegns in winter time; the fire is burning on the hearth in the middle of the hall and all inside is warm, while outside the wintry storms of rain and snow are raging; and a sparrow flies swiftly through the hall. It enters in at one door and quickly flies out through the other. For the few moments it is inside, the storm and wintry tempest cannot touch it, but after the briefest moment of calm, it flits from your sight, out of the wintry storm and into it again. So this life of man appears but for a moment; what follows or indeed what went before, we know not at all.'

The company in the royal or noble hall provided the audience for a literature which mirrored the age: heroic lays recited by professional bards. The surviving fragments include one major epic, *Beowulf*. As we have it, this is a relatively late and sophisticated work, perhaps written for a clerical audience. Yet it lays before us the heroic, essentially pagan world of the seventh-century aristocracy, transmuted by Christianity but not effaced. Its hero, Beowulf, is an exile who takes service with Hrothgar, king of the Danes. A generous giver of treasure and splendid weapons, Hrothgar attracts to his court noble warriors who make him powerful. But the political world of the poem is violent and unstable: a king who loses support will quickly perish, and his

Detail of the Sutton Hoo Sceptre. This unique object may have been the personal sceptre of Raedwald, king of the East Angles and one of the English *Bretwaldas* or over-kings.

kingdom with him. The ethos is one of loyalty and feud: 'It is better for everyone that he avenge his friend, rather than mourn him long . . . let he who can win glory before death.' Beowulf fights with monsters and dragons, inhabitants of a pre-Christian mental world. When he is killed, his followers lay him with rich treasures in a mound overlooking the sea, just as the East Angles had done for their king on the headland at Sutton Hoo:

> Then the warriors rode around the barrow
>
> . . . .
> They praised his manhood and the prowess of his hands,
> They raised his name; it is right a man
> Should be lavish in honouring his lord and friend.
>
> . . . . . .
> They said that he was of all the world's kings
> The gentlest of men, and the most gracious,
> The kindest to his people, the keenest for fame.

But there was more to early Anglo-Saxon society than warfare, savage loyalties, and ostentatious splendour. In some ways this was a surprisingly orderly world. The institutions which made the English state so exceptionally strong in the central Middle Ages have roots in the seventh century or even earlier: the efficiency of 'local government' was one important reason why new overlords could establish power so quickly. By the tenth century, English counties were divided for legal and administrative purposes into areas called 'hundreds'. In some at least of the early kingdoms, hundreds were formed out of larger but equally coherent districts, great blocks of fifty to a hundred square miles which apparently existed by the mid-seventh century. These have long been recognized in Kent, but recent research has detected them also in Northumbria, Mercia, Wessex, Sussex, and Surrey. The origin of this startlingly comprehensive system for dividing up the countryside is one of the great unsolved problems in early English history. Was it, as many believe, a Romano-Celtic survival? Was it created by one of the shadowy sixth-century *Bretwaldas*? Or did it develop spontaneously in the various kingdoms, reflecting common elements in the settlers' social background? Whatever the answer, it remains an oddly stable substratum in an unstable political world.

At the heart of each early district was a royal manor house or *tun*, run by a local official but visited by the king and his retinue at more or less frequent intervals. Each modern county contains several such sites, some given away by place-names such as Kingston, others less obvious. It was these 'central places', not towns or even villages, which were the main local foci of early and mid-Saxon society. The scattered inhabitants of the district looked for law and government to the king's great hall with its surrounding buildings. Here too they paid their dues and other public burdens in accordance with a complex system of assessment. Land was reckoned in 'hides', each notionally the area needed to support a free peasant cultivator and his family, and often an actual farm unit. Obligations, it seems, were assessed by the hide, and hides were grouped into multiples of twenty or more which owed obligations of a specialized kind. The king's deputy at the centre might thus receive renders of grain from some groups of hides, of calves or foals from others, and of honey, mead, or lesser commodities from others again.

Thus the early administrative districts were organized for exploitation as well as for jurisdiction. A system of economically specialized zones suited the under-developed countryside, with its sharp geographical contrasts and large areas of uncleared common pasture. So it is not surprising that when mid-Saxon kings granted away blocks of land, these early 'manors' often preserved the internal structure of the districts from which they were formed. Hence the 'multiple estate', the federation of distinct 'vills' or townships linked to one manorial centre, which was still prominent in many parts of England in the twelfth and thirteenth centuries. Some historians have recently argued that this type of organization (which certainly resembles that of early Wales) was of Celtic origin. Some continuity in rural organization is quite likely, but perhaps only in a sense so broad that it ceases to mean much. It was growth and social change, not conquest, which eventually made the 'multiple estate' obsolete. Granted that the British peasants were not all driven out, and that their way of life was probably not so very different from the invaders', it would be surprising if a pattern which suited existing resources had *not* continued.

This pattern also suited a peasant population which was dispersed, unstructured, and relatively small. The most prominent figure in the early sources is the free peasant farmer or *ceorl* (modern English 'churl', but without its derogatory sense), typically cultivating one hide of land. This does not mean that all seventh- and eighth-century farmers were so 'free' that they had no lord save the king. After the Conversion kings granted blocks of land to churches, as they had probably done to lay followers (at least on a temporary basis) from earlier still. The origin of the 'manor' as a private unit of jurisdiction and revenue is obscure, but some historians place it near the very beginnings of English society. The medieval division of estates into 'demesne' (exploited directly by the lord) and peasant land is recorded by the late seventh century, and much of the manpower on demesnes was provided by slaves. But in the early stages it seems likely that lesser lords, like kings, drew revenue from smallholders without greatly altering their way of life or farming methods. There is no evidence for the hierarchical, thoroughly dependent groups of tenants who existed by the tenth century; nor for the organized 'village communities' which seem so closely linked to strong lordship in the twelfth and thirteenth centuries. Archaeology suggests that most farmsteads in mid-Saxon England were either isolated or in little clusters, and even the nucleated settlements lack any sign of the orderly streets, greens, and plot-boundaries familiar from later village topography. It now seems likely that medieval common-field systems, with holdings intermixed in scattered strips, result from several centuries of evolution. In seventh-century England the integrated 'village community' was still in the future.

Into this very traditional society of kings, warriors, and farmers there came in 597 an alien influence—the Christian Church. The conversion of the English was initiated by Pope Gregory the Great, who according to tradition had seen English youths in Rome and pronounced them 'not Angles but angels'. Gregory knew that King Æthelberht of Kent had a Christian Frankish queen; thus it was to Kent that he sent the first mission, headed by a Roman monk named Augustine. Æthelberht, hesitant at first, soon converted, and Augustine founded a monastery at Canterbury. Misjudging the survival of Romano-British life, Gregory had planned archbishoprics based in London and York, but political realities were acknowledged in 601 when Augustine was enthroned as first Archbishop of Canterbury. Initially, success seemed rapid. In 604 a see was founded at Rochester; the East Saxons were converted, and a cathedral dedicated to St. Paul was built for them in London. Meanwhile several monasteries were built in Kent, their churches closely modelled on Roman prototypes.

But the skin-deep conversion of a king and his household was a shaky foundation at best. The East Saxons soon apostatized and expelled their bishop. Despite his baptism King Raedwald of the East Angles remained ambivalent, for Bede reports that he maintained simultaneously a church and a pagan shrine. In Northumbria the story is similar. King Edwin received the Roman missionary Paulinus, and was baptized with his thegns in 627. But on his defeat and death only five years later, his successors apostatized and Paulinus had to flee. The Church had speedily gained a foothold in the English courts; but a broader

An early monastic enclosure or 'cashel' at Kiltiernan,
County Galway, Ireland. The typical Celtic monastery had a circular
outer boundary, with an inner precinct for the main buildings.
Round monastic sites also existed in Wales and Cornwall,
where they are often identified by the place-name element *llan*.

basis was needed if it was to rise above the ebb and flow of
political fortunes.

Surprisingly, it was not the Gregorian mission which was
most successful in this respect but the primitive, isolated Celtic
Church. The Christians of Wales and Cornwall probably had
some influence on the English, but it was scarcely very significant. Augustine, who seems to have been a rather proud,
humourless man, offended the Welsh bishops and no co-
operation resulted. The mission which achieved so much among
the northern English came rather from Ireland to Scotland, and
thence to Northumbria.

Thanks to St. Patrick and his followers, Ireland was largely
Christian by the early sixth century. Monasteries multiplied, so
much so that the whole Irish Church came to be organized along
monastic lines. 'Provinces' were based on monasteries and were
ruled by abbots; bishops performed their normal spiritual
functions, but they lacked formal dioceses and were under the
abbots' authority. Hence the typical Irish missionary was the
wandering bishop owing obedience to a community at home.
The Irish houses were to reach a level of wealth and sophistication far surpassing their counterparts in Wales, and already in
the sixth and seventh centuries they were sending missionaries
to Gaul, Germany, Scotland, and England. One named Columba

went to Scotland, converted the northern Picts (the southern Picts were already Christian), and in c.563 founded a monastery on the island of Iona. When the Christian King Oswald won control of Northumbria in 633 it was naturally to Iona that he turned for a missionary, for his exile had been spent among the Irish of western Scotland.

The simple, wandering life of the Irish bishops and monks brought them in touch with the people at large. Aidan, Oswald's bishop, had the qualities needed to convert Northumbria permanently. After building a monastery on the island of Lindisfarne, he set up a church in each royal vill from which to preach to the countryside around. Bede says that he always travelled on foot, thus meeting passers-by on equal terms. Several monasteries were founded, and soon the Northumbrian Church was strong enough to branch out into other kingdoms. Penda of Mercia remained pagan but allowed a mission from Lindisfarne to work in his realm, and his son Peada was baptized in 653. The over-kingship of Oswald and then of Oswy helped the Northumbrian Church to spread. In 635 Oswald's influence caused Cynegils of Wessex to accept baptism from a missionary named Birinus, who became first bishop of the West Saxons. Thanks to Oswy, the East Saxons re-converted and received a Northumbrian bishop named Cedd, who had been trained in the Irish Church. By 660 only the men of Sussex and the Isle of Wight remained pagan, and soon they too were converted.

The zeal of the Irish missionaries had achieved much; in the long run the authority of the Roman Church was bound to count for more. If Pope Gregory's aims were to be realized, the Celtic Church in English kingdoms had to accept the discipline of Rome. The main sticking-point was an issue which now seems absurdly trivial—on what day should Easter be celebrated? In their long isolation, the Celts had adopted computations which differed from those used at Rome. When the two Churches came into contact, the results could be inconvenient: at the Northumbrian court the Irish-trained King Oswy sometimes celebrated Easter while his Kentish-trained wife was still observing Lent. The question itself had a deep religious and symbolic importance; for the future of the English Church, resolving it was more important still. At the Synod of Whitby (664), King Oswy of Northumbria came down in favour of the Roman party, and the few Celtic die-hards returned to Iona. This was the turning-point: the Church through all the English kingdoms could now become a united and uniting force under one primate.

None the less, the Church was beset with problems in the 660s.

The Ardagh chalice: one of the most striking illustrations
of the richness and sophistication which Irish monastic culture
attained during the first millennium AD.

Organization was haphazard; there were far too few bishops,
and some were invalidly consecrated. Others died in a plague in
664, which also made the East Saxons apostatize again. But in 669
the pope sent a new archbishop, a native of Asia Minor named
Theodore. This surprising candidate (only chosen when several
others had refused) was just what was needed: a firm admini-
strator. During his thirty-year reign, he rationalized the diocesan
structure, which had been fluid everywhere and perhaps almost
absent from kingdoms converted by the monastically-organized
Irish. Bishops with invalid orders were disciplined, and dubious
authorities either ratified or annulled: all acts of the Welsh
bishops, for instance, were declared void. A synod held at
Hertford in 672 established the first basic canons for Church
government.

Most churchmen accepted Theodore's rulings with good
grace, but not the formidable Wilfrid, bishop of Ripon and then
of York. Wilfrid was firmly orthodox and had championed the
Roman Easter at Whitby, but he resented any threat to his power
in the Northumbrian Church. His stormy relations with Theodore and successive kings involved two expulsions, two appeals
to Rome, exile, and imprisonment. Meanwhile he managed to
preach to the Frisians, convert Sussex, and found monasteries in

Mercia. With his retinue and huge wealth, Wilfrid seems an extraordinary mixture of saint and secular nobleman. Only a young and essentially aristocratic Church could have produced such a figure.

Theodore's reign was a golden age for monasteries. On the one hand, the great Celtic houses such as Lindisfarne and Whitby were increasingly influenced by Roman ways, though the old values lived on: in St. Cuthbert the solitude and austere devotion of the Irish missionaries was combined with Roman attitudes to monastic life and discipline. On the other hand, many new houses founded in these years would be counted for centuries among the greatest in Britain. In some ways the most important of these were Wearmouth and Jarrow, founded by Benedict Biscop, a Northumbrian nobleman turned monk. Biscop had been five times to Rome, and his twin monasteries brought to Northumbria the culture of the Mediterranean Church. Their most celebrated member, Bede himself, describes how Biscop had a church built by Gaulish masons 'in the Roman manner which he always loved', filled it with rich pictures and furnishings, and built up a great library from Continental sources.

Impressive though these achievements were, there was also a need to provide some permanent basis for the Church's work in the countryside: it is hard to believe that the conversion of the peasantry had hitherto been more than superficial. Many will find it surprising that here, too, the first stages were achieved by monastic or quasi-monastic bodies. With hindsight it seems obvious that missionary work and pastoral care are activities for priests, not monks. But in the seventh and eighth centuries this line was not quite so firmly drawn, even outside the Celtic Church. The English word *mynster* (monastery) was used for institutions ranging from true Benedictine houses to small, loose-knit communities of priests. Rules varied greatly (Biscop composed his own for Jarrow), and so did standards; we really have very little idea of what life was like in all but the greatest houses. But it is becoming clear that by 750 England contained hundreds of small 'minsters' with genuine and important pastoral functions, serving what may be called the first English parochial system.

The 'old minsters', as they came to be called, were older than the mass of ordinary local churches, and served much larger areas. Most of the sources are late, and show them as near-obsolete establishments with only residual authority. Hence we know little of their pastoral work, except that it existed. It appears that the collegiate priests, or deputies in the case of strict

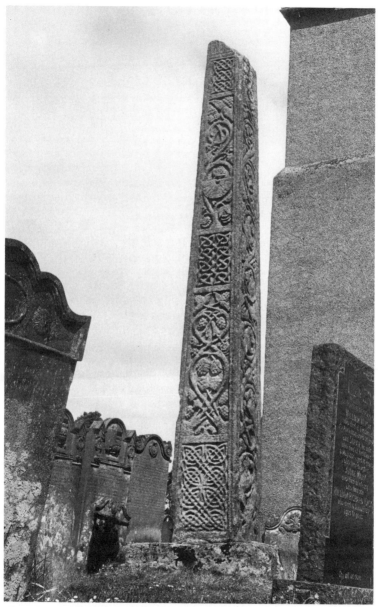

The early eighth-century Bewcastle Cross. With its runic inscriptions and mixture of English and Celtic decoration, this is perhaps the finest surviving monument of the Celtic mission to Northumbria.

monks, travelled about within a defined 'parish' preaching to local communities. The 'parishioners' of the minster owed it their tithes, and were obliged to bring to it their children for baptism and their dead for burial. So complex a system could not have evolved so quickly without royal patronage. Paulinus and Aidan preached from their kings' vills (see p. 73), and it is no surprise to find many minster churches sited at royal *tuns* (see p. 74). Tithe-duty was probably based on existing tax assessments, and some kings may have founded several minsters as an act of policy, as Oswy of Northumbria seems to have done in 655. Kings had an organized system of local government; so, therefore, did the Church. Though eventually smothered by the thousands of little churches which sprang up within them, minster 'parishes' moulded the whole future development of the Church in the English countryside.

If kings helped the Church to grow, the Church also enhanced the status of kings. The grandsons of pagan war-leaders were coming to see themselves as God's appointed deputies; a few generations later, the crowning of a new king became something very like an episcopal consecration. With Christianity, too, came literacy: kings could revise and formulate tribal custom to resemble the legislation of the civilized world. Æthelberht of Kent, says Bede, made his laws 'according to the custom of the Romans'. Æthelberht's code, and the later seventh-century codes from Kent and Wessex, suggest a mixture of local tradition with borrowings from the Continent. Whatever their practical usefulness (which is doubtful), the kings who made them clearly wanted to seem sophisticated: lawgivers in the classical mould. As the kingdoms were opened more and more to influences from Rome and Gaul, the nature of kingship changed. It was becoming important for rulers to uphold justice and direct the internal affairs of their kingdoms, not merely to win battles. Even the seventh-century codes, with their long lists of fines and penalties, suggest an impressive range of royal authority.

Also with the first English churches, we start to glimpse the first English towns. Possibly sixth-century rulers had set up headquarters in the Roman towns and forts; certainly seventh- and eighth-century rulers favoured them as sites for cathedrals and minsters. Canterbury, York, Winchester, and Worcester cathedrals were all built within Roman defences, and in 635 the first bishop of Wessex was given the Roman fort at Dorchester-on-Thames, called by Bede a *civitas*, to found his see. Royal halls and churches built on abandoned ruins are not in themselves towns. None the less, the most highly-organized communities of the age were surely the cathedrals and minsters; craftsmen, tradesmen, servants, and beggars all gravitated to their doors. It is no coincidence that the first hints of reawakening urban life are associated with major churches, both in Roman towns and on the more numerous sites with no pre-English origins. The first archaeological evidence for Anglo-Saxon settlement in Canterbury is slightly later than the building of Augustine's cathedral there. At Northampton, recent excavations have shown that the nucleus of the town was an eighth-century minster church and hall, with associated buildings. A late ninth-century translation of Bede's term *urbana loca* is not, as we would expect, 'towns', but 'minster-places'. Scores of English towns began as minsters with lay settlements converging on their gates.

The Mercian Supremacy

England in the early eighth century was a more sophisticated place than it had been in the early seventh. A united English kingdom was still far away, but the English were now starting to become aware of themselves as an ethnic and cultural unity. Bede may have felt this more keenly than anyone: it is easy to forget how significant is the very title of his greatest work, *The Ecclesiastical History of the English People*. It was because he saw the common destiny of his race fulfilled in the united English Church that he could think of an 'English people'. But are there any signs that secular government was also becoming more comprehensive? This is a hard question to answer, not least because there are more sources. On the one hand, institutions and concepts which show the strong side of eighth-century kingship may not be new, but merely recorded for the first time. On the other hand, the dynastic turmoils which show its weak side may not be new either: it is possible that Bede and his contemporaries glossed over such matters. This at least can be said: as *Bretwaldas* on the old pattern the eighth-century Mercian kings were as mighty as their forerunners; and they lived in a world of greater literacy and legality, of firmer-entrenched rights, which made their power more stable and more capable of development.

Æthelbald of Mercia (716–57) inherited much of the influence won by Wulfhere. Written charters recording royal grants were now appearing in some quantity, so we can see how kings liked to style themselves. Æthelbald's titles are impressive, but perhaps not wholly new. 'King not only of the Mercians but of all the

Carving at Breedon-on-the-Hill, Leicestershire. This is a rare example of architectural ornament from a Mercian minster of Offa's time.

provinces called by the general name Southern English', as one charter calls him, echoes Bede's statement that the early over-kings 'held sway over all the provinces south of the River Humber'. The claim can be supported to the extent that charters show him influencing Kentish affairs and controlling London. But Wessex remained independent, as did Northumbria under Bede's patron King Ceolwulf: Mercian supremacy was never to go north of the Humber.

Æthelbald's successor Offa (757–96) was the most powerful English king before Alfred. His position once secured (which took some years), his conduct in all the kingdoms except

Northumbria and Wessex seems to have been more that of a direct ruler than a remote overlord. Earlier kings had suppressed small royal dynasties, but Offa suppressed great ones. He had full control over Kent (with a brief interlude in the late 770s), and treated its king as his servant. Once he annulled a grant by King Egbert of Kent, 'saying that it was wrong that his minister should have presumed to give land . . . without his witness'. After an unsuccessful coup against Offa's successor in 798, the ancient Kentish dynasty was extinguished for ever. The last king of Sussex appears as one of Offa's *duces*; in Surrey, which had been West Saxon territory, we find Offa confirming a grant by a Mercian noble. In East Anglia (though here the dynasty reappeared later), the *Chronicle* notes laconically for 794: 'In this year Offa, king of Mercia, ordered [King] Æthelberht's head to be struck off.' In Wessex, royal power and tradition were stronger: the kingdom only recognized Mercian protection between 786 and 802, and even then the lordship seems to have been of a much vaguer kind than in Kent.

Offa is the first ruler whose charters use the simple, unqualified title 'king of the English'. His status is emphasized by a famous letter to him from the great Frankish king, Charlemagne. Charlemagne addresses him as an equal, 'his dearest brother', and speaks of 'the various episcopal sees of your kingdom and Æthelred's' as though Offa of Mercia and Æthelred of Northumbria were the only kings in England. The Frankish connection is important (though possibly too much has been made of this one document: there had always been plenty of contact between Gaul and the southern English). Offa would certainly have liked to be thought another Charlemagne, and whatever the reality of royal power, its status certainly rose in line with developments

Silver penny of King Offa. As well as providing a better currency, Offa's coins were of a higher artistic quality than any which had circulated in England since the Romans left.

abroad. In 787 Offa had his son Egfrith made king of the Mercians by a solemn consecration which Northumbria copied nine years later. The semi-sacred character of kingship was becoming stronger.

This did not make dynasties more stable. Succession was uncertain: long after Offa, kings would still be 'chosen' from the royal stock. Any vaguely eligible candidate with forces behind him could aim at the throne, and Mercia, Wessex, and Northumbria were all torn by dynastic feuds during the eighth century. In his efforts to secure the succession, Offa seems to have been as ruthless towards relatives as he was towards neighbours. When his son Egfrith died shortly after Offa himself, the Northumbrian scholar Alcuin saw it as a judgement: 'The vengeance for the blood shed by the father has now reached the son; for you know very well how much blood his father shed to secure the kingdom on his son.'

Much of this shows Offa in a savage light, but some important institutions did start to take shape under the Mercian kings. The Church was now firmly established with lands and privileges. Its assemblies were solemn affairs, recorded in writing. Æthelbald and Offa were often involved in Church councils and sometimes presided over them; their thegns and ministers witnessed decisions. The way Church business was conducted can hardly have failed to heighten the sense of precedent and legality. Though the context is ecclesiastical, such assemblies must have helped to transform the *ad hoc* band of warriors around a seventh-century king into the formal 'Witan' or grand council which we find in late Saxon England.

The concept of 'bookland' (land for which a written charter gave legal title) was now well established. Most eighth-century charters, at least the surviving ones, are grants to churches, but they reflect a society in which rights in the land and local interests were winning ground against traditional values. The eighth-century aristocracy begin to seem a little less like warriors, a little more like country gentlemen, and evidence starts to appear for family houses and family churches. Little is known of the houses, though one has been excavated at Goltho, Lincolnshire: a mid-ninth-century defended enclosure containing a hall, kitchen, chamber, and outbuildings. For the churches there is more evidence: hereditary 'private' minsters, controlled by families of noble patrons, often figure in eighth-century sources. All this is equally true to the mightiest lord of all. Earlier kings had had their royal vills, but Offa seems to have tried to make his residence at Tamworth a kind of national headquarters or 'capital'. Near Tamworth was the Mercian cathedral of Lichfield, which Offa managed to have raised for several years into an archbishopric. If this was partly for political reasons, there was much to be said for a metropolitan church near the 'metropolis' of Offa's kingdom.

The duty of landowners to help in the building of bridges and fortifications first appears in a document of 749, and is usually stipulated in later grants of land. This is significant in an age which produced massive public works of at least two kinds: one long-famous, the other only recently understood. The first is, of course, Offa's Dyke, so called by an ancient and probably correct tradition. Recent excavations suggest that this enormous earthwork was a continuous barrier between England and Wales, running from sea to sea. Offa is known to have raided into Wales, but the Dyke must be a defensive rather than an offensive work, built to stop a Welsh counter-attack when plans for conquest had been abandoned. But the fact that it exists at all is proof of the huge resources which Offa commanded.

The charter references to 'fortress-work' imply fortified strong-holds rather than dykes. It is well known that Alfred and his heirs developed a network of large communal fortresses or *burhs* to protect Wessex against the Vikings. Archaeology has recently begun to suggest that some *burhs* are a century or more older, and may have been founded to defend Mercia in its years of greatness. In most cases (for instance Bedford, where Offa is said to have been buried), the evidence is still only topographical, and therefore inconclusive. But at Hereford, excavation has revealed an eighth-century defended circuit pre-dating later Saxon enlargements, and less conclusive evidence for defences of Offa's period has been found at Tamworth. Several of the late ninth-century Wessex *burhs* may also have earlier origins; some, such as Wareham (Dorset), Dorchester (Dorset), and Oxford, are certainly on sites which were important in the eighth century or before.

We have seen two factors in the emergence of towns: churches and fortresses. The third, in the long run the biggest, is trade. Offa lived in an age when foreign and internal trade were both expanding. The clearest sign is the appearance of a systematic coinage. Until c.600, only foreign gold coins had circulated in England. The crude silver coins minted by seventh- and eighth-century kings were unreliable, and usually of localized circulation. A new Frankish currency of silver pennies was the model for a better coinage, and an East Anglian king seems to have used it slightly before Offa. But when Offa's beautiful pennies did appear, they quickly drove out older issues and gained a wider circulation than any currency since Roman times. Perhaps the most interesting point is that Offa's coins have been found not only in large hoards, but also in small, scattered groups. Evidently, they were used for small-scale transactions at a local level: money was becoming of general importance in the English economy.

A dispute with Offa in 789 caused Charlemagne to close Frankish ports to English merchants. Hence it seems that English merchants normally used such ports: Charlemagne's realm and Offa's were part of a growing world of international commerce. Trading centres were appearing throughout northern Europe. Excavations on the huge settlements of Hedeby in Denmark and Birke in Sweden have produced finds suggesting that in the eighth century England and the Viking lands belonged to the same international trading community. In England, commercial settlements such as these were often linked to existing royal and ecclesiastical centres, and their names often include the element -*wic* (from Latin *vicus*). *Hamwih* was the precursor of modern Southampton. It lay at the junction of the Test and Itchen near a royal vill called Hampton, and its name labels it as the *Ham-wic* associated with the *Ham-tun*. Here excavation has disclosed a settlement of at least 30 hectares, probably first occupied in about the 720s, with artefacts suggesting wide European contacts. Others were probably Ipswich (*Gips-wic*), a major pottery-producing centre, Sandwich, and Fordwich. Roman towns started to regain economic as well as hierarchical importance. A commercial suburb developed at York (*Eofor-wic*), where Frisian merchants are recorded; at Canterbury excavation has revealed eighth-century houses, and a market is mentioned in 786. Most important was London, which Bede could describe in *c*.730 as 'an *emporium* of many people coming by land and sea'. This commercial zone has proved hard to find, though it now seems that the Roman and medieval waterfronts at Billingsgate include a mid-Saxon clay bank. Wherever it lay, it must have been large and important: *Lunden-wic* is mentioned in the late seventh century, and eighth-century sources refer to tolls and tax-gatherers at its port.

The eighth century was a rather unsettled time for the English Church. Lay foundation and patronage of minsters had brought its own problems. Hereditary interest was not necessarily a bad thing: in the hands of a responsible family, a monastery could expect both security and prosperity. But not all proprietors were responsible; while some minsters, if we can believe Bede, were simply 'fronts' for tax evasion. Bede was not alone in worrying about lax standards. Æthelbald, Offa, and his successor Cenwulf (796–821) participated in a series of much-needed reforming synods. Monks were forbidden to live like lay nobles; drunkenness and secular songs in monasteries were condemned. In 786, Offa held the only council in the Anglo-Saxon period to be attended by papal legates. But if the growth of Church government enhanced royal dignity, it also raised the pretensions of bishops. Relations between Church and State were not always easy, especially with a king like Æthelbald who seems to have combined monastic reform with robbing minsters and seducing nuns. Dealings between the king and the Archbishop of Canterbury tended to be complicated by the strong anti-Mercian feeling in Kent. Archbishop Jaenbert was outraged when Offa raised Lichfield to an archiepiscopal see, and the scheme was abandoned after the king's death on the grounds that it had been prompted by enmity towards the people of Kent.

On the positive side, the English Church did produce one outstanding scholar, Alcuin. A product of the cathedral school at York, he was a leading figure in Charlemagne's court and took a central part in Charlemagne's great revival of classical learning

The minster church at Brixworth, Northamptonshire. This is by far the most important eighth-century building remaining in England; it is possible that Brixworth was the unidentified *Clofesho* where several synods met under the Mercian kings.

and education. It is significant, especially in the context of Charlemagne's letter to Offa, that the dominant intellectual of late eighth-century Europe was an Englishman. But it must be remembered that Alcuin, like Bede before him, was a Northumbrian: we know very little about Mercian culture. Probably this simply means that much has been lost. Mercia had no Bede to record its achievements, and its greatest monasteries were sacked by the Vikings. Fragments of decorative art, such as the sculptures in the minster of Breedon-on-the-Hill, suggest sumptuous physical surroundings. A noble monument to the age of Æthelbald and Offa is the great minster church of Brixworth, Northamptonshire. It is a sign of how much we do *not* know that this monastery fails to appear in any early document, unless it is the lost *Clofesho* where the Mercian synods were held.

The most impressive fact about the eighth-century Church is that the English were now taking Christianity to their original homelands on the Continent. The mission began, oddly enough, through St. Wilfrid's quarrel with Archbishop Theodore. Setting out in 678 to state his case at Rome, Wilfrid travelled through pagan Frisia and spent a year preaching. The Frisians were well known to the English from their merchants, and Wilfrid opened the way to more ambitious missionary work. A group of Northumbrians landed in Frisia in 690. Among them was Willibrord, who took the lead and was consecrated Archbishop of Frisia in 695. He established his cathedral at Utrecht, and the organized Church of Frankish Frisia developed quickly. Willibrord's work was supplemented by a West Saxon mission led by St. Boniface. Between his arrival in 718 and his murder by pagans in 754, Boniface preached among the Frisians, Germans, and Franks, setting up a see at Maine. As well as converting pagan areas Boniface had great influence on the Frankish Church as a whole, regulating it and bringing it under papal guidance. Throughout his career he relied on books, recruits, and advice from England, and there survives a large correspondence with friends at home. Much of the work which transformed the stagnant Frankish Church into the expanding Church of the Crolingian revival was done by English men and women.

The Viking Invasions and the Rise of the House of Wessex

Mercian power did not long outlast Offa. His successor, King Cenwulf, kept hold of Kent and Sussex and even gained some new territory from the northern Welsh, but Wessex slipped from his grasp in 802. A new dynasty of overlords was about to appear, this time West Saxon. In 825 Egbert of Wessex won a decisive victory near Swindon, expelled a Mercian under-king from Kent, and annexed Kent, Essex, Surrey, and Sussex. Four years later, Mercia itself fell to Egbert, and even Northumbria acknowledged his lordship. The reversal is spectacular, and shows that Offa's dynasty had done little to stabilize English politics. Nor could Egbert: by his death in 839 Mercia was independent once again. The old interplay of dynasties seemed to be continuing much as ever. But under the year 789 the *Anglo-Saxon Chronicle* contains an ominous entry: the first breath of a storm that was to sweep away all rivals to the house of Wessex, and with them some of the best achievements of English civilization:

In this year Beorhtric [king of Wessex] took to wife Eadburh, daughter of King Offa. And in his days came first three ships of Norwegians from Hörthaland: and then the reeve rode thither and tried to compel them to go to the royal manor, for he did not know what they were: and then they slew him. These were the first ships of the Danes to come to England.

This Viking landing was a minor affair, though there are other references soon afterwards to 'sea-borne pagans' attacking the south coast. More serious, and incomparably more distressing, were raids in the north, for they involved the successive plundering of Lindisfarne (793), Jarrow (794), and Iona (795). England had been safe from foreign attacks for two centuries; the reaction to the sudden desecration of three of its most holy places is easily imagined. These were, however, isolated incidents, and it was a generation before the Viking nuisance became a major threat. But a big raid on Kent in 835 opened three decades in which attacks came almost yearly, and which ended with the arrival of a full-scale invading army.

The dramatic expansion of the Norwegians and Danes is a European phenomenon, of which the raids on England and Ireland were only one part. Two races were involved (the word *Viking*, 'pirate', was coined by their victims and refers equally to both), and several motives. They were far from being total barbarians, and by the 840s they had been heavily involved in trade for some generations. It was, indeed, this trade which opened up regular contact with the nations to the west and south. Population grew, and it became hard to find a reasonable living at home. Many adventurers must have heard stories of the fertile lands with monasteries full of easy plunder, and it is surprising rather than otherwise that the early raids were not followed up more quickly. The fall of the Danish royal dynasty in

854 left a power vacuum, with no strong king who could unite warriors and prevent them from dispersing on foreign exploits.

These factors help to explain why raiders descended in such numbers on European countries from the 850s onwards, and why casual plundering gave way to a policy of conquest and settlement. There seem to have been two main routes: one around the north of Scotland to the Western Isles and so southwards, the other to the east and south coasts of England and to Gaul. Hence the raids and settlements in Ireland, Scotland, Wales, and Cornwall were mainly Norwegian, while those in the English and Frankish lands were mainly Danish.

In 865 the Danish 'Great Army', led by Halfdan and Ivarr the Boneless, landed in East Anglia. After a few months' stay it turned northwards into Northumbria, which happened to be split by a dynastic dispute, and captured York in 867. Both the rival kings perished, and the Danes set up their own nominee to rule Northumbria as a client state. The army then advanced into Mercia, but on meeting opposition it withdrew to York without an open fight, and in 869 descended again on East Anglia. The inhabitants were defeated in battle, and their king Edmund (soon to be venerated as St. Edmund the Martyr) became the victim of a ritual murder. Within three years, the once-great kingdoms of Northumbria and East Anglia had ceased to exist.

In 870 the Danish army camped at Reading and prepared to invade Wessex. But here the opposition was better organized. After Egbert's death the West Saxons were ruled by his son Æthelwulf, an unambitious but capable man. Æthelwulf's main achievement seems to have been to avoid the kind of family feuding which had ruined other dynasties: his four sons succeeded peacefully in order of age. When the Vikings attacked, the third son, Æthelred, was on the throne; the name of his brother and heir, Alfred, was to become the greatest in Anglo-Saxon history.

It was a combined force under Æthelred and Alfred which met the Danes on the Berkshire Downs and inflicted their first serious defeat. But the English success was short-lived. The Danes withdrew to Reading, but almost immediately advanced again and defeated Æthelred and Alfred near Basingstoke. In April 871 a new Danish army landed. Invasion of Wessex seemed imminent, and its defenders had nowhere to turn for help. In the midst of this crises Æthelred died, and his brother became king of the West Saxons.

Alfred the Great (871–99) is known to everyone as the king who saved England against seemingly hopeless odds. This is not quite how contemporaries would have seen it. In political terms at least, 'England' still did not mean very much. The first writer known to use *Angelcynn* (literally '[the land of] the English folk') was Alfred himself, and *Englaland* does not appear for another century. It was not a foregone conclusion that the other kingdoms would accept West Saxon lordship, or even prefer it to the Danes. They might well have chosen kings of their own, and there was always a danger that English rivals, exiles, or disaffected groups would enlist Viking support. The destruction of the other dynasties did not automatically make Alfred king of all the English; he and his heirs achieved this through a mixture of military success, tactful diplomacy, and good luck.

The reign started badly, and after a year of minor defeats Alfred had to buy the Danes off. They left Wessex alone for five years, during which they invaded Mercia, expelled King Burgred, and replaced him with their own nominee: a third ancient kingdom had gone for good. The Great Army now split into two halves. One, led by Halfdan, turned north and began dividing up Yorkshire for permanent settlement. The other, led by Guthrum, Oscytel, and Anund, turned south, and in 875–6 launched another attack on Wessex. At first their success was limited; in 877 they withdrew again to partition out Mercia, and another group split off to colonize Lincolnshire, Nottinghamshire, Derbyshire, and Leicestershire.

Thus it was a much-reduced force which attacked Wessex for the third time in 878. However, a surprise attack on Chippenham gave them the upper hand; much of Wiltshire and Hampshire submitted, and Alfred was driven back to a refuge at Athelney in the Somerset marshes. The position seemed hopeless, but Alfred bided his time in his fortress and gathered troops. Early in May, says the near-contemporary writer of the *Chronicle*, 'he rode to *Ecgbrihtesstan* [Egbert's Stone] . . . and came to meet him there all

The Alfred jewel. This object, found near Alfred's refuge at Athelney, is inscribed 'Alfred had me made' and almost certainly belonged to the king. Of gold, rock-crystal, and enamel, it illustrates the wealth of the West Saxon court.

the men of Somerset and Wiltshire and part of Hampshire . . . and they rejoiced to see him. And one day later he went from those camps to Iley Oak, and one day later to Edington; and there he fought against the entire host, and put it to flight.'

The victory was sudden but decisive. The Danish leader Guthrum accepted baptism with several of his captains, and the two kings settled peace terms. These recognized the Danish occupation of much of England as a *fait accompli*. The frontier ran roughly north-westwards from London to Chester; Guthrum was to withdraw with his troops behind this line, where he was to be recognized as king of an independent kingdom. By the autumn of 880 the Danes had left Wessex and begun the systematic settlement of East Anglia.

This was not the end of the conflict. In 886 Alfred captured London, apparently after defeating a Danish garrison. In 893 a big Danish army landed in the Thames estuary and raided through England during the next three years, but this time it made little impression on Wessex. Alfred had been busy, both in securing the safety of his own kingdom and in consolidating his lordship over the other territory west and south of the Danish frontier. For the first task, he seems to have improved both the army and the navy. Kings had long been entitled to levies of troops raised in accordance with the land assessment in hides. Alfred's reorganization, by which only half of the army was to be on service at any one time, foreshadows the later 'select fyrd' or militia: it must have produced a smaller but more efficient host. An obvious way of combating sea-borne raiders was with more ships, and Alfred is said to have built vessels much bigger than the Vikings', carrying sixty oars or more.

The most important element in his programme (certainly the one which saved Wessex from further inland raids) makes Alfred the first English town planner. By the late 880s Wessex was covered with a network of public strongholds, several of which have a regular grid of streets and can only be described as planned fortified towns. A document called the *Burghal Hidage* lists thirty of these *burhs*, with three more which may be later additions. Perhaps the most impressive case is Winchester, where a new grid ignoring the Roman streets was laid out within the Roman walls. The same linearity can be seen at Oxford, Chichester, Wareham, and others. Planning was remarkably systematic, and it seems that the surveyors used a standard 66-foot measure for setting out the streets. The larger *burhs* were more than just fortresses, and soon acquired an important role in the local rural economy. Manning the defences was the responsibility of neighbouring landowners, who were able in return to use the defended area for their own purposes. Often they built 'town houses' in the *burh* to store their produce for marketing: Domesday Book records several links between urban tenements and rural manors. Traders and craftsmen followed, and the strongholds of the late ninth century became the thriving towns of the tenth. Defence happened to coincide with the needs of a growing economy; thus Alfred has his unexpected but permanent memorial in the road systems of several modern towns.

One important reason for Alfred's long-term success was the tact with which he treated his neighbours. In Mercia especially, it was dangerous to wound local pride. Alfred left affairs there in the hands of the old royal council, headed by a Mercian nobleman named Æthelred who became his son-in-law, and when he took London in 886 he immediately handed it over to Mercian control. Thus treated, Æthelred was staunchly loyal to the Crown, and after Alfred's death he and his wife Æthelflaed led Mercian offensives against the Danes. If Alfred was more truly 'king of the English' than anyone before him, it was not just through military strength or because no rivals remained: people genuinely wanted him because they knew that he and his family were just and considerate rulers.

But there remained the problem of the Danes and the damage they had done. Some of it was irreparable: whatever happened now, the world of Bede and Offa had gone for ever. The size of the Danish Great Army may be disputed, but it is impossible to deny the evidence of three kingdoms destroyed, dioceses disrupted, innumerable monasteries plundered, charters and other documents almost completely lost for much of eastern England. The ruin of monasteries was perhaps the most serious, for the great houses had been the main repositories of learning and culture, while the small ones were still mainly responsible for pastoral care in the countryside.

In the Danelaw (as the area behind Guthrum's frontier came to be known) the Danish soldiers quickly established a society of their own. Yorkshire, Lincolnshire, Leicestershire, and to a lesser extent East Anglia are full of place-names ending in *-by*, *-thorp*, and other Scandinavian elements. This impact is startling: it shows both that the army was very large, and that it distributed itself widely over the countryside. Even when the Danelaw was Christianized and brought under English rule it retained striking peculiarities, with its own systems of manorial organization, land measurement, law, and social differentiation. Tenth-century kings had the problem of reconciling the claims of a united kingdom with customs very different from those of the English.

England badly needed a revival of literacy and learning, and to this Alfred devoted his last ten years. Like Charlemagne, he carried out his programme of education through a circle of court intellectuals. In some ways his own contribution to this project is the most remarkable of Alfred's achievements. He was the only English king before Henry VIII who wrote books. Lamenting the destruction of manuscripts and the decay of scholarship, he learnt Latin and translated works into English for his subjects' benefit. Among the many translations which his circle produced (and which include, significantly, Bede's *Ecclesiastical History*), three are probably Alfred's own work. It is also believed that the *Anglo-Saxon Chronicle*, as we now have it, may have been first compiled at Alfred's court. For priests, a good Latin education became once again necessary for high office. It is hard to know how well Alfred's Renaissance succeeded, but it must have provided more literate priests and a more learned laity: good foundations for the monastic reform of two generations later. Alfred was lucky that future events caused so many of his various schemes to bear fruit. Even allowing for this, he remains the outstanding figure of early English history.

The reigns of Edward the Elder (899–924), Athelstan (924–39), and Edmund (939–46) were dominated by the reconquest of the Danelaw. This half-century was the formative period for national kingship. Dynastic feuds were avoided, partly through Alfred's careful provision for the succession and partly through some lucky chances. In 902 a dangerous split was averted when Edward's cousin, who had sought Danish help to win the crown, was killed in battle. Athelstan succeeded smoothly in 924 because he was both the rightful heir to Wessex and had been educated in his Mercian aunt's household. By the mid-century there was no serious possibility that Mercia, still less any other kingdom, could revert to an older dynasty. The royal house of Wessex was the royal house of England.

The campaigns of Edward's reign were mainly directed by the king himself in partnership with his sister Æthelflaed, 'the Lady of the Mercians'. The English offensive began when a Danish raid into Mercia was defeated in 910. Over the next eight years, Edward pushed into the Danelaw while his sister kept the Danes busy on their Mercian frontier. Æthelflaed was now threatened from two directions, for Norwegian Vikings from Ireland had begun attacking the west coast. Her main achievement was to build a series of new Mercian *burhs*: on the east frontier against the Danes, on the west frontier against the Welsh, and in the north-west to block Norwegian raids on Tamworth from the Dee and Mersey. In 917 Æthelflaed took Derby, giving Edward a chance to invade East Anglia while the enemy was occupied. By 918 all the southern Danelaw had fallen to Edward, though isolated Danish armies were holding out in Stamford, Leicester, Nottingham, and Lincoln. Leicester submitted to Æthelflaed, but her death soon afterwards forced Edward to halt the campaign while he secured Mercia. Returning swiftly, he took Stamford, Nottingham, and Lincoln, and by the end of 920 the English frontier was fixed at the Humber.

Meanwhile, Edward was forming links with his other non-English neighbours. In 918 he received the 'submissions' of the Welsh kings of Gwynedd and Dyfed. In 923, says the *Chronicle*, 'the king of Scots and the whole Scottish nation accepted him as father and lord: so also did Raegnald and the sons of Eadwulf and all the inhabitants of Northumbria, both English and Danish, Norwegians and others; together with the king of the Strathclyde Welsh and all his subjects'. These were the first in a series of such 'submissions', culminating in an extraordinary spectacle in 973 when eight 'British kings' swore fealty to Edward's grandson Edgar and rowed him on the River Dee.

It must be emphasized that these were personal submissions to the kings to whom they were made: they involved the acceptance of lordship and protection, not the permanent surrender of independence. In fact, Scotland and Wales were both advancing towards their own internal unity. In *c.*850 Kenneth Mac Alpin, king of the Scots, had annexed the Pictish kingdom, and over the next two centuries Scotland developed under Scottish (as against Pictish) rule. In Wales, politics were transformed by the sudden expansion of Gwynedd from the late ninth century onwards, leaving only Dyfed of the smaller kingdoms. The Anglo-Saxons never conquered Wales or Scotland, and in each a native power had emerged dominant by 1066. None the less, Wales was much influenced both by England and by the Vikings.

Among the many groups competing for land in tenth-century Britain was a new one—the Norwegians from Ireland. They had no fondness for the Danes, and their main object was to gain control of the northern Danelaw. In 918 a force led by Raegnald attacked Scotland, based itself in Northumbria, and the following year took York, where Raegnald established himself as king. The Norse kingdom was to last, with interruptions, for thirty-five years, during which trade grew and the twin Norse cities of York and Dublin expanded fast. Excavation at York has revealed streets of timber houses and shops, laid out by the Danes and redeveloped by Raegnald's followers. During the reigns of Athelstan and Edmund, the enemies of the English were the Norwegians more than the Danes.

In 920 Edmund had accepted Raegnald's fealty and thus acknowledged his status. But when a new Norse king tried to seize his inheritance in 926, Athelstan attacked and captured York, destroyed its defences, and received the submission of the kings of Scotland and Strathclyde. Six years later, relations between Athelstan and the Scots broke down. Fearing invasion, the various rivals of the English made common cause. But in 937 the English army under Athelstan defeated a combined force of Norse, Scots, and Strathclyde Welsh. Athelstan was now at the height of his power, king of the English and Danes and in some sense overlord of the British. He was respected by foreign powers, and formed marriage alliances with the French and German royal families. His charters show the Welsh princes regularly attending his court; Hywel Dda, king of Dyfed in Athelstan's time, imitated English silver pennies and issued laws modelled on English codes.

But much still depended on the individual king. Soon after Athelstan's death in 939, a Norse army returned under Olaf Guthfrithson. The new king Edmund was forced to recognize Olaf as king of York and its dependent territories. Olaf died in 941, and during the next four years Edmund recovered the northern Danelaw and ravaged Strathclyde. Especially interesting here is a contemporary poem in which Edmund features as liberator of the Danes from their Norse oppressors: the great-grandsons of Alfred's enemies could identify with the English Crown rather than with their fellow Scandinavians. But in 947, the year after Edmund's death, York fell yet again to a Norse king, Eric Bloodaxe. The next six years saw a confused struggle between Eric, the new English king, Eadred, and a Norwegian rival named Olaf Sihtricson. In 954 Eadred invaded Northumbria, this time for good, and the last king of York was driven out and killed.

From nearly fifty years of complex warfare the house of Wessex had emerged triumphant. The tranquil reign of Edgar (959–75) proves that more had been created than mere military power. Edgar was not a conqueror: one historian has written that 'his part in history was to maintain the peace established in England by earlier kings'. But this was no mean achievement: the kingdom was young, and it is with Edgar that the main developments in late Saxon kingship come into focus.

Ceded to Scotland c. 975

LOTHIAN

STRATHCLYDE

NORTHUMBRIA

Bamburgh

North

English Frontier 927

Sea

Carlisle

Eamont

Isle of Man

KINGDOM

York

OF YORK

English Frontier, 920

Dublin

Manchester

Runcorn   Thelwall

Bakewell

Davenport

Eddisbury

Chester

Lincoln

LAND OF THE

ENGLISH   FIVE BOROUGHS

English Frontier, 917

Stafford

Tamworth

EAST

Thetford

MERCIA

Bedford

ANGLIA

Cambridge

Buckingham

Cricklade

Hertford

Malmesbury

Wallingford

Maldon

Bath

London

W E S S E X

Winchester

Canterbury

Lydford

Exeter

Southampton   Porchester   Hastings

Wareham

Chichester

▨	Norse settlements
▨	Danish settlements
—	Boundary of Guthrum's Kingdom

0   50   100 *miles*
0   50   100   150 *km.*

England in the tenth century

From Athelstan onwards, kings made laws more frequently
and went into more detail. They cover a wide range of subjects—
peace-keeping, the suppression of thieves, the hierarchy of
churches, the conduct of merchants and markets, to name only a
few. The emphasis is on unity: Edgar's codes make allowance for
local custom, especially in the Danelaw, but insist that 'the
secular law shall stand in each folk as can best be established'. By
the early eleventh century the trying of most serious crimes was

reserved to the Crown, and there was a concept of a national peace which it was the king's duty and right to maintain. Royal authority was spread wider, and went deeper, than in any other tenth-century European country of comparable size.

Laws and charters were issued at meetings of the 'Witan' or royal council. Its development can be traced by means of the witness lists attached to charters. In the tenth century it was much bigger and probably more formal than the councils of earlier kings, and included numerous men described as 'ministers' or thegns. Some nineteenth-century historians tried too hard to see the Witan as a 'proto-parliament': it was in no sense a democratic body, nor did it impose 'constitutional' restraints on the king. But it was important. In the Witan new kings were chosen, solemn public acts were ratified, and business was discussed. It was composed of nobles, bishops, and many men of influence in their own localities. From Athelstan's reign onwards, the enlarged Witan was an established institution and a force to be reckoned with.

The king's will operated through a much-improved system of local government. During the tenth century, the regional anomalies of England were progressively reduced to a single framework of 'shires'. Some had existed for a century or more, and many were based on still older boundaries. But it was essentially under Edgar that the English counties stabilized in the form which lasted until 1974, exactly a thousand years later. The shires were entrusted to a group of leading magnates, the aldermen. In ninth-century Wessex there had been an alderman for each shire, but by a gradual process, which seems to start under Athelstan, the number of aldermen fell and their status rose. By Edgar's reign the alderman was becoming less like a local official, and more like his successor the eleventh-century earl. But he still remained in regular touch with the government of the shires under his care.

For legal and administrative purposes the shires were broken down into subdivisions, called 'hundreds' in most counties, and 'wapentakes' in the northern Danelaw. Each hundred had its own court for settling local business, and communal obligations to provide troops and oarsmen came to be assessed by the hundred. Even this was not the bottom of the ladder: for law enforcement the population was organized into groups of ten mutually-responsible households or 'tithings'. The weight of royal government reached the individual peasant through a structure of remarkable complexity. How much was new in the tenth century is hard to say. The principle of the hundred appears in earlier law codes, and it seems likely that late Saxon hundreds were often or usually based on older territories. But the system was rationalized and improved by Alfred's successors, and under Edgar it emerges clearly in its developed form.

Another mark of royal strength was the coinage. Even before Alfred, the three coin-issuing authorities (the kings of Wessex and Mercia and the Archbishop of Canterbury) had agreed on a standard currency of silver pennies. Decrees issued by Athelstan between 924 and 939 order that 'one coinage shall run throughout the land'. He and his heirs managed to maintain uniformity remarkably well, and all coins were minted by strictly-controlled moneyers in the *burhs*. In *c*.973 Edgar designed a new coinage of pennies, which remained the basis of the English currency until long after the Conquest. The excellence of the coins shows a degree of control which was, once again, unique in contemporary Europe.

Edgar's main personal achievement was his encouragement of monastic reform. True Benedictine monasticism seems to have been almost dead in early tenth-century England. Several great and innumerable small minsters had been destroyed by the Danes, while those which survived had tended more and more towards the loose, secular life-style that Bede had long ago deplored. Groups of minster priests lived in separate houses with their wives and children; in their everyday existence they came closer to cathedral canons than to monks. A successful reconstruction of the English Church would need models for the new monasticism, and money to build the new monasteries. The first was provided by the great European reform movement, of which the English reform was essentially a part; the second was provided by Edgar and his nobility. The prime movers were three great churchmen, St. Dunstan, St. Æthelwold, and St. Oswold.

The monastic reform in England began in the early 940s, and under royal patronage: Glastonbury, given to Dunstan by King Edmund, and Abingdon, given to Æthelwold by King Eadred, were the first of the 'new' houses. But Edmund and Eadred were both lukewarm, while the next king, Eadwig, had a personal grudge against Dunstan. This had productive consequences, for Dunstan was exiled abroad and gained a wide knowledge of European monasticism. Times changed with Edgar's accession in 959: Dunstan became Archbishop of Canterbury, and Æthelwold bishop of Winchester. Oswold, the youngest of the three, had spent some time in the French monastery of Fleury. Dunstan persuaded Edgar to give him the bishopric of Worcester, and soon afterwards Oswold built a monastery at Westbury-on-Trym. Over the next half-century some fifty houses were founded or refounded under the influence of Glastonbury, Abingdon, and Westbury.

The monks in the new monasteries followed a way of life based on the rule of St. Benedict, with elaborations in ritual and daily routine in line with Continental practice. In c.970 the various traditions were combined in the *Regularis Concordia*, one rule for all the English houses to follow. Edgar's part was crucial: he gave the weight of his authority to the movement, and all the new monasteries were under his direct patronage. The expulsion of secular priests from the old minsters to make way for monks, which first happened at Winchester in 964, would have been difficult without royal backing. Edgar gave generously, and expected others to do likewise: by the 970s there are signs that the drain on aristocratic funds was becoming resented. None the less, to found a monastery was once again a socially prestigious act.

The new houses were wealthy, respected, and endowed with treasures and fine buildings. Literary sources hint at the richness of English art under Edgar. A number of the magnificent illuminated books survive, but only fragments of the gold, enamel, and ivory ornaments, and almost none of the major buildings. Fate has been unkind to late Anglo-Saxon architecture, for all the greatest churches were rebuilt after the Conquest. As enlarged in the tenth century, the Old Minster at Winchester was 250 feet long, with side-chapels, elaborate western towers, and carved and painted friezes. But it must be stressed that this spiritual and material regeneration touched only a fraction (probably under 10 per cent) of the old communities: the others continued in their former ways. Thus at the Norman Conquest the Benedictine houses co-existed with an unknown number of small secular minsters, relics of the pre-Viking English Church.

If the new monasticism owed much to Europe, it was distinctively English in its relations with the state and society at large. By 1000 most English bishops were monks, and both bishops and abbots deliberated with lay magnates in the Witan. Great churchmen were among the most valued advisers of the last Anglo-Saxon kings. Equally, Church reform added lustre to a king who, perhaps more than any of his predecessors, set store by the sacred character of his office. Edgar's coronation in 973 was postponed until he reached thirty, the minimum canonical age for ordination to the priesthood. The climax of the ceremony was not the crowning, but the anointing with holy oil which

Odda's chapel, Deerhurst: the private church of a late Saxon thegn. Inscription dated 1056 states: 'Earl Odda had this royal hall built and dedicated in honour of the Holy Trinity for the soul of his brother Ælfric'. View of north side of nave, with chancel incorporated in late medieval farmhouse.

conferred near-priestly status and set the king above human judgement. As the homilist Ælfric of Eynsham put it, 'no man can make himself king, but the people have the free will to choose him to be king who is most pleasing to them. But once he has been consecrated king he has power over the people, and they may not shake his yoke from their necks.' The frontispiece of the Winchester New Minster foundation charter shows Edgar as he wanted to be seen: crowned, standing between two saints, and offering his gift to the heavenly king through whom earthly kings rule.

Æthelred and Cnut: the Decline of the English Monarchy

The next two reigns would show that there were still great limitations on the national monarchy. A new king could not count on loyalty before he had won it, as was shown when Edgar died in 975 leaving two sons under age. The elder, Edward, became unpopular, and many nobles preferred his brother Æthelred. Edward was crowned, but four years later he was murdered at Corfe. There can be little doubt that Æthelred's supporters were responsible, and the murder was a fitting start for an unhappy reign. Æthelred 'the Unready' (979–1016) has always had a bad press (though his famous nickname has lost its original meaning, which involved the pun *Æthelræd Unræd*, 'Noble-Counsel No-Counsel'). Probably he did lack the qualities which were still so important for kingship: the knack of putting trust in the right places and commanding trust in others. On the other hand, law and justice continued to develop in his reign under the guidance of the learned Archbishop Wulfstan. If it had not been for a new problem—the return of the Vikings—the English state might have held together as well as it had done under Edgar.

The new raiders were even more dangerous than their ninth-century ancestors. By the 970s the Danish king, Harold Bluetooth, who had gained control of both Denmark and Norway, was creating a formidable army of highly-trained professional soldiers. In 988 Harold was deposed by his son Swein, who maintained his father's army and built large fortresses to house military communities. One of these has been excavated at Trelleborg in Denmark. It consists of a large circular earthwork enclosing groups of great boat-shaped halls, all planned with mathematical precision. Both Trelleborg and the Danish sagas suggest a degree of co-ordination and discipline which the English army would have found it hard to match.

The attacks began within a year or two of Æthelred's accession. At first they were on a fairly small scale, but in 991 a large Danish force defeated Alderman Byrhtnoth and the Essex militia at Maldon, and had to be bought off with a large payment. The pattern was repeated after heavy raids in 994, 997, and 1002. It is for these payments that Æthelred's reign is now so notorious. Huge numbers of his pennies have been found in Scandinavia, and several Swedish tombstones commemorate mercenaries who went to England and enriched themselves with tribute. In the 990s, as in 1066, England's wealth was also its danger.

How was Æthelred to cope? One measure was to prevent the harbouring of Vikings by his neighbours, and for geographical reasons the young duchy of Normandy was the most important of these. The Normans were only a few generations away from their own Viking ancestors, and had sometimes opened their ports to raiders returning from England. But in 991 King Æthelred and Duke Richard made a treaty against aiding each other's enemies, and ten years later Æthelred married the duke's daughter. So began the fateful association of Normandy and England.

Hitherto the king's internal policy does not seem to have been very different from that of his predecessors. He inherited a powerful, well-established aristocracy, and his early charters show him building up support with grants of land just as Eadwig and Edgar had done. But from 1002 the Viking threat became rapidly more severe, and exposed a basic weakness in royal power. The king's lands, and probably his activities generally, were still heavily concentrated in Wessex. The resources with which he could buy support in the north and east were very limited—and these were just the areas where support was most needed to be bought. They still had separatist tendencies, and contained many people who remembered their Danish origins. Æthelred's later charters show a shift of patronage into the Midlands and eastern England, and new men of non-Wessex origin become prominent. The king was struggling to hold England united and in a state of defence. His ineptitudes may have made the task harder, but nobody would have found it easy.

The strain on the government was demonstrated when, in 1002, Æthelred and his council ordered a massacre of all the Danes living in England. This extraordinary command cannot have been fully enforced—in some areas the population was largely Danish—but it hints at something approaching national hysteria. We know that, when the Danes in Oxford took refuge in St. Frideswide's minster church, the citizens burnt it down. This massacre almost certainly prompted the Danish invasion of the following year, led by King Swein himself. Swein sacked Norwich, but his East Anglian campaign involved heavy losses and in 1005 he withdrew to Denmark. Next year he returned, led his army through Berkshire, Wiltshire, and Hampshire, and once again had to be bought off with a large payment. In the

A late Anglo-Saxon drawing of a wheeled plough, pulled by a team of oxen.

ensuing respite the government built a new fleet, but early in 1009 eighty of the ships were burnt through the treason of an English captain. On the heels of this misfortune, another Danish army landed, led by Thorkill the Tall and Hemming. In 1010 they burnt Oxford, and then moved to East Anglia from which they raided into Kent the following year. The campaign ended unexpectedly in 1012 when Thorkill changed sides, disgusted by his own army's brutal murder of Archbishop Ælfheah. This brought forty-five ships into Æthelred's service; the rest of the army left England.

The feebleness of England's defences was now clear to all, and when Swein returned in 1013 it was with the intention of conquest. Disillusioned with Æthelred's government, the men of the Danelaw welcomed a Danish king and accepted Swein almost immediately. By the end of the year he had taken Oxford, Winchester, and London, and Æthelred had fled to exile in Normandy. In February 1014 Swein died; his son Harold succeeded to his Scandinavian empire, but the army in England accepted Harold's younger brother Cnut as their king. Meanwhile Æthelred had returned, and by spring he was fielding an expedition against the Danes. Caught unprepared, Cnut withdrew to Denmark. In 1015 he was back with a bigger force, to find that Æthelred's son Edmund Ironside had taken control of the northern Danelaw in defiance of his father. During the next few months Cnut recovered Northumbria and then moved towards London. But before the Danish forces arrived Æthelred was dead and Edmund had been proclaimed king. Even in Wessex, however, many men accepted Cnut's lordship without a struggle. Edmund rallied his forces, and for a little while it seemed that the Danes might still be driven back. But in the autumn of 1016 Cnut won a decisive battle at Ashingdon in Essex. The treaty which followed left Edmund with only Wessex, and when he died shortly afterwards Cnut became king of all England.

King Cnut (1016–35) had to deal with problems which were not dissimilar to those which faced King William fifty years later. Like William, Cnut set out to rule not as a conqueror but as a rightful English king. He married Æthelred's widow, and acted ruthlessly to secure the throne: several leading English were killed, including Æthelred's eldest surviving son. Once secure, Cnut adopted with enthusiasm the traditional attributes of civilized kingship. He issued laws and founded monasteries; in the words of a chronicler of the next century, he changed himself 'from a wild man into a most Christian king'. Yet he was still a

Dane, and on his brother's death in 1019 he inherited a great northern empire of which England was only part. During the 1020s he became more and more involved in Danish affairs. The breadth of Cnut's involvements is the main reason for his changes in England, which were relatively few, but in the end damaging.

Naturally he had many followers eager for rewards. There was no full-scale replacement of the English landowning class such as occurred after 1066, but a good many Danes joined the aristocracy. An alien and therefore rather insecure king, Cnut kept a regiment of household troops or 'housecarls' who were a considerable burden on the country. After thirty years of paying to keep the Danes away, landowners now had to pay to support a Danish standing army.

Cnut also had to make English government function during his long absences abroad. In 1017 he divided the kingdom into four earldoms—Northumbria, East Anglia, Mercia, and Wessex. This ran obvious risks of reviving local separatist feeling, especially since the Northumbrian and East Anglian earls were both Danes. By the end of the reign the most important figures were Siward earl of Northumbria, Leofric earl of Mercia (whose wife was Lady Godiva of Coventry fame), and Godwin earl of Wessex. Godwin's origins are obscure, but by the 1030s he and his family were the wealthiest and most powerful laymen below the king. Cnut's earldoms are largely responsible for the power politics which dominate the last thirty years of Anglo-Saxon history.

The End of the Anglo-Saxon Kingdom

When Cnut died in 1035 there were several possible successors. The Wessex dynasty was represented by Æthelred's younger sons Edward and Alfred, now at the Norman court, and by Edmund Ironside's son who was exiled in Hungary. Cnut had two sons by two wives: Harold, by Ælfgyfu of Northampton, and Harthacnut, by Emma the widow of Æthelred. Cnut had wanted Harthacnut to succeed to his whole empire. But while Harthacnut delayed in Denmark the Witan appointed Harold as regent (despite the opposition of both Emma and Godwin), and in 1037 made him king. The previous year, the English prince Alfred had unwisely visited England and died of injuries inflicted at Godwin's instigation. Harthacnut was recalled after Harold's death in 1040, but when he died two years later the Danish royal line ended. Almost everyone now wanted to restore the ancient dynasty of Wessex. Æthelred's son Edward had been living for a year at the English court, and in 1042 he was elected king.

Edward 'the Confessor' (1042–66) was not the most able of kings. He was tactless in his dealings with the nobility, especially in promoting Norman favourites acquired during his exile. Always ascetic, he turned more and more to religion in his later years, and was to be venerated as the principal English royal saint. But despite his personal shortcomings, he inherited the strongest government in eleventh-century Europe. The reason for this strength lay partly in institutions which were centuries old, partly in the very disruptions of the last sixty years.

Local government had developed since Edgar's day. On the one hand, the great earldoms consolidated under Cnut had given huge territorial power to a few men. An insecure king now had to face the threat of over-mighty subjects. On the other hand, an invaluable new official had appeared to carry out royal policy in the localities. During Æthelred's reign one of the king's local bailiffs ('reeves') in each shire had come to be known as the 'shire-reeve' or sheriff. He was the king's chief executive agent in the shire, and gradually assumed more and more of the alderman's functions. The sheriff was responsible for collecting royal revenues and the profits of justice, but he also belonged to the growing community of local thegns. In the shire court he could announce the king's will to the gentry of the shire, take a big part in day-to-day business, and add the weight of royal authority to action against oppressive magnates. The shire court and the sheriff are among the most important Anglo-Saxon legacies to later medieval government.

A highly efficient tax system had evolved as a direct result of England's weakness under Æthelred. The huge sums paid to the Danes in the 990s had to be raised from the country. The 'Danegeld', as it came to be called, was based on the ancient method of assessing land in hides, and was raised at a fixed rate of so much per hide. Between 1012 and 1051 it was levied yearly by the successive kings, though now for maintaining their standing armies. The complex system of assessment developed for this purpose is the basis of the later Domesday Book, and it is an extraordinary tribute to the early eleventh-century English bureaucracy that the Norman kings continued to raise Danegeld for nearly a century after the Conquest.

This period also saw a new type of official document: the royal writ. Writs were possibly issued by Æthelred and certainly by Cnut, but the earliest which now survive as originals are from

Edward's reign. In its initial form, the writ was a brief notification to the shire-earl and the sheriff or bishop that a grant of land had been made and should be witnessed in the shire court. A typical example reads:

Edward the king greets Harold the earl and Tofi his sheriff and all his thegns in Somerset in friendly fashion. And I make known that Alfred has sold to Giso the bishop the land of Lutton peacefully and quietly: he did this in my presence at Parret, and in the presence of Edith my wife, Harold the earl and many others who were there present with us. We also wish that the same bishop shall hold that land with all its appurtenances which the bishop possesses with sac and soc as freely as any of his predecessors as bishops ever did anything. And if anything be taken away from it unjustly we ask that it may be restored. Nor shall it be done otherwise.

This combined efficiency with a new means of authentication: a pendent wax seal, stamped from a die kept in the king's household. As title-deeds, writs provided useful supplements to the old formal charters, which were unwieldy and easily forged. They also provided a means for the king to make his will known quickly and clearly in the shires. The Conqueror soon adapted the writ for issuing orders, and all the more important types of post-Conquest royal document are descended from it.

When ordering a taxation or issuing a writ, the king would have consulted his secretariat. Edward the Confessor, like kings since Alfred at the latest, had a clerical staff of priests, headed by a chief clerk whose office developed into that of the medieval chancellor. One of their duties was to keep records: from the late Anglo-Saxon period comes evidence of very detailed surveys recording land-tenure, numbers of hides, and tax obligations. Some remarks by Bede suggest that even the seventh-century Northumbrian kings had enough precise information to grant land in exact numbers of hides; while from the eighth century a document called the *Tribal Hidage* lists the names and hidages of the peoples, provinces, and tribes dependent on Mercia. So we can be confident that ninth- and tenth-century kings had fiscal records of some kind, though how detailed is impossible to say. By Edward the Confessor's reign, the royal secretariat possessed rolls which listed the hidages of shires and hundreds, the amount of royal land they contained, and perhaps even the names, owners, and values of individual manors. We know this not from the documents themselves (though a few fragments survive), but from Domesday Book. The great survey of 1086 could scarcely have been compiled so quickly and so thoroughly if the commissioners had not had access to earlier lists. The loss of the pre-Conquest public records is tragic, but the mere knowledge that they existed says much for the quality of Edward's administration.

If English government changed greatly between the reigns of Alfred and Edward, so too did English society. The mid-ninth to mid-eleventh centuries saw rapid growth in the population and economy. Before Domesday Book there are no statistics, but written, archaeological, and topographical evidence gives some strong hints that many aspects of later English society crystallized in these years. Not surprisingly, more people meant bigger towns. By the Conquest there were English towns in a sense that we would understand today: large concentrations of people with markets and tradesmen, groups of craftsmen in specialized quarters, guilds and regulations, numerous churches, and in some cases rapidly expanding suburbs. The late Saxon law codes recognize trading centres or 'ports' (not necessarily coastal) and large boroughs, rated according to the number of moneyers they were allowed to contain. The towns included most of the *burhs* and many minster centres, but they were not confined to places of ancient importance. We cannot even guess at the number of local markets, but a good many which first appear in the thirteenth century may be older than they seem.

The countryside was also changing, though it is hard to trace the changes clearly. Topographical studies suggest a process of settlement nucleation in the more populous areas, with the inhabitants of scattered farms clustering into villages. At the same time, agriculture was becoming more complex and more integrated, so that by 1066 many parts of England had 'common fields', farmed by peasants with intermingled holdings, and therefore probably with corporately-agreed cropping patterns. The early development of field systems is now a controversial subject, but it is in the tenth century that we can first detect the basic contrast between the open-field zone of Midland England and the surrounding 'wood-pasture' areas. Much remains uncertain about the relationship between changes in settlement form, agriculture, and land-holding, but it seems that the process went through several stages and continued well beyond the Conquest. There are also suggestions that sometimes these were not spontaneous developments, but rearrangements planned from above. Peasant society was becoming more stratified and cohesive, and lords were making greater demands on their tenants.

One reason is that there were more manors and more manorial lords. Except in retarded areas, most of the old 'multiple estates' had fragmented by the eleventh century into units correspond-

ing in size to modern rural parishes. Population grew, cultivation expanded, and the components of the old 'extensive'
systems became self-contained entities. Many more charters
survive from the tenth century than from the eighth and ninth
together; most of them grant smaller units of land, and the
proportion in favour of laymen is higher. The class of small
thegns had broadened into a rural squirearchy, and Domesday
Book shows that in 1066 England contained hundreds of
manorial lords.

This is the context in which most parish churches were
founded. Just as kings and bishops had built minsters in the
seventh and eighth centuries, so thegns built manorial churches
in the tenth and eleventh. There were *some* private churches from
a relatively early date (Bede mentions a bishop consecrating one
in the 690s), but both documents and archaeology suggest that
the majority were founded after 900, perhaps even after 950.
Pastoral organization must have been chaotic: the minster
parishes were slowly decaying, and more and more of the manors
within them were acquiring rival churches of their own, served
by manorial priests. Eleventh-century churches (both before and
after the Conquest) were in effect 'owned' by their lords, and
their functions were determined on tenurial rather than pastoral
lines: the church's function was to serve the needs of the lord, his
household, and tenants. We can scarcely speak of anything so
formal as a 'parochial system', though the raw materials were
there: probably more than half the parish churches existing in
1700 were founded before 1066.

So the familiar landmarks of rural England—villages, manor
houses, churches—took shape mainly in the late Saxon period.
For Archbishop Wulfstan, writing in *c.*1010, the last two were
normal marks of thegnhood: 'If a *ceorl* prospered so that he
possessed fully five hides of land of his own, a church and a
kitchen, a bell and a fortress-gate, a seat and special office in the
king's hall, he was worthy thereafter to be called a thegn.' The
'fortress-gate' in this famous passage leads to a question which
has become needlessly controversial: were there castles in
pre-Conquest England? One writer, equating private castles
with feudalism and convinced that late Saxon England was
non-feudal, argues that it contained no fortresses beyond the
communal *burhs*. But if a strongly-fortified manor house counts
as a castle, the existence of castles says little about a society
except that it included a land-based aristocracy of some status. In
fact excavation now proves that fortified houses *did* exist, and
complex manorial buildings surrounded by banks and ditches of

*c.*1000–20 have been found at Sulgrave, Northamptonshire, and Goltho, Lincolnshire. These sites show that ordinary late Saxon thegns' residences could be as imposing as most manor houses of the twelfth and early thirteenth centuries.

Warfare was becoming more professional, and equipment consequently more expensive. By the end of the tenth century, a system of military service had developed in which every five hides was responsible for providing and equipping one man for the *fyrd* (militia). This acknowledged that the average farmer could not reasonably be expected to kit himself out from his own resources, and by implication raised the status of the fighting man. Five hides, according to Wulfstan, was a thegn's minimum estate, and armour and weapons had become another mark of thegnhood. The fully-armed late Saxon warrior was something more than a *ceorl* turned soldier.

By Æthelred's reign the monastic reform was running out of steam. Burton Abbey in Staffordshire (1004) and Eynsham Abbey in Oxfordshire (1005) were the last great foundations, and the general political disruption and draining of resources soon put a stop to large-scale patronage and building. Edward's piety did, however, produce one building project, the most ambitious that England had ever seen. In about 1050 he began to rebuild the old minster church at Westminster on a scale worthy of the English monarchy. Architecture in England was stagnant, but in

Westminster Abbey and its precincts c.1100: a reconstruction from archaeological and documentary evidence and surviving buildings (after Gem and Ball, 1980). In the foreground is the Abbey Church, built by Edward the Confessor and destroyed in the thirteenth and fourteenth centuries. Westminster Hall, in the background, was rebuilt by William II.

Normandy its development during the last forty years had been spectacular: the finest buildings of Edgar's day would have looked unimpressive beside the abbey churches of Bernay and Caen. So for Westminster Abbey Edward naturally looked to Norman architects, though his church as eventually built was magnificent and innovative even by their standards, and probably owed something to English decorative traditions. It is somewhat ironic that the last great monument of the house of Wessex was mainly a product of Norman culture.

The final years of Anglo-Saxon history are dominated by Godwin's family and the problem of the succession. Edward had married Godwin's daughter, but it was known that he was vowed to celibacy and would never produce an heir. Edward, son of Edmund Ironside, returned from Hungary with his infant son in 1057 but died almost immediately. The young prince Edgar was the legitimate heir, but nobody can have viewed with much enthusiasm the prospect of a child on the throne. The Norwegian king, Magnus, and after him his son Harold Hardrada, saw themselves as the heirs to Cnut's empire, including England. Neither candidate is likely to have appealed much to King Edward: his eyes, if they were turned anywhere, were turned across the Channel. The duchy of Normandy, where he had lived in exile for twenty-five years, had developed fast in strength and internal organization. In 1035 Duke Robert had been succeeded by his bastard son William, then a boy of seven. We will never know for certain if Edward promised his throne to William, but we can say that this is exactly the course which we might expect of him.

Edward had never forgiven Godwin for his brother's murder, and the tension between them came to a head in 1051. One of Edward's Norman friends became involved in a brawl at Dover, and several men were killed. Edward ordered Godwin, as earl of Wessex, to sack Dover in retribution. Godwin refused and raised troops against the king, who summoned the Mercian and Northumbrian earls with their full forces. Conflict was avoided; as a contemporary put it, 'some of them considered it would be great folly if they joined battle, because well-nigh all the noblest in England were present in those two companies, and they were convinced they would be leving the country open to the invasion of our enemies'. Godwin's support crumbled, and he and his family went into exile. Over the next year Edward increased the Norman element at court, but in 1052 Godwin returned with a large fleet and the king was obliged to be more compliant. The Norman archbishop fled home, and several of his fellow countrymen were banished at Godwin's request.

Godwin now enjoyed virtually supreme power, but in 1053 he died. His successor in the earldom of Wessex was his son Harold, destined to be the last Anglo-Saxon king. When Earl Siward of Northumbria died two years later, his earldom went to Harold's brother Tostig. Thanks to the activities of King Gruffydd of Gwynedd, the standing of Godwin's sons soon rose yet higher. Gruffydd, who had recently made himself supreme in Wales, allied with the exiled heir to the Mercian earldom and launched a series of attacks into English territory, in the course of which Hereford was sacked and burnt. The combined forces of Harold and Tostig drove Gruffydd back into Wales, and in 1063 caused his downfall and death. With this success behind him, Harold was the outstanding figure in England. Despite his lack of royal ancestry, he seemed an obvious candidate for the throne.

But in 1064, or perhaps early in 1065, Harold visited Duke William in Normandy. He went, say the Norman sources, as Edward's ambassador, to swear an oath confirming an earlier promise of the English crown. It is possible, but on the whole unlikely, that the story of the oath is a Norman invention. But there is a third explanation, the one which the English artists of the Bayeux Tapestry may secretly be trying to give us: Harold falls into William's hands by mischance, is forced to swear the

King Edward the Confessor receives Earl Harold on his return from Normandy. A detail from the Bayeux Tapestry. This unique embroidery frieze measures 70m by 50cm. It was probably commissioned by Odo of Bayeux and made in a Canterbury workshop.

oath, and returns shamefacedly to a horrified King Edward. Whichever version is true (and on balance the Norman one may have the best claim after all), many contemporaries believed that William had right on his side as well as might.

The events of the last two years moved quickly. During 1065 Northumbria rebelled against Earl Tostig. Harold mediated, but the local nominee was upheld: Tostig went into exile, henceforth his brother's enemy. On 5 January 1066 King Edward died. Urgent military need overrode legality, and the Witan elected Harold as king. This was the signal for his two adult rivals. Harold Hardrada of Norway was the first to move: aided by the exiled Tostig, he invaded Northumbria during the summer and occupied York. Harold, who was awaiting the expected invasion from Normandy, was forced to move north. At Stamford Bridge near York he met and defeated the Norwegian forces on 25 September. Hardrada and Tostig were both killed, and King Harold recovered Northumbria.

Meanwhile Duke William's fleet, which had been delayed by bad weather, landed at Pevensey on 28 September. Harold rushed southwards; but the preparations which he had made two months earlier had fallen apart, and the core of his army was exhausted. On 14 October 1066, the English and Norman armies met near Hastings. Harold's forces gathered on the crest of a hill and formed a wall of shields. The battle lasted all day, and at first the English position seemed strong. Apparently it was lost through lack of discipline rather than lack of force. Sections of Harold's army seem to have been enticed down the slope in pursuit of real or feigned retreats, and then cut off and over-whelmed. Gradually the English troops were broken up; the centre held until dusk, but the outcome was already clear when Harold fell on the spot marked in later centuries by the high altar of Battle Abbey.

William advanced to Dover and then to Canterbury, where he received the submission of Winchester. But his main objective was London, for there the core of the English resistance had gathered under Edgar Atheling. Meeting opposition at London Bridge, William encircled the city leaving a trail of devastation. Meanwhile the Atheling's party was crumbling, and when William reached Berkhamsted the English nobles, headed by Edgar himself, met him and offered their fealty. Alfred's family had survived Danes, Norsemen, and Danes again, but at last a foreign dynasty had supplanted it for good.

JOHN GILLINGHAM

3. *The Early Middle Ages*

(1066–1290)

1066 and All That

ON Christmas Day 1066 Duke William of Normandy was acclaimed king in Westminster Abbey. It was an electrifying moment. The shouts of acclamation—in English as well as in French—alarmed the Norman guards stationed outside the abbey. Believing that inside the church something had gone horribly wrong, they set fire to the neighbouring houses. Half a century later, a Norman monk recalled the chaos of that day. 'As the fire spread rapidly, the people in the church were thrown into confusion and crowds of them rushed outside, some to fight the flames, others to take the chance to go looting. Only the monks, the bishops and a few clergy remained before the altar. Though they were terrified, they managed to carry on and complete the consecration of the king who was trembling violently.'

Despite his victory at Hastings, despite the surrender of London and Winchester, William's position was still a precarious one and he had good reason to tremble. It was to take at least another five years before he could feel fairly confident that the conquest had been completed. There were risings against Norman rule in every year from 1067 to 1070: in Kent, in the south-west, in the Welsh marches, in the Fenland, and in the north. The Normans had to live like an army of occupation, living, eating, and sleeping together in operational units. They had to build castles—strong points from which a few men could dominate a subject population. There may well have been no more than 10,000 Normans living in the midst of a hostile population of one or two million. This is not to say that every single Englishman actively opposed the Normans. Unquestionably there were many who co-operated with them; it was this which made possible the successful Norman take-over of so many Anglo-Saxon institutions. But there is plenty of evidence to show that the English resented becoming an oppressed majority in their own country. The years of insecurity were to have a profound effect on subsequent history. They meant that England received not just a new royal family but also a new ruling class, a new culture and language. Probably no other conquest in European history has had such disastrous consequences for the defeated.

Almost certainly this had not been William's original intention. In the early days many Englishmen were able to offer their submission and retain their lands. Yet by 1086 something had clearly changed. Domesday Book is a record of a land deeply marked by the scars of conquest. In 1086 there were only two surviving English lords of any account. More than 4,000 thegns had lost their lands and been replaced by a group of less than 200 barons. A few of the new landlords were Bretons and men from Flanders and Lorraine but most were Normans. In the case of the Church we can put a date to William's anti-English policy. In 1070 he had some English bishops deposed and thereafter appointed no Englishman to either bishopric or abbey. In military matters, the harrying of the north during the winter of 1069–70 also suggests ruthlessness on a new scale at about this time. In Yorkshire this meant that between 1066 and 1086 land values fell by as much as two-thirds. But whenever and however it occurred it is certain that by 1086 the Anglo-Saxon aristocracy was no more and its place had been taken by a new Norman élite. Naturally this new élite retained its old lands on the Continent; the result was that England and Normandy, once two separate states, now became a single cross-Channel political community, sharing not only a ruling dynasty, but also a single Anglo-Norman aristocracy. Given the advantages of water transport, the Channel no more divided England from Normandy than the Thames divided Middlesex from Surrey. From now on, until 1204, the histories of England and Normandy were inextricably interwoven.

Since Normandy was a principality ruled by a duke who owed homage to the king of France this also meant that from now on 'English' politics became part of French politics. But the French connection went deeper still. The Normans, being Frenchmen, brought with them to England the French language and French culture. Moreover, we are not dealing with a single massive input of 'Frenchness' in the generation after 1066 followed by a gradual reassertion of 'Englishness'. The Norman Conquest of 1066 was followed by an Angevin conquest of 1153–4; although this did not involve the settlement of a Loire Valley aristocracy in England, the effect of the arrival of the court of Henry II and

Aerial photograph of Old Sarum: a graphic illustration of the problems facing the first post-Conquest generation. The Norman cathedral huddles close to the castle, itself built to defend a group of men too small to need the full extent of the prehistoric ramparts.

Eleanor of Aquitaine was to reinforce the dominance of French culture.

Whereas in 1066 less than 30 percent of Winchester property owners had non-English names, by 1207 the proportion had risen to over 80 per cent, mostly French names like William, Robert, and Richard. This receptiveness to Continental influence means that at this time it is the foreignness of English art that is most striking. In ecclesiastical architecture, for example, the European terms 'Romanesque' and 'Gothic' describe the fashionable styles much better than 'Norman' and 'Early English'. Although churches built in England, like manuscripts illuminated in England, often contain some recognizably English elements, the designs which the architects and artists were adapting came from abroad, sometimes from the Mediterranean world (Italy, Sicily, or even Byzantium), usually from France. It was a French architect, William of Sens, who was called in to rebuild the choir of Canterbury Cathedral after the fire of 1174. Similarly Henry III's rebuilding of Westminster Abbey was heavily influenced by French models. Indeed so great was the pre-eminence of France in the fields of music, literature, and architecture, that French became a truly international rather than just a national language, a language spoken—and written—by anyone who wanted to consider himself civilized. Thus, in thirteenth-century England, French became, if anything, even more important than it had been before. Throughout most of the period covered by this chapter a well-educated Englishman was trilingual. English would be his mother tongue; he would have some knowledge of Latin, and he would speak fluent French. In this cosmopolitan society French was vital. It was the practical language of law and estate management as well as the language of song and verse, of *chanson* and romance. The Norman Conquest, in other words, ushered in a period during which England, like the kingdom of Jerusalem, can fairly be described as a part of France overseas, *Outremer*; in political terms, it was a French colony (though not, of course, one that belonged to the French king) until the early thirteenth century and a cultural colony thereafter.

It is hardly surprising, then, that generations of patriotic Englishmen should have looked upon the battle of Hastings as a national catastrophe. Yet even if we do not, as E. A. Freeman did, describe Paris as 'beastly', it can still be argued that the Norman Conquest was the greatest disaster in English history. Not because it was predatory and destructive—though, of course, like any conquest it was both—but because of the problem of '1066 and All That'. With 1066 as the most famous date in English history the Norman Conquest is a 'blessedly well-known landmark'. It is devastatingly easy to see it as a 'new beginning' or a 'significant turning-point'. Almost everything that happened in late eleventh-century England has been discussed in terms of the impact of the Norman Conquest. But the second half of the eleventh century was a period of rapid development throughout Europe. Countries which suffered no Norman Conquest were, none the less, transformed. So there is the problem. In some respects 1066 wrought great changes; in other respects, great changes occurred but can hardly be ascribed to the Conquest; in yet others, the most striking feature is not change at all, but continuity.

The main problem facing the historian of this period, however, is posed not by a single dramatic event, but by a social and cultural process of great complexity. This is the tremendous proliferation of written records which occurred during the twelfth and thirteenth centuries. Many more documents than ever before were written and many more were preserved.

Whereas from the whole of the Anglo-Saxon period about 2,000 writs and charters survive, from the thirteenth century alone there are uncounted tens of thousands. Of course the 2,000 Anglo-Saxon documents were only the tip of the iceberg; many more did not survive. But this is true also of the thirteenth century. It has, for example, been estimated that as many as eight million charters could have been produced for thirteenth-century smallholders and peasants alone. Even if this were to be a rather generous estimate, it would still be true that whole classes of the population, serfs for example, were now concerned with documents in ways that previously they had not been. Whereas in the reign of Edward the Confessor only the king is known to have possessed a seal, in Edward I's reign even serfs were required by statute to have them. At the centre of this development, and to some extent its motor, lay the king's government. The king possessed permanently organized writing offices, the chancery, and then the exchequer too: they were becoming busier and busier. In Henry III's reign, we can measure the amount of sealing wax which the chancery used. In the late 1220s it was getting through 3.63 lb. per week; by the late 1260s the amount had gone up to 31.9 lb. per week. Not only was the government issuing more documents than ever before; it was also systematically making copies and keeping them. Here the key date is 1199. In that year the chancery clerks began to keep copies, on rolls of parchment, of most of the letters—and certainly of all the important ones—sent out under the great seal. The survival of the chancery enrolments means that from 1199 historians know a great deal more about the routine of government than ever before.

These are developments of fundamental importance. The proliferation of records involved a shift from habitually memorizing things to writing them down. It meant that the whole population was now, in a sense, 'participating in literacy'; even if they could not themselves read they became accustomed to seeing day-to-day business transacted through the medium of writing. Clearly this development of a literate mentality is closely linked with the cultural movement commonly known as the twelfth-century Renaissance. At first the powerhouses of the new learning all lay abroad in the towns and cathedrals of Italy and France; but by the late twelfth century there were some schools of higher learning in England and by the 1220s two universities, first at Oxford and then at Cambridge, had been established. At Oxford there were schools where men could learn severely practical subjects such as conveyancing, administration, and

Durham Cathedral, built in the early twelfth century. The Romanesque pillars and arches of the interior contrast strongly with the later Gothic style used, for example, at Salisbury.

elementary legal procedure. And throughout England the signs point to an increasing number of schools at all levels.

But are these profound developments associated with revolutionary changes in other aspects of social organization? Clearly, the production of all these written records means that society is becoming more bureaucratic, but does this mean that the relationships between classes are being conserved or being altered? Is the economic system changing? Is the political system changing? Or are both merely being more elaborately recorded?

These are not questions which it is easy to answer. The cumulative nature of the evidence tends to deceive. For example, a particular form of relationship between men may first be clearly documented in the thirteenth century. But does this mean that the relationship itself originated in that century? Or that these types of relationship were first fixed in writing then? Or only that this is the earliest period from which the relevant documents happen to have survived? A case in point is the fact that the earliest known examples of a type of document known as the 'indenture of retainer' date from the thirteenth century. The indenture records the terms on which a man was engaged to serve his lord; it would normally specify his wages and, if it was a long-service contract, his retaining fee. On the basis of these documents, historians have decided that the 'indentured retainer' and the 'contract army' both came into existence towards the end of the thirteenth century, and that they were characteristic of the later Middle Ages, the period of 'bastard feudalism'. Yet there is clear, though indirect, evidence that both contract armies and retainers receiving fees and wages were in existence at least as early as 1100. And in general in this chapter it will be argued that there was a much higher degree of continuity in economic, political, and social organization than is often supposed. But first, before going any further, it will be useful to give a brief outline of the main events, concentrating on those events which were of greatest concern to kings.

William I (1066–1087)

After 1071, William's hold on England was fairly secure. The Welsh and the Scots gave him little trouble. Scandinavian rulers continued to look upon England with acquisitive eyes but the ever-present threat of another Viking invasion never quite materialized. From 1071 to the end of his reign most of William's attention was taken up by war and diplomacy on the Continent.

Normandy was his homeland and far more vulnerable to sudden attack than was his island kingdom. Several of William's neighbours were alarmed by his new power and took every opportunity to diminish it. At their head were King Philip of France, and Count Fulk le Rechin of Anjou. Their best opportunities were provided by William's eldest son Robert (b. 1054). Recognized as the heir to Normandy as long ago as 1066, he had never been allowed to enjoy either money or power, and from 1078 onwards he became involved in a series of intrigues against his father. In quarrels between the king of France and the duke of Normandy the natural battlefield was the Vexin, a disputed territory lying on the north bank of the Seine between Rouen and Paris. The county of Maine, which William had conquered in 1063, played a similar role in the hostilities between Normandy and Anjou. Maine was to remain a bone of contention for the next two generations; the Vexin for much longer still (until 1203). Thus already in William's reign it is possible to see the political pattern which was to dominate the next century: the intermingling of family dissension and frontier dispute. In this context the circumstances of William's death are revealing. The garrison of the French fortress of Mantes made a raid into Normandy. William retaliated and while his troops sacked Mantes (July 1087) he received the injury from which he died. Robert was in rebellion at the time and chose to remain at the court of King Philip, while his younger brother William dutifully, and pointedly, was to be found in attendance at his father's bedside. On 9 September 1087, William I died. His body was carried to his great church of St. Stephen at Caen. Towards the end of his life he had grown very fat and when the attendants tried to force the body into the stone sarcophagus, it burst, filling the church with a foul smell. It was an unfortunate ending to the career of an unusually fortunate and competent king.

William II (1087–1100)

Whatever William's last wishes may have been, there was a strong presumption that the eldest son should have his father's patrimony, that is those lands which the father himself had inherited. Thus, despite his rebellion, Robert succeeded to Normandy. But a man's acquisition, the land he himself had obtained whether by purchase, marriage, or conquest, could more easily be used to provide for other members of his family. Thus England, the Conqueror's vast acquisition, was used to provide for his younger son, William. Naturally, Robert objected to this and perhaps, if it had not been for his rebellion, he would have succeeded to England as well.

What is clear is that the customs governing the succession to the throne were still flexible; they could—should—be bent in order to take account of political realities, for example the characters of the rival candidates. Thus those influential men, Archbishop Lanfranc of Canterbury among them, who decided to accept William Rufus as king of England, may well have judged that he would make a better ruler than his elder brother. In view of Robert's record both before and after 1087 this would have been a reasonable judgement, yet within a few months of his accession Rufus found himself opposed by a powerful coalition of great barons, the magnates. According to the Anglo-Norman chronicler Orderic Vitalis, the rebels' objective was to reunite England and Normandy, not for the sake of some principle of constitutional law but in order to ease their own political problems. Their dilemma was summed up in the words which Orderic placed in the mouth of the greatest of them, Odo of Bayeux. 'How can we give proper service to two distant and mutually hostile lords? If we serve Duke Robert well we shall offend his brother William and he will deprive us of our revenues and honours in England. On the other hand if we obey King William, Duke Robert will deprive us of our patrimonies in Normandy.' This was an argument which appealed to powerful vested interests and could very easily have unseated Rufus. If there were to be just one ruler of the joint Anglo-Norman realm then the elder brother's claim was difficult to deny. Fortunately for Rufus, his brother's case went almost by default: Robert stayed in Normandy, leaving his supporters in the lurch. None the less the 1088 revolt, despite its swift collapse, does reveal just how precarious was the position of a king of England who was not also duke of Normandy.

Taking the forty-eight years (1087–1135) of the reigns of William II and Henry I as a whole, it can be seen that the rebellions (1088, 1095, 1101, 1102) cluster in the two periods (some fifteen years in all) when the king was not duke, that is 1087–96 and 1100–6. Obviously, it was not in the king's interest that England and Normandy should be under separate rulers. But neither was it in the interest of the aristocracy. As Odo of Bayeux's speech makes plain they had too much at risk to welcome instability. Whenever the cross-Channel kingdom did break up into its constituent parts this ushered in a period of conflict which was only settled when one ruler ousted the other.

The Gothic interior of Salisbury Cathedral, which was built in the generation after 1220. The Gothic style is in stark contrast with the Romanesque of earlier periods, seen for example in Durham Cathedral; but both churches testify to the wealth and ambition of their builders.

Thus the primary concern of a king of England was to win and hold Normandy.

In 1089 Rufus laid claim to the duchy. With English silver he was able to buy support and he campaigned there with some success. But his hold on England still remained insecure; he faced a conspiracy in 1095. Next year the tension was resolved, at any rate temporarily, in a totally unforeseeable manner. The astonishing success of Pope Urban II's preaching tour created a climate of opinion in which thousands decided to join an expedition aimed at recovering Jerusalem from the Muslims. For Robert Curthose this offered an honourable and exciting way out of his increasingly difficult domestic political position. In order to equip himself and his retinue for the long march, he pawned Normandy to William for 10,000 marks.

The new duke's next task was to recover Maine and the Vexin, lost during Robert's slack rule. By 1099, this had been successfully accomplished. Rufus had restored his father's kingdom to its former frontiers; indeed in Scotland, by installing Edgar on the throne in 1097, he intervened more effectively than even his father had done.

Yet for all his success as a generous leader of soldiers, William's reputation has remained consistently low. Unfortunately for him, the history of the time was written almost entirely by monks and they did not like him. Serious-minded churchmen, accustomed to the conventional piety and sober discretion of his father's court, were appalled by Rufus's, by its ostentatious extravagance, by its gaiety, and by the new fashions—long hair for example—which seemed to them to be both effeminate and licentious. Rufus never married. According to the Welsh *Chronicle of Princes*, 'he used concubines and because of that died without an heir'. He may have been sceptical of the claims of religion—at any rate this is how contemporaries portrayed him; undoubtedly he treated the Church as a rich corporation which needed soaking. He was rarely in a hurry to appoint bishops and abbots, for during vacancies he could help himself to the Church's revenues. In carrying out these profitable policies Rufus relied on the ingenious aid of a quick-witted and worldly clerk, Ranulf Flambard, whom he eventually made bishop of Durham.

Above all, Rufus's reputation has suffered because in 1093, when he thought he was dying, he appointed a saintly scholar Anselm of Bec as Archbishop of Canterbury (after having kept the see vacant for four years). What made this appointment so disastrous from William's point of view was the fact that it

Eleventh-century knights ride into the attack. Note the different ways of using the lance. The vigour of this scene reminds us that the Bayeux Tapestry is a major work of English art.

occurred at a time when a European movement for Church reform—the Gregorian reform—had created a controversial atmosphere in which holy men were only too likely to become political radicals. In 1095 William called a council at Rockingham to deal with the matters in dispute between him and Anselm. To the consternation of all, Archbishop Anselm appealed to Rome, arguing that as Archbishop of Canterbury he could not be judged in a secular court. The rise of the Papacy in the second half of the eleventh century, with its claim to the first loyalty of prelates, had brought a new and disturbing element on to the political stage. If churchmen were to believe that their obligations to God, as defined by the vicar of St. Peter, were to override their duty to the king, then the customary structure of the world would have been turned upside down.

Anselm's case in favour of an autonomous spiritual hierarchy was a well-reasoned one; in this respect he can be said to have had the better of the argument. But Rufus had a case too; not only that, he had power—pitted against the material resources available to a masterful king, a scholarly Archbishop of Canterbury was in a very weak position indeed. William continued to harass the archbishop, and never showed any sympathy for his attempts to reform the Church. Eventually Anselm could bear it no longer. In 1097 he sailed from Dover, leaving the estates of Canterbury to be taken into the king's hand. In the short run the king had gained from the quarrel. In 1100 he enjoyed the revenues of three bishoprics and twelve abbeys. Nor was there as yet any sign that the arguments had undermined men's belief in the awesome powers of an anointed king. Even Eadmer, the Canterbury monk who wrote a *Life of Anselm*, remarked of Rufus that 'the wind and the sea seemed to obey him'. Indeed, Eadmer went on, 'in war and in the acquisition of territory he enjoyed such success that you would think the whole world smiling upon him'. Whether, in reality, William II's position in 1100 was quite so strong is another matter; it suited moralistic chroniclers to portray him as a self-confident, boastful king who was struck down just when he seemed to be at the very pinnacle of success. During the summer of 1100 everyone must have known that the peaceful interlude of Duke Robert's absence was about to end. The crusader was on his way home, accompanied by a rich wife and basking in the prestige due to a man who had fought his way into the Holy City. When Curthose reclaimed his inheritance, who could tell what would happen or what line the Anglo-Norman magnates would take? As it happened, on 2 August 1100 a hunting accident in the New Forest brought the life of this forceful and much-maligned king to an abrupt end. Also, as it happened, William's younger brother was in the New Forest on the day the king died.

Henry I (1100–1135)

As soon as he knew Rufus was dead Henry moved fast. He rode to Winchester and took possession of the treasury. Then he went straight on to Westminster where he was crowned on 5 August. This speed of action has prompted speculation that Henry knew that his brother was going to die, that he had 'arranged the accident'. But no contemporary makes the charge and if Henry had planned so cold-blooded a crime his timing is likely to have been different. The impending war between Rufus and Curthose could be expected to end with the defeat and perhaps the elimination of one of them. In other words a delayed assassination would have opened up to the assassin the prospect of obtaining *both* England *and* Normandy. As it was, Rufus's death in August 1100 meant that Henry had to act with phenomenal speed merely to seize control of just one of the two parts of the Anglo-Norman realm. A man capable of waiting for so long before he struck would surely have waited a year or two longer.

A few weeks later, Robert arrived back in Normandy. Henry had to prepare to meet the inevitable invasion. His policy was to

Indenture with seals. This indenture records an agreement made in the 1220s between a lord and the men of Freiston and Butterwick (Lincolnshire). The fifty or so villagers whose seals are attached clearly lived in a society which was already thoroughly accustomed to using written legal documents.

buy support by granting favours and wide-ranging concessions. This was a policy proclaimed on the day of his coronation, when he issued a charter of liberties denouncing his brother's oppressive practices and promising good government. On the other hand the urgent need to organize his defences meant that Henry could not afford to cause too much confusion. This was a time for gestures and manifestos, but it was not the moment to overturn a whole regime. The reality of the situation was that his elder brother had left him a ready-made court and administration and Henry had little choice but to take them over.

When Duke Robert landed at Portsmouth in July 1101, many of the greatest barons in England, led by Robert of Bellême and his brothers, flocked to his side. But Rufus's court circle, Robert of Meulan at their head, remained loyal to Henry; so also did the English Church. Both sides drew back and negotiated. Henry was to keep England and pay his brother a pension of £2,000 a year.

Having survived the crisis of 1101, Henry set about ensuring that it would not recur. The essential first step was the overthrow of the house of Montgomery (Bellême). In 1102 he captured Robert of Bellême's chief strongholds in the Welsh marches and then banished him. Two years later he confiscated the lands of William of Mortain. But Earls Robert and William, like others in their position, possessed in their Norman properties a base from which to organize the recovery of their English lands. By perpetuating the separation of England and Normandy the treaty of 1101 had ensured the continuance of political instability. So in a rerun of the history of the previous reign we find a king of England, first on the defensive, then going over to the attack. At the battle of Tinchebray (1106) the issue was decided. Duke Robert himself was captured and spent the last twenty-eight years of his life as his brother's prisoner.

Although in the first years of his reign Henry was preoccupied with Norman affairs, he was not as free to concentrate on them as he would have liked. Traditional royal rights over the Church were threatened by the new ideas associated with the Gregorian reform movement. The reformers did not only wish to purify the moral and spiritual life of the clergy; in order to do this, they believed that it was also necessary to free the Church from secular control. The most hated symbol of this control was lay investiture, a ceremony in which a new abbot or bishop received the ring and staff of office from the hands of the secular prince who had appointed him. Although the first papal decree against lay investiture had been issued as long ago as 1059 and more prohibitions had been published since, no one in England seems to have been aware of their existence until Anselm returned in the autumn of 1100. While in exile he had learned of the papal attitude to lay investiture. Thus although he himself had been invested by Rufus in 1093 he now refused either to do homage to Henry or to consecrate those prelates whom Henry had invested. This placed the king in a difficult position. Bishops and abbots were great landowners and key figures in central and local administration; he needed their assistance and had to be sure of their loyalty. On the other hand, unlike Rufus, he was unwilling to provoke a quarrel, so for years he found it more convenient to postpone the problem rather than try to solve it. Not until 1107 was the matter settled.

Henry renounced lay investiture, but prelates were to continue to do homage for their fiefs. In practice, the king's wishes continued to be the decisive factor in the making of bishops. To some extent, it can be said that Henry gave up the form but preserved the reality of control. When Anselm died in 1109 he kept the see of Canterbury vacant for five years. Yet he had lost something and he knew it. In the fierce war of propaganda which accompanied the 'Investiture Contest' the Gregorians had insisted that the king was a layman, nothing more, and as such he was inferior to all priests, for priests were concerned with the soul and the king only with the body. The Church could no longer tolerate the old idea that anointed kings were sacred deputies of God. In giving up lay investiture Henry was acknowledging the secular nature of his office. It was an important moment in the history of kingship.

Once Normandy had been conquered and a compromise solution found to the investiture dispute, Henry's main concern was to hold on to what he had. Recognizing the threat that could come from an alienated aristocracy, he was careful to close the gap between court and magnates which Rufus had allowed to develop. In Orderic's words, 'he treated the magnates with honour and generosity, adding to their wealth and estates, and by placating them in this way, he won their loyalty.' A direct threat to Henry's position came from the claim of Curthose's young son, William Clito (b. 1102) that he, not Henry, was the rightful duke of Normandy. This rival claim, coupled with Normandy's long land frontier, meant that the duchy remained the most vulnerable part of his empire. After 1106 Henry spent more than half the rest of his reign there in opposition to the traditional enemies of the Norman dukes, notably Louis VI of France (king 1108–37), and Fulk V of Anjou (count 1109–28). He organized a protective ring of alliances—no less than eight of his illegitimate daughters were married to neighbouring princes, from Alexander of Scotland in the north to Rotrou count of Perche in the south. This diplomatic pattern lends some slight credibility to William of Malmesbury's assertion that for Henry sex was a matter not of pleasure but of policy. The end result of all this activity was that Henry kept Normandy and for this reason, since it turned out to be a struggle which only maintained the status quo, historians have not been inclined to take it very seriously. But for Henry it was a very serious business indeed, a war for survival which at least once, in 1118–19, he came perilously close to losing.

The preoccupation with the defence of Normandy was a serious matter in England too, and not just for the great landowners who held estates on the Continent. Castles, garrisons, diplomacy, and war all cost a great deal of money. The connection is spelt out in the *Anglo-Saxon Chronicle*'s entry for 1118: 'King Henry spent the whole of this year in Normandy on account of the war with the king of France, count of Anjou and count of Flanders . . . England paid dearly for this in numerous taxes from which there was no relief all year.' The king's long absences and his urgent need for money were the motors behind the increasing elaboration and sophistication of the machinery of government. While the king was away, England was admin-

The Anglo–Norman realm 1066–1154

istered by a vice-regal committee. Twice a year this committee met 'at the exchequer', that is, it met to audit the accounts of the sheriffs over the famous chequered cloth. Most of the routine administrative work, in particular the collection of revenue, was supervised by Roger of Salisbury, a man who—in contrast to the flamboyant Flambard—seems to have been the archetypal bureaucrat, competent and discreet.

The death of William, his only legitimate son, in 1120 in the wreck of the White Ship brought Henry's whole carefully-contrived edifice tumbling down. From then on, the succession problem dominated the politics of the reign. Less than three months after William's death, Henry married a new wife but the heir so desperately hoped for was never born. So although Henry is said to have acknowledged more than twenty bastards, he was survived by only one legitimate child, his daughter Matilda. When her husband, Emperor Henry V of Germany, died in 1125, Henry recalled her to his court and made the barons swear to accept her as heir to the Anglo-Norman realm. Then in 1127 Henry received a fresh shock. William Clito was recognized as count of Flanders. If he were able to employ the wealth of Flanders in pursuit of his claim to Normandy, then the outlook for his uncle was black indeed. At this critical juncture Henry approached Fulk V of Anjou with a proposal for a marriage alliance between Matilda and Fulk's son and heir, Geoffrey Plantagenet. In June 1128 Matilda, somewhat against her will, was married to the fourteen-year-old youth. Unquestionably, Count Fulk had scored a diplomatic triumph: the first vital step in the Angevin take-over of the Anglo-Norman realm.

By 1135 Henry I was quarrelling openly and violently with Geoffrey and Matilda. This had the effect of driving those magnates who were loyal to Henry into opposition to the Angevins. When the old king died these magnates would inevitably find it difficult to come to terms with his designated heirs. In this sense it was Henry himself who provoked the succession dispute which followed his death. Even at the end of his life he still wanted his daughter and son-in-law to succeed, but he had been unable to bring himself to take the measures which would have enabled them to do so. Henry I had been an outstandingly able and successful king, the master politician of his age, but even he failed to cope with the tensions of the succession question. It was for this reason that Henry of Huntingdon portrayed Henry as a king in a permanent state of anxiety. 'Each of his triumphs only made him worry lest he lose what he had gained; therefore though he seemed to be the most fortunate of kings, he was in truth the most miserable.'

Stephen (1135–1154)

When the news came that Henry I lay dying, the old king's chosen heirs were in their own dominions, either in Anjou or in

Maine. But his nephew, Stephen of Blois, was in his county of Boulogne. From there, it was but a day-trip to the south-east of England. This accident of geography gave Stephen a head start. Having first secured the support of the Londoners he then rode to Winchester, where his brother, Henry of Blois, was bishop. With Henry's help he obtained both the treasury at Winchester, and Roger of Salisbury's acceptance of his claim to be king. Then all that remained was to persuade the Archbishop of Canterbury to anoint him. This was done by arguing that the oath to Matilda—which they had all sworn—was void because it had been exacted by force, and by spreading a fictitious story about the old King's deathbed change of mind. On 22 December 1135, Stephen was crowned and anointed king at Westminster.

The political structure of the Anglo-Norman realm meant that once Stephen had been recognized as king in England, he was in a very strong position in Normandy as well. From then on, the Norman barons could give their allegiance to someone else only at the risk of losing their English estates. Above all those with most to lose felt that they had to support Stephen. So, right from the start of their campaign to win their inheritance, Geoffrey and Matilda found themselves opposed by the most powerful magnates of the Anglo-Norman state.

The first two and a half years of Stephen's reign passed peacefully enough: indeed they were rather more trouble-free than the opening years of both his predecessors' reigns had been. The first serious blow came in the summer of 1138 when Robert of Gloucester decided to join his half-sister's cause. Robert's defection not only meant that Stephen lost control of some important strong points in Normandy, it was also a signal that the Angevins were on the point of carrying the struggle to England. As Stephen waited for the blow to fall he began to lose his grip on the situation.

He offended his brother Henry of Blois by not making him Archbishop of Canterbury; he arrested three influential 'civil service' bishops, including Roger of Salisbury, and thus enabled Henry of Blois to claim that ecclesiastical liberties had been infringed. In the autumn of 1139, when the Empress—as Matilda was commonly known—landed at Arundel and seemed to be in Stephen's grasp, he allowed her to go free to join Robert of Gloucester at Bristol when the ruthless, if unchivalrous, thing to do was to imprison her. From now on there were two rival courts in England. The civil war was well and truly joined.

In February 1141 Stephen rashly accepted battle at Lincoln, and fought on bravely when he might have escaped. As a result, he was captured and put in prison in Bristol. Henry of Blois, now acting as papal legate, openly went over to the Empress's side and in the summer she was able to enter London. But she spurned the peace terms worked out by the legate and offended the Londoners by her tactless behaviour. When Stephen's queen, Matilda of Boulogne, advanced towards the city, the Londoners took up arms and drove the Empress out. Thus, the planned coronation at Westminster never took place. Matilda never became queen of England. A few months later Robert of Gloucester was captured and since he was the mainstay of her party Matilda had to agree to an exchange of prisoners: Stephen for Robert. The Empress had thrown away a won position; England remained a divided country.

In Normandy, events had taken a very different course. Geoffrey of Anjou stayed behind to maintain the pressure on the duchy—and to look after his own interests in Anjou. A series of campaigns from 1141 to 1144 ended with the surrender of Rouen and Geoffrey's formal investiture as duke. But the count of Anjou's single-minded concentration on the conquest of Normandy led·to him turning his back on England.

Here the civil war settled down into a kind of routine. Neither side could make much headway at a time when the art of war revolved around castles, and the defenders generally held the

The capture of a castle by escalade – as seen by the St. Albans chronicler, Matthew Paris, probably the best-known English artist of the thirteenth century.

advantage. In October 1147 Robert of Gloucester died. Disheartened, the Empress left England early in 1148, never to return.

In 1150 Geoffrey of Anjou associated his son Henry with him in the rule of the duchy. Next year this arrangement was legitimized when Louis VII (king of France 1137–80), in return for concessions in the Vexin, decided to recognize Henry as duke. At this point, it must have looked as though the old link between England and Normandy had at last been broken. Yet neither side would give up its claims and though there seemed to be a stalemate in England, on the Continent the situation turned out to be remarkably fluid. Geoffrey of Anjou died, still under forty, leaving his eldest son in control of both Normandy and Anjou. In March 1152 Louis VII divorced his wife, Eleanor of Aquitaine. Eight weeks later she married Henry Plantagenet, who in consequence could now add control of the vast duchy of Aquitaine to his other Continental possessions.

Henry's marriage was a great coup—yet it also gave fresh hope to Stephen. Louis VII organized a grand coalition of all Henry's rivals. As a result, the summer of 1152 saw Henry fighting on four fronts at once—in Aquitaine, in Normandy, against rebels in Anjou, and against Stephen in England. One well-informed Norman chronicler tells us that the betting was that Henry would not survive. At this juncture, his decision to sail to England and carry the fight to Stephen impressed contemporaries by its sheer audacity. Even so there was little Henry could do to break the stalemate in England and his whole position was still precariously over-extended when the death of Stephen's heir, Eustace, in August 1153 transformed everything. Stephen's second son, William, had never expected to be king and so the way was opened for a negotiated settlement.

The barons on both sides had long been anxious for peace. Their landed estates made them too vulnerable to the ravages of war for them to be in favour of protracted hostilities. At times they had ignored the wishes of the chief protagonists and made local truces of their own. So there was a general sense of relief when Stephen and Henry bowed to the wishes of their advisers.

By the treaty of Westminster (December 1153) it was agreed that Stephen should hold the kingdom for life and that he should adopt Henry as his heir. William was to inherit all Stephen's baronial lands. This, in essence, was a repeat of the peace terms proposed by Henry of Blois in 1141. Matilda's inability to be magnanimous in victory had cost the country another twelve years of civil war. Now at last Stephen could rule unchallenged but he was a tired man and did not live long to enjoy it. On 25

October 1154 he died and was buried by the side of his wife and elder son in the monastery they had founded at Faversham.

Stephen must take some responsibility for the troubles of his reign. He was a competent army commander and a brave knight—but perhaps too gallant for his own good. It is true that he was faced by a disputed succession, but then so were all his predecessors; disputed successions were the norm. Stephen of Blois was a more attractive character than any of the Norman kings: but he lacked their masterfulness. Without it he was unable to dominate either his court or his kingdom. Moreover he spent very little time in Normandy; only one visit, in 1137, during his entire reign. This stands in marked contrast to the itineraries of his predecessors and, in view of the 'cross-Channel structure' of the Anglo-Norman aristocracy, was certainly a mistake. In this sense the ruler from the house of Blois can be said to have failed because he was too 'English' a king to realize that England was only a part of a greater whole.

Henry II (1154–1189)

Henry took over without difficulty; it was the first undisputed succession to the English throne for over a hundred years. As lord of an empire stretching from the Scottish border to the Pyrenees he was potentially the most powerful ruler in Europe, richer even than the emperor and completely overshadowing the king of France, the nominal suzerain of his Continental possessions. Although England provided him with great wealth as well as a royal title, the heart of the empire lay elsewhere, in Anjou, the land of his fathers.

In England his first task was to make good the losses suffered during Stephen's reign. By 1158 this had been achieved. The most dramatic example came in 1157 when he used diplomatic pressure to force the young king of Scotland, Malcolm IV, to restore Cumberland, Westmorland, and Northumbria to the English Crown. In Wales, however, Henry found in Owain of Gwynedd and Rhys of Deheubarth two well-established princes whom it was impossible to browbeat. In 1157 and 1165, force of arms proved equally unavailing in the face of a combination of Welsh guerrilla tactics and torrential summer rain. After 1165 Henry's attitude to the Welsh princes was much more accommodating. As early as 1155 he had toyed with the idea of conquering Ireland. Not until 1169–70, however, did the move into Ireland take place, first by some lords from the Welsh march and then (in

The continental dominions of Henry II

1171–2) by Henry himself. As the long delay makes plain, in the king's eyes there were matters much more urgent than the Irish question.

Out of the thirty-four years of his reign, Henry II spent twenty-one on the Continent. Socially and culturally England was a bit of a backwater compared with the French parts of the Angevin dominion. The prosperous communities which lived in the valleys of the Seine, Loire, and Garonne river systems were centres of learning, art, architecture, poetry, and music. Aquitaine and Anjou produced two of the essential commodities of medieval commerce: wine and salt. These could be exchanged for English cloth and this trade must have brought great profit to the prince who ruled over both producers and consumers. As duke of Normandy, duke 'of Aquitaine, and count of Anjou Henry had inherited the claims of his predecessors to lordship over neighbouring territories. These claims led to intervention in Nantes (1156) where he installed his brother, Geoffrey, as count; an expedition against Toulouse in 1159 which resulted in the capture of Cahors and the Quercy; the recovery of the Norman Vexin in 1160; and finally, as a result of repeated invasions after 1166, the occupation of Brittany and the installation of his son Geoffrey as duke.

Yet ironically it is not for his successes that Henry is best remembered, but for his dubious part in the murder of Thomas Becket. In June 1162 Becket was consecrated Archbishop of Canterbury. In the eyes of respectable churchmen Becket, who had been chancellor since 1155, did not deserve the highest ecclesiastical post in the land. He set out to prove, to an astonished world, that he was the best of all possible archbishops. Right from the start, he went out of his way to oppose the king who, chiefly out of friendship, had promoted him. Inevitably it was not long before Henry began to react like a man betrayed. In the mid-twelfth century Church–State relations bristled with problems which could be, and normally were, shelved by men of goodwill but which could provide a field-day for men who were determined to quarrel. Henry chose the question of 'criminous clerks' as the issue on which to settle accounts with his archbishop. Like many laymen, Henry resented the way in which clerks who committed felonies could escape capital punishment by claiming trial in an ecclesiastical court. At a council held at Westminster in October 1163 Henry demanded that criminous clerks should be unfrocked by the Church and handed over to the lay courts for punishment. In opposing this, Becket carried his episcopal colleagues with him but when Pope Alexander III asked him to adopt a more conciliatory line, Henry summoned a council to Clarendon (January 1164). He presented the bishops with a clear statement of the king's customary rights over the Church—the Constitutions of Clarendon—and required from them a promise to observe these customs in good faith. Taken by surprise, Becket argued for two days and then gave in. But no sooner had the rest of the bishops followed his example than Becket repented of his weakness. Thoroughly exasperated, Henry now decided to destroy Becket. The archbishop was found guilty and sentenced to the forfeiture of his estates. In a hopeless position Becket fled across the Channel and appealed to the pope. By taking a stand on principle and then wavering Becket had reduced the English Church to confusion.

With Becket in exile Henry concentrated on more important matters for the next five years: Brittany was conquered and the English judicial system overhauled. Then in 1169 the question of the coronation of the heir to the throne, Prince Henry, led to the interminable negotiations between king, pope, and archbishop being treated as a matter of urgency. In 1170 Becket returned to England determined to punish those who had taken part in the young king's coronation. His enemies lost no time in telling Henry of the archbishop's ostentatious behaviour. 'Will no one rid me of this turbulent priest?' Henry's heated words were taken all too literally by four of his knights. Anxious to win the king's favour they rushed off to Canterbury; and there, on 29 December 1170, Becket was murdered in his own cathedral. The deed shocked Christendom and secured Becket's canonization in record time. In popular memory the archbishop came to symbolize resistance to the oppressive authority of the State, but in reality everyone was better off with him out of the way. Once the storm of protest had died down it became apparent that the king's hold on his vast empire had in no way been shaken by the Becket controversy. In the early 1170s Henry stood at the height of his power.

By this date Henry II had already decided that after his death his dominions should be partitioned between his three eldest

Two scenes from the life and death of Thomas Becket.
(*left*) Henry II listens to complaints about Becket's continuing intransigence. (*right*) The archbishop's murder.

sons. Henry was to have his father's inheritance, namely Anjou, Normandy, and England; Richard was to have his mother's inheritance, Aquitaine; Geoffrey was to have the acquisition, Brittany. For the moment there was nothing for John but later, in 1185, he was granted his father's other major acquisition, Ireland. By then Henry II's partition plans had already run into difficulties. The trouble was that they aroused expectations which, while he retained all real power in his own hands, he could not satisfy. Thus from 1173 onwards Henry was plagued by rebellious sons. The rebels, moreover, could always count on a warm welcome at the court of the king of France. After 1180 this was a serious matter for in that year the mild-mannered Louis VII was succeeded by his son Philip II Augustus, an unscrupulous politician determined to destroy the Angevin Empire. The deaths of two of his sons, the young King Henry in 1183 and Geoffrey in 1186, ought to have simplified Henry's problems, but this was offset by the old King's obvious preference for John, a preference which alarmed Richard. An alliance between Richard and Philip brought Henry to his knees and, defeated, the old king died at Chinon on 6 July 1189.

Only in the last weeks of his life had the task of ruling his immense territories been too much for Henry. He rode ceaselessly from one corner of his empire to another, almost giving an impression of being everywhere at once—an impression that helped to keep men loyal. Although the central government offices, chamber, chancery, and military household, travelled around with him, the sheer size of the empire inevitably stimulated the further development of localized administrations which could deal with routine matters of justice and finance in his absence. Thus in England, as elsewhere, government became increasingly complex and bureaucratic. This development, taken together with Henry's interest in rational reform, has led to him being regarded as the founder of the English common law, and as a great and creative king, but in his own eyes these were matters of secondary importance. To him what really mattered was family politics and he died believing that he had failed. But for over thirty years he had succeeded.

Richard I (1189–1199)

Richard's alliance with Philip Augustus meant that his position as heir to all his father's rights and dominions was unchallengeable. John remained lord of Ireland; in time, Brittany would belong to Geoffrey's posthumous son Arthur, now two years old. The rest was at Richard's disposal.

But Richard had no wish to stay long in England. He had been made duke of Aquitaine in 1172 and since then had spent most of his life on the Continent. Even after he became king of England he was well aware that he ruled much more than England. In consequence he, like his father, had wider interests and greater responsibilities. One aspect of this was the assistance he gave to the kingdom of Jerusalem, a kingdom ruled by a daughter of the junior branch of the house of Anjou now married to one of his Aquitanian vassals. In November 1187, as soon as he heard the news of Saladin's overwhelming victory at Hattin, Richard took the cross. Delayed by his involvement in the family quarrels at the end of his father's reign, he was now determined to leave

Thirteenth-century psalter. In terms of armour there was not much difference between the thirteenth-century knight and his eleventh-century counterpart; note, however, mittens, leggings, and the helmet's extra protection for the face. But twelfth- and thirteenth-century developments – the crusading movement and the cult of chivalry – have clearly made an impression on the artist.

for the East as soon as he had raised enough money and arranged for the secure government of all his dominions during a prolonged absence.

In July 1190 he and Philip Augustus set out on the Third Crusade. Not until March 1194 did Richard again set foot on English soil. In the meantime he had taken both a fleet and an army to the other end of the Mediterranean. Although unable to recapture Jerusalem, he achieved an astonishing amount against a great opponent, Saladin. On crusade Richard tackled and solved far greater logistical problems than ever confronted other warrior-kings of England, William I, Edward III, or Henry V. The treaty of Jaffa which he negotiated in 1192 enabled the crusader states to survive for another century.

During his absence on crusade there had been some disturbances in England in 1191 but his contingency plans restored stable government. King Philip, after his own return to France, tried to take advantage of Richard's continued absence, but without success. If Richard had returned from crusade as he expected in January 1193 he would have found his empire intact.

The damage was done while he was held captive in Germany. He stayed in prison for more than a year (December 1192–February 1194) and—for all anyone knew in 1193—might have had to stay there much longer. Even in these inauspicious circumstances Richard's agents in England were able to contain his younger brother's treacherous revolt. The real losses were suffered on the Continent, in particular in Normandy where Philip overran the Vexin and came close to capturing Rouen itself.

Richard was released in February 1194 after payment of 100,000 marks, the first two-thirds of the king's ransom. After a brief visit to England (March–May 1194) he returned to the Continent and devoted the next five years to the hard grind of recovering the territory lost so rapidly while he was in prison. By the end of 1198 Richard's skilful diplomacy, fine generalship, and, above all, his greater resources meant that he had succeeded in recapturing almost everything that had been lost. Then, in April 1199, Richard died as the result of a wound suffered at the siege of Chalus-Chabrol (near Limoges) where he was engaged in suppressing a rebellion led by the count of Angoulême and the viscount of Limoges. In the Angevin–Capetian struggle this was to be the decisive turning-point.

One of the marks of Richard's greatness had been his ability to choose ministers; above all, Hubert Walter in England. As justiciar, Archbishop of Canterbury, and papal legate Hubert

al ke nule riens ne dura

e deffint mue; z bñ li faut

A tournament mêlée. This crowded representation
illustrates the practical value of this medieval war-game:
a mock-battle contested by teams of knights.

Walter stood for harmonious co-operation between king and
Church. In England, as in the other provinces of the Angevin
Empire, Richard's long absences meant the continuing development, under Walter's supervision, of an effective machinery of
central government. From the point of view of Richard's
subjects, this meant increasingly heavy taxation, but there is no
evidence to suggest that the financial burdens of war had
brought the Angevin Empire to the point of economic collapse.

John (1199–1216)

Richard left no legitimate children, and when he died the
different parts of the Angevin Empire chose different successors.
The barons of England and Normandy opted for John; Anjou,
Maine, and Touraine preferred Arthur of Brittany, now twelve
years old; Aquitaine continued to be held—on John's behalf—by
his mother, Eleanor (d. 1204). By May 1200 John had ousted
Arthur and had established himself as lord of all the Angevin

dominions, though at a heavy price—the cession of the Vexin and Evreux to King Philip (treaty of Le Goulet, January 1200). Later that year his first marriage was annulled and he married Isabella of Angoulême. There were great strategic advantages to be gained from marrying the heiress to Angoulême and had John given her fiancé, Hugh of Lusignan, adequate compensation, all might yet have been well. As it was, this marriage set in motion a train of events which led to Hugh appealing to the court of France and, in 1202, to Philip's declaration that all John's Continental dominions—the lands which he held as fiefs of the king of France—were forfeit. The sentence still had to be

Cauterizing a wound with red-hot instruments which an assistant is seen heating in the lower part of the drawing. (From a twelfth-century medical treatise given by a doctor, Master Herebert, to Durham cathedral priory)

enforced. In 1152 Henry II had resisted Louis VII's attempt to execute a similar verdict. In 1203–4, however, John failed where his father had succeeded. By his tactless treatment of the leading barons of Anjou and Poitou he threw away all the advantages he won when he captured Arthur at Mirebeau (July 1202); the well-founded rumour that he was responsible for his nephew's murder (April 1203) further undermined an already shaky reputation. In an atmosphere of suspicion and fear John found it impossible to organize an effective defence. In December 1203 he threw in the towel and withdrew to England. Philip overran Normandy, Anjou, Maine, Touraine, and all of Poitou except for La Rochelle. These humiliating military reverses earned for John a new nickname. 'Lackland' now became 'Softsword'.

Until December 1203 John, like his father and brother, spent most of his reign in his Continental possessions. After that date he became, by force of circumstances, an English king. Not since Stephen's reign had the country seen so much of its ruler, but there was little pleasure or profit to be got from a king who constantly suspected that men were plotting against him. The weight of John's presence was even felt in the north where men were not accustomed to visits from kings of England. The extent of their resentment can be measured by the number of northerners who opposed John in 1215–16. Undoubtedly he faced genuine problems. He was duty-bound to try to recover his lost inheritance, but the conquests of 1203–4 meant that the French king was now a much more formidable opponent. An unusually high rate of inflation meant that many families and religious houses were in financial difficulties and they found it easier to blame the king than to understand the underlying economic forces. Inflation tended to erode the real value of royal revenues. As a result, John levied frequent taxes and tightened up the laws governing the forest (a profitable but highly unpopular source of income).

John also quarrelled with the Church. A disputed election to the see of Canterbury in 1205 led to a clash with Innocent III. In 1208 Innocent laid an interdict on England and Wales; all church services were suspended and remained so for six years. In 1209 John himself was excommunicated. Neither John nor lay society in general seem to have been very worried by this state of affairs; indeed since John's response to the interdict was to confiscate the estates of the Church it even helped to ease his financial problem. But in 1212 a baronial plot and Philip's plans to cross the Channel served to remind John that an excommunicated king was particularly vulnerable to rebellion and invasion. So he decided to make peace with the Church in order to have a free hand to deal with his more dangerous enemies. By agreeing to hold England as a fief of the Papacy in May 1213 he completely won over Innocent and assured himself of the pope's support in the coming struggles.

All now turned on the outcome of John's attempt to recover his lost lands. In 1214 he led an expedition to Poitou but the defeat of his allies at the battle of Bouvines (July 1214) entailed both the failure of his Continental strategy and the onset of rebellion in England. But rebels had genuine problems too. Leadership was normally provided by a discontented member of the royal family. After the elimination of Arthur, John faced no such rivals. His own sons were too young. The only possible candidate was Louis, son of Philip Augustus, but a Capetian prince was hardly an attractive anti-king. So the rebels devised a new kind of focus for revolt: a programme of reform. In June 1215, after they had captured London, the rebels forced John to accept the terms laid out in a document later to be known as Magna Carta. In essence it was a hostile commentary on some of the more objectionable features of the last sixty years of Angevin rule. As such it was clearly unacceptable to John who regarded the agreement made at Runnymede merely as a means of buying time. Attempts to implement Magna Carta only led to further quarrels. In the end the rebels had to invite Louis to take the throne. In May 1216 he entered London. When John died, in October 1216, shortly after losing part of his baggage train in quicksands in the Wash, the country was torn in two by a civil war which was going badly for the Angevins.

A dramatic moment during the battle of Bouvines (1214). King Philip of France is unhorsed. If he had stayed on the ground many of John's troubles might have been solved. Note the variety of weapon carried by the heavily-armed knights: sword, lance, bow.

Magna Carta. Although as a peace treaty the charter of 1215 was a failure, as a statement of law it was always taken seriously. After John's death it was amended and reissued in 1216, 1217, and 1225. Because the reissue of 1217 was accompanied by the publication of a second, smaller charter dealing with forest law, it became known as the large charter, *Magna Carta.*

John possessed qualities which have endeared him to some modern historians. He took a close interest in the details of governmental and legal business, but in his own day this counted for little. It is a mistake to see him as a busier king than his predecessors. The survival of chancery records from 1199 onwards permits historians to look, for the first time, into the daily routine of the king's government at work. As a result they have sometimes given the impression that John was unusually competent. In fact he was a very poor king, incompetent where it really mattered, in the management of his more powerful subjects.

Henry III (1216–1272)

The minority council which governed in the name of John's nine-year-old son, Henry, was soon vouchsafed that success in war, both on land (the battle of Lincoln, May 1217) and at sea (the battle of Dover, August 1217), which had been denied his father. Under the impact of these defeats, support for Louis dwindled rapidly. In September 1217 he accepted the treaty of Lambeth and withdrew.

It was not until 1232 that Henry began to rule in his own right. Minorities tended to be periods of unstable government; but, on the whole, the men, above all Hubert de Burgh, who kept Henry in political tutelage until he was in his mid-twenties, did remarkably well. Most of the struggles for power took place in the council chamber; appeals to arms were rare and very brief. As part of a series of conciliatory moves Magna Carta was amended and reissued. But while the lords of the council concentrated on their own rivalries and on events in England and Wales, they were understandably less concerned about the king's overseas inheritance. None of them had estates in Poitou and Gascony. In 1224, during one such domestic quarrel, their old Capetian enemy, now King Louis VIII, walked into Poitou, captured La Rochelle, and threatened Gascony. An expedition in 1225 consolidated the position in Gascony but made no serious attempt to recover Poitou. Subsequent expeditions, in 1230 and 1242, were on a more ambitious scale but ended ingloriously. After 1224, only Gascony remained of the lands which Henry III's ancestors had once held in France. The effect of this was to reverse the territorial balance of the twelfth century. Once England had been one of the provinces in the Angevin orbit; now it became the

The town seal of Faversham. The loss of Normandy (1204) meant that the Channel became a front line of defence. Thus the representation of a ship manned for war on this seal was an apt symbol for one of the members of the thirteenth century confederation of Cinque Ports.

indisputable centre of the Plantagenet dominions. Eventually, by the treaty of Paris (1259), Henry gave up his claims to Normandy, Anjou, and Poitou, and did homage to Louis IX for Gascony.

Realistically speaking, the treaty of Paris was Henry III's greatest political success but he accepted the generous terms offered by Louis IX only with great reluctance and in the hope of extricating himself from his other difficulties. Chief among these was the fact that a sworn confederation of the most powerful magnates in the country was threatening to take up arms against him. Henry had faced opposition on and off since 1233. Time and again, the bone of contention had been his choice of friends and advisers; these were the men who obtained the lion's share of the patronage at the king's disposal. The problem was aggravated by the fact that many of his favourites were not English—this at a time when English politics were becoming increasingly insular. Henry was a good family man, happily married (since 1236) to Eleanor of Provence, and ready to provide generously for his wife's relatives. Then, when life in France became difficult for his half-brothers, the Lusignans—his mother's children by her second marriage—he welcomed them to England and from 1247 onwards they constantly soured the atmosphere.

Equally controversial was the king's scheme for providing for Edmund, his own second son. In 1252 the pope offered the kingdom of Sicily to Henry and in 1254 he accepted on Edmund's behalf. Unfortunately, Sicily was actually held by Manfred, an illegitimate son of the Hohenstaufen Emperor Frederick II. Not only did Henry agree that he would finance the island's conquest, he also promised to meet the pope's existing debts—and the pope had already spent a fortune, some 135,000 marks, in fighting Manfred. It was an absurd commitment and in 1258 it ended with the barons taking the government out of the king's hands and initiating a far-reaching programme of reform: the Provisions of Oxford (October 1258) and the Provisions of Westminster (October 1259). But taking power out of the hands of an adult king, and handing it to an elected aristocratic council, was a revolutionary step. For the next five years England teetered on the brink of civil war. When, in the spring of 1264, war finally came, the issues at stake had been narrowed down to one question. Was, or was not, the king free to choose foreigners to be his counsellors? Ironically, the man who had been most adamant in insisting that in the last resort it was the barons, acting in the name of 'the community of the realm', who should decide, was himself born a foreigner, Simon de Montfort. By this time, Simon had long been a powerful member of 'the commun-

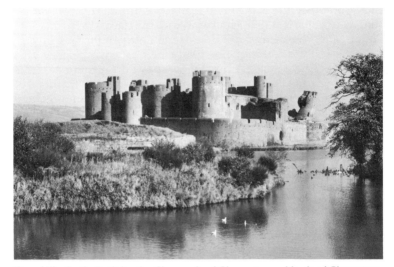

Caerphilly Castle. Built by the Clare earls of Gloucester and lords of Glamorgan this great concentric fortress, with the most elaborate water defences in Britain, was begun in 1271 – a baronial stronghold on the scale of Edward I's famous Welsh castles.

ity': earl of Leicester since 1231, husband of the king's sister since 1238. In 1264 Earl Simon won the battle of Lewes, but next year was himself defeated, killed, and dismembered at the battle of Evesham. In the last years of Henry III's reign the full restoration of royal authority was combined with the recognition, in the statute of Marlborough (1267), that the 'customs of the realm' including both Charters of Liberties and even some of the Provisions of Westminster, should be upheld. Feeling uncomfortable in this atmosphere of moderation, the victor of Evesham, Edward, the heir to the throne, went off on crusade, leaving his father free to concentrate on rebuilding Westminster Abbey.

Edward I (1272–1307)

In 1272 Edward I was in Sicily, on his way back from crusade, when he heard the news that his father had died and that he had been proclaimed king. He returned home at a leisurely pace. In Paris, choosing his words carefully, he did homage to Philip III for his lands in France: 'I do you homage for all the lands which I ought to hold of you.' He then turned south to Gascony where he stayed in 1273–4. He visited Gascony again in 1286–9. He was the last Plantagenet king to hold court at Bordeaux and when he left, in July 1289, it marked the end of an era. Yet the history of English rule in Gascony is by no means a straightforward story of decline. In 1279, for example, the French at last handed over the Agenais, as they were bound to do under the terms of the treaty of Paris. The Agenais was an important wine-growing area and its cession further strengthened the rapidly-developing commercial links between Bordeaux and London. The Bordeaux wine customs, farmed for only £300 a year in the 1240s, were worth over £6,000 sixty years later. In return the Gascons imported English cloth, leather, and corn. A mutual interest in an expanding trade riveted the two communities together.

In October 1274, soon after his return to England, Edward launched an inquiry into the activities of both royal and baronial officials. Like similar earlier investigations it uncovered an enormous number of grievances and in trying to remedy some of these, the king's advisers, headed by his chancellor, Robert Burnell, were led on to issue new laws on a wide range of subjects. But even in the most prolific period of legislation (1275–90) there was no attempt to codify English law in the manner of a Justinian and the statutes were quite as much concerned with the rights of the king as with the liberties of the subject.

From 1276 to 1284 Edward's main preoccupation was with Wales. Initially his plan was to cut Llywelyn ap Gruffydd down to size and then hand the Welsh prince's lands to his brothers Dafydd and Gruffydd. But after the victorious campaign of 1277 he imposed a peace treaty which the Welsh found humiliating and failed to give Dafydd the rewards he had expected. In 1282 the Welsh rebelled. In the war of 1282–3 Llywelyn was killed and Dafydd captured. He was then put on trial and executed as a traitor, the first man since 1076 to forfeit his life for rebellion. Unlike the campaign of 1277, the war of 1282–3 had been intended as a war of conquest; given Edward's enormous preponderance of resources, it was not too difficult a task.

Whereas the conquest of Wales can be seen as the culmination of centuries of warfare, relations between the kingdoms of England and Scotland were exceptionally good for most of the thirteenth century. But in 1286 Alexander III was killed by a fall from his horse and his only granddaughter, Margaret, the 'Maid of Norway', was recognized as heir to the throne. Edward I proposed that she should marry his own son and heir, Edward. The Scottish magnates agreed to this proposal (treaty of Birgham, July 1290) but at the same time insisted that Scotland should retain its own laws and customs.

Sadly, the six-year-old Margaret died in Orkney (September 1290). Edward seized the opportunity to assert his overlordship and his right to adjudicate between the contenders for the throne. After complicated legal arguments he decided in favour of John Balliol; on St. Andrew's Day 1292 the new king was enthroned at Scone. Up to this point Edward was justified in claiming that his actions had helped to maintain peace and order in Scotland; but from now on his domineering treatment of the Scots was to provoke a long and disastrous war.

Wales and the Marches

Eleventh-century Wales was a collection of small kingdoms in a mountainous country. These were kingdoms without stable borders. They expanded and contracted in accordance with law (the custom of sharing the inheritance between sons) and politics (the ambitions and military fortunes of individual rulers). Although English kings traditionally claimed an overall supremacy here, they had done little to transform that ill-defined overlordship into lasting military and administrative control. At first it looked as though the impetus of the Norman Conquest of England would carry the newcomers right through Wales. The Norman earls of Hereford, Shrewsbury, and Chester were, in effect, licensed to take whatever they could. But after a period of rapid advance in 1067–75, they found their progress impeded by the nature of the terrain. As a result, their colonizing efforts were long confined to the lowlands and river valleys, particularly in the south. There were indeed periods when Welsh princes recovered the initiative and resumed control of lands they had earlier lost. Not until the reign of Edward I was the Norman Conquest of Wales complete. Thus throughout this period Wales was a land of war, a land of castles. Welsh princes and Anglo-Norman marcher lords made war and peace and both therefore enjoyed what later constitutional lawyers would call 'sovereign' powers.

For most of this period the conquest was a piecemeal affair, undertaken and carried through by individual Anglo-Norman baronial families: the Clares, the Mortimers, the Lacys, the Braoses. The lands which they conquered were, in effect, 'private' lordships, outside the normal framework of English governance. None the less, these families remained subjects of the king of England and occasionally they were reminded of this fact in summary fashion. In 1102 Henry I broke the sons of Roger of Montgomery, earl of Shrewsbury, and dismembered their father's marcher 'empire'. In 1208–11 John drove William de Braose to destruction. The groundwork of conquest and colonization was left to the marcher lords, but the overall strategy remained in royal hands. It was, for example, the kings who determined what relations with the native princes should be: a matter which became increasingly vital as some Welsh kingdoms were eliminated and the surviving ones became increasingly consolidated.

By the second half of the twelfth century the rulers of Deheubarth, particularly the Lord Rhys, and of Gwynedd were outstanding. In the thirteenth century two princes of Gwynedd, Llywelyn the Great and his grandson, Llywelyn ap Gruffydd, managed, by force and diplomacy, to bring all the other Welsh dynasties under their authority. Indeed in the treaty of Montgomery (1267) Llywelyn ap Gruffydd was able to persuade a reluctant English king, Henry III, to acknowledge both his territorial gains and his new title, 'Prince of Wales'.

But eight years earlier another treaty had sealed the fate of Wales. In 1259 by the treaty of Paris Henry III accepted the loss of most of his Continental possessions. Peace with France meant that for the first time a king of England could, if he wanted to, concentrate his attention on his British neighbours. There followed Edward's conquest and a massive programme of castle building. By the statute of Wales (1284) the newly-acquired lands were divided into shires on the English model: Flint, Anglesey, Merioneth, and Caernarfon. As for Welsh laws and customs, Edward announced: 'certain of them we have abolished; some we have allowed, some we have corrected, others we have added'. What this meant in effect was that English common law had been introduced into Wales.

There were revolts in 1287 and 1294–5 but the castles proved their worth. Flint, Rhuddlan, Aberystwyth, Builth, Conway, Caernarfon, Criccieth, Harlech, and Beaumaris—resounding names, and resoundingly expensive to build and maintain. This was the high premium Edward paid to insure his conquests against the fire of rebellion.

The contrast between, on the one hand, the piecemeal conquest of the south and east and, on the other, the sudden defeat which overwhelmed the north and west left an enduring mark on the political geography of Wales. The Edwardian conquests were largely retained in Crown lands; the rest remained divided into the numerous large lordships collectively known as the march of Wales. As for Prince Llywelyn, killed in an English trap at Irfon Bridge in 1282, his fate was to become a cult figure for some twentieth-century Welsh nationalists.

Scotland

In contrast to fragmented Wales, in the eleventh century much of Scotland, in particular the south and east—the wealthiest part—was ruled by one king, the king of the Scots. Ever since Athelstan's reign, the king of the Scots had occasionally recognized English overlordship, but that was as far as the connection went—or was likely to go. On the one hand the king of the Scots was too powerful to have much to fear from the kind of 'private enterprise' invasions which marked the advance of Anglo-Norman barons into Wales and even Ireland. On the other, his land was too poor and he was generally too distant a figure to be of much interest to the kings of England. Besides, although it might not be too difficult to launch a successful expedition against the Scots, the dual problem of conquering and controlling so remote a country seemed—and probably was—insoluble to kings whose own bases lay in the Thames Valley and further south.

Nor were the Scots obsessed by the problem of the English. Apart from a temporary success when King David (1124–53) took advantage of the civil war of Stephen's reign to acquire Northumbria (held from 1149 to 1157), the border with England effectively remained where it had been established in the eleventh century. Much more significant was the kingdom's extension to include the far north and much of the western seaboard (Caithness, Ross, Moray, Argyll, Galloway). The culmination of this expansionist policy came when the king of Norway ceded the Western Isles (treaty of Perth, 1266). Scottish advance here was materially assisted by the stability and continuity of leadership provided by three successive kings: William I (1165–1214), Alexander II (1214–49), and Alexander III (1249–86).

Territorial expansion in the Highlands was matched by internal development in the Lowlands. Here, burghs, abbeys, and cathedrals were founded; castles were built and royal sheriffdoms formed in order to reduce the kingdom to manageable administrative units; royal moneyers began to mint silver pennies (enjoying parity with English sterling) and import duties were collected. The marriages made by its rulers show that in the twelfth and thirteenth centuries Scotland was increasingly becoming part of a 'European' political scene. What was most remarkable about all these developments was that they involved very little war. So long as no English king conceived the unrealistic ambition of conquering Scotland, there was no reason for that to change.

Government

The most important component of government remained the king himself. His character still counted for more than any other single factor—as is obvious from the contrast between Edward I's reign and the reigns of both his father and son. But naturally the king could not govern alone. Wherever he went he was followed by a great crowd: courtiers, officials, servants, traders, petitioners, and hangers-on of every description.

At the centre of the crowd that followed him was the king's household. In part this was an elaborate domestic service: cooks, butlers, larderers, grooms, tent-keepers, carters, pack-horse drivers, and the bearer of the king's bed. There were also the men who looked after his hunt, the keepers of the hounds, the horn-blowers, the archers. Then there were the men whose work

From the Bayeux Tapestry. Harold Godwineson riding with hawk and hounds. Nearly all nobles enjoyed hunting – an activity which combined pleasure with meat procurement, pest control, and weapon training. In part it was the king's avid pursuit of this pleasure which, by 1200, had led to an estimated one-third of the English countryside being designated 'forest'.

was political and administrative as well as domestic. Some of them had fairly well-defined functions. The chancellor was responsible for the king's seal and the chancery clerks. Treasurer and chamberlains looked after the king's money and valuables. Constables and marshals were in charge of military organization. But the household, like the king, was omnicompetent and any great household officer, the steward for example, was likely to find himself entrusted with essential political and military tasks.

Some of these officials were clerks. Until the 1340s the chancellor and the treasurer always were. But many of them were laymen: the chamberlains, the stewards, the constables, the marshals—as also, at a local level, were the sheriffs. Medieval kings of England did not depend exclusively, or even primarily, upon clerks for the administrative skills necessary to rule a country. Nor did they rely on a group of royal officials whose interests were pitted against the interests of the great land-holders, the magnates. On the contrary, the king's household normally included some of the most powerful barons. Servants in the king's household, they were also lords of great estates and masters in their own houses. Through their influence the authority of the Crown was carried into the localities. This informal power system was often reinforced by the appointment of members of the household to local offices. Under Rufus, Hamo 'the steward' was sheriff of Kent; Urse d'Abetôt was constable of the household and sheriff of Worcester. Throughout the twelfth and thirteenth centuries household knights continued to be employed as sheriffs.

Here, in the king's household, lay the mainspring of government. This is as true of 1279, the year of Edward I's Household Ordinance, as it is of 1136, the approximate date of the earliest surviving description of the king's household, the *Constitutio domus regis*. Moreover there is no reason to believe that the household of the *Constitutio* was significantly different from William I's household, or indeed, from Cnut's household.

Similarly the king's household was the hub of military organization. It has long been accepted that the armies of Edward I's reign were essentially 'the household in arms'. The household cavalry constituted a professional task force capable of responding quickly if trouble blew up unexpectedly. In the event of a major campaign, it could be rapidly expanded. Household knights were often made responsible for mobilizing and commanding large infantry contingents. The household men, the *familiares*, were paid annual fees and then daily wages according to the number of days they served. This, it used to be thought, was a far cry from the Norman period when armies were basically 'feudal hosts', made up of the quotas of knights which tenants-in-chief mustered when summoned to perform their military service to the Crown. But close study of the much more fragmentary evidence for the period around 1100 has demonstrated that not only is it difficult to find the 'feudal host' in action, but also that all the essential features of the Edwardian system were already in existence—the retaining fees, the daily wages, the framework for planned expansion, the use of household troops both as garrisons for key castles and as the main field armies (composed of knights and mounted archers), the employment of household knights as commanders of supplementary forces. There is no reason to believe that the tasks which Cnut's housecarls were called upon to perform were fundamentally different.

For practical purposes there was an upper limit on the size of the royal household in peacetime; transport and catering problems were alone sufficient to see to that. To some extent, forward planning of the royal itinerary helped; when they knew in advance where the household was going to be then merchants could arrange to be there with their wares. But the presence of the king imposed a near-intolerable burden on any district through which he passed. The demands made by the household

From the Bayeux Tapestry. Medieval governments spent more on war than on anything else. This scene gives a rare artist's impression of the careful preparations which preceded any major campaign.

had a dramatic effect on local foodstocks and prices; it created a situation wide open to abuse. This is how Eadmer, a monk of Canterbury, described the household of William Rufus, a king of whom he disapproved. 'Those who attended his court made a practice of plundering and destroying everything; they laid waste all the territory through which they passed. Consequently when it became known that the king was coming everyone fled to the woods.' In Edward I's reign there is still the same combination of planning and plunder. An official letter announcing that he intended to spend Easter at Nottingham asked that local people should be comforted by being assured that the king would go as fast as he had come.

Thus it was both for political reasons—in order to make his presence felt—and for economic reasons—to make his presence no longer felt—that the king travelled constantly. The sheer size of their dominions meant that in this respect the Angevins had to work harder than their predecessors, though John's political failures did at least have the effect of easing his travel problems. After 1203 the royal itinerary became increasingly confined to England and, in Edward I's case, to North Wales as well. After 1289 no king visited Gascony. At the same time the roads leading in and out of London became gradually more important. By 1300 the king's itinerary was no longer dominated, as John's had still been, by the restless move from palace to hunting lodge in 'central Wessex', the old heartland of the West Saxon kings.

Yet while political and economic considerations made the court mobile, there was another feature of the age which pointed in the opposite direction: the seemingly inexorable development of bureaucracy. Given the practical limitations on household size, what would happen as the king's secretarial and financial officers grew ever more numerous? Inevitably not all of them could continue to travel everywhere with their lord. Some were bound to settle down in a convenient place. By 1066 indeed this point had already been reached. There was already a permanent royal treasury at Winchester, a depository for fiscal records as well as for silver, and this required a permanent staff to guard and oversee it. By 1290 there were many more settled officials, both clerks and laymen, in the chancery and exchequer, and they were settled at Westminster, not Winchester. But this bureaucratic growth had not altered the fundamental political facts of life: the king still itinerated; he still took with him a seal, a secretariat, and financial experts—and it was within this mobile group, not at Westminster, that the most important political and administrative decisions were taken. In 1290, as in 1066, the saddle remained the chief seat of government, both in war and in peace. There was still no capital but the king's highway.

Nor had bureaucratic growth altered the basic fact that the political stability of the realm still depended primarily on the king's ability to manage the small, but immensely powerful, aristocratic establishment—as is made clear by the events of Henry III's and Edward II's reign. On what terms did the tenants-in-chief hold their estates from the king? They were expected—as they had been in Anglo-Saxon England—to serve and aid the king: essentially this meant political service and, in times of war, military service; in certain circumstances they could be asked to give him financial aid. In addition, a tenant-in-chief's heir had to pay a duty, known as a relief, in order to enter into his inheritance, while if he—or she—were under age then the king took the estates into his custody, to do with them very much as he pleased (subject to certain conventions). In these circumstances the king controlled his ward's marriage. If there were no direct heirs, then after provision had been made for the widow—whose re-marriage was also subject to Crown control—the king could grant the land out again to whomever he pleased. This degree of control over the inheritances and marriages of the wealthiest people in the kingdom meant that the king's powers of patronage were immense. He not only had offices at his disposal, he also had heirs, heiresses, and widows. Thus, for example, when Richard I gave William Marshal the heiress of the earldom of Pembroke, in effect he made William a millionaire overnight. No political leader in the Western world of today has anything remotely approaching the power of patronage in the hands of a medieval king. It is not surprising that the king's court was the focal point of the whole political system, a turbulent, lively, tense, factious place in which men—and a few women—pushed and jostled each other in desperate attempts to catch the king's eye. Not surprisingly it was a twelfth-century literary convention to describe a courtier's life as sheer hell—but standing at the mouth of hell there were hundreds only too keen to enter. In these circumstances patronage was one of the strongest cards in the king's hand. It mattered how he played it, and a king who played it badly would soon find himself in trouble.

The essential features of this patronage system were already in existence during the reign of William Rufus. This much is clear from the terms of the Coronation Charter issued by Henry I in 1100. It is also clear that the system was still in existence during the reign of Edward I. Magna Carta had clarified it and, to some extent, even modified it. After 1215, for example, baronial reliefs were fixed at a rate of £100. None the less, the laws governing inheritance, wardship, and marriage could still be manipulated to suit a king's personal predilections, whether it was to provide for his own family, as with Edward I, or to enrich favourites, as with Edward II. What is less clear is whether the system was already there in 1066. Most historians would probably say that it was not. But it is surely significant that Cnut and, probably, Æthelred the Unready were already making promises broadly similar to those contained in the charter of 1100.

Patronage was lucrative. Men offered money in order to obtain what the king had to offer: offices (from the chancellorship down), succession to estates, custody of land, wardship, and marriage—or even nothing more concrete than the king's goodwill. All of these were to be had at a price, and the price was negotiable. Here was an area in which a king could hope to raise money by consistently driving harder bargains. In these circumstances any document which told the king how rich his tenants were would naturally be immensely valuable. Domesday Book is just such a record—and it showed that half the value of the whole country was in the hands of less than two hundred men. By fining these men heavily when they were in political trouble or by offering them what they wanted, though at a price, the king had found a practical method of soaking the rich. Of course the information had to be kept up to date and throughout the twelfth and thirteenth centuries the Crown found ways of ensuring that it was. For example, one of the surviving documents produced by Henry II's administration is the delightfully named 'Roll of Ladies, boys and girls'. Thus to a hostile observer like Gerald of Wales the king appeared to be 'a robber permanently on the prowl, always probing, always looking for the weak spot where there is something for him to steal'. Gerald was talking of the position under the Angevins but it may be that Lucy, widowed countess of Chester, offering Henry I 500 marks for the privilege of remaining single for five years, would have concurred. The fact that most of the influential people in the realm were semi-permanently in their debt gave kings a powerful political lever—and one which they regularly employed. In 1295, for example, Edward I used the threat of debt collection to force a group of reluctant magnates to go to Gascony.

The earliest surviving detailed account of royal revenues, the pipe roll of 1129–30, shows just how lucrative patronage could be. In this financial year Henry I is recorded as having collected about £3,600 from agreements of this kind. This is about 15 per cent of his recorded revenue and more than he got from taxation. But the arithmetic of the pipe roll tells us a good deal more than this. In 1129–30 the total sum due as a result of agreements made in this and previous years was almost £26,000, that is only 14 per cent of the amount due was actually collected. William de Pont de l'Arche, for example, had offered 1,000 marks for a chamberlainship and in 1129–30 he paid 100 marks. This meant that if the king were satisfied with William's behaviour, then payment of further instalments might be suspended or pardoned. The expectation that the exchequer would not press too hard had the effect of encouraging men to bid highly. But a man who fell out of favour would find that he had to pay up promptly—or get into even worse trouble. This, for example, was the fate which befell William de Braose in John's reign. In other words, collecting only a small proportion of the amount due was not an indication of chronic government inefficiency but rather of a further refinement of an infinitely flexible system of patronage.

Masterful kings always had their hands in their subjects' pockets. Edward I was known as *Le Roi Coveytous* just as William I had 'loved greediness above all'. At a more abstract level, as early as the twelfth century it was asserted that royal power can be measured in financial terms. In the words of Richard Fitz Neal, bishop of London, Treasurer of England, and author of *The Dialogue of the Exchequer*, a work dating from the 1170s, 'the power of princes fluctuates according to the ebb and flow of their cash resources'. The pipe roll of 1129–30—a record of the accounts presented at the exchequer by sheriffs and other officials in that year—shows an exchequer system already working very much along the lines described in *The Dialogue*. But the financial system itself certainly pre-dated the pipe roll. In broad outline—annual renders made by sheriffs to the treasury—it is an Anglo-Saxon system. In 1066 and 1086 the renders produced by some large royal manors were still paid in kind. By 1129–30 it is clear that a widespread commutation into money rents had taken place. This was in line with general European development. The more the sheriffs' renders were made in cash, the greater the need for an easily followed but quick method of making calculations in pounds, shillings, and pence. Thus the chequered table cloth (from which the word exchequer is derived) served as a simplified abacus, on which the king's *calculator* did sums by moving counters from square to square like a croupier. The earliest reference to the exchequer dates from 1110. Twice a year a group of the most powerful and trusted men in the realm met in order to audit the sheriffs' accounts. When the king was in Normandy they would meet, as the vice-regal committee 'at the exchequer', in the king's absence. Presumably a similarly-composed committee had met for a similar purpose when Cnut was in Denmark.

But this is speculation. It is only when we reach 1129–30 that some degree of precision is possible. Even here, however, we have to be careful. An exchequer record, a pipe roll, tells almost nothing about those sums which were paid into and out of the chamber. Certainly these sums cannot be quantified, though in view of the fact that the chamber was the financial office of the itinerant household it is likely that they were large. For example it was estimated that by 1187 Henry II had paid 30,000 marks into his Jerusalem bank account though there is no sign of this money in the pipe rolls of his reign. In the absence of twelfth-century chamber records, it is not easy to estimate total royal revenue. Thus, the low pipe roll totals in the early years of Henry II's reign may be very largely a reflection of the new king's preference for chamber finance, a very natural preference for an Angevin prince, all of whose forefathers had managed perfectly well without an exchequer. After all, when it came to minting coins the Angevins introduced Angevin practice into both England and Normandy. But, whatever the difficulties, analysis of the only surviving pipe roll of Henry I's reign is undoubtedly revealing.

In 1129–30, £22,865 was paid into the treasury. Out of this total almost £12,000 comes under the heading of 'land and associated profits'. Just under £3,000 can be described as taxation, nearly all of this (almost £2,500) being Danegeld, as the geld (see p. 163) was commonly called in the twelfth century. Another £7,200 can be described as the profits of feudal lordship and jurisdiction: this included about £1,000 from ecclesiastical vacancies; £2,400 from judicial fines; and the £3,600 from agreements mentioned earlier. Thus over half the recorded revenue came from land; about a third from lordship and jurisdiction; and only some 13 per cent from taxation. If we compare this with the state of royal revenues in the early years of Edward I's reign then some significant differences emerge. In very rough terms, land accounted for about a third of the total; lordship and jurisdiction may well have provided less than 10 per cent, while taxation (including customs duties) accounted for over a half. Land, lordship, and jurisdiction became relatively less important; taxation became much more important. Even allowing for the likelihood that tax revenue in 1129–30 was rather less than usual (because the geld was the only tax levied that year), this broad generalization would still hold.

Though the royal lands were immensely lucrative in 1130, a comparison with Domesday Book suggests that they were already a declining asset. In 1086 the total recorded value of the king's lands and boroughs was almost £14,000, while by 1129–30 it had gone down to less than £10,700. It seems that the stock of royal lands was dwindling faster than it was being replenished by forfeitures and reversions to the Crown (escheats). Kings had to grant land to powerful men. They did so in order to reward and encourage loyalty, particularly early in their reigns when faced with the problems of disputed succession. This process continued, but was to some extent offset by attempts to manage the royal estates more efficiently. The success of these managerial reforms, begun under Hubert Walter, then continued by John's and Henry III's ministers, can be measured by the fact that Edward I was still able to enjoy a revenue from land of some £13,000 a year. (In view of the inflation in the previous one hundred and fifty years, however, this means that real income from this source was a good deal less than it had been in 1129–30. Equally £20,000 under Henry I was probably worth more than £40,000 under Edward I.)

The geld, the hide—the unit of land on which the geld was assessed—and the fiscal machinery through which the geld was collected, are all further examples of those rights which the Norman kings inherited from the Anglo-Saxons. Even though at two shillings on the hide the geld contributed only 10 per cent of Henry I's recorded income, it was clearly a valuable royal asset. By 1129–30 it had become an annual tax and one which could occasionally be levied at a higher rate (moreover geld exemptions could be granted as political favours, adding yet another string to the bow of royal patronage). But the geld was levied only twice by Henry II, in 1155–6 and 1161–2. Instead he developed other levies, the aid of knights (scutage: assessed on knights' fees) and the aid of boroughs and cities (tallage: assessed on a valuation of movable property). By John's reign, scutages and tallages between them constituted a more or less annual tax which adequately compensated the Crown for the withering away of the geld. But the geld was not quite dead. Under a new name, carucage, and a revised assessment it was revived and levied four times between 1194 and 1220.

By this date, however, the government had discovered a new and altogether more productive form of tax, assessed not on land but on an estimate of a man's revenues and movable property. Probably based on the ecclesiastical tithe, it was initially used in 1166, 1185, and 1188 for a pious purpose—the financial support of the Holy Land. John certainly levied this tax on movables in 1207, and may have done so in 1203. An account of the 1207 tax survives and the figures which it discloses are astonishing. Levied at the rate of 1/13 it produced no less than £60,000—a sum far and away in excess of the yield of other taxes. (Yet in 1194 this same tax had been levied at the rate of ¼—the heaviest rate in the long history of the tax—in order to contribute to Richard's ransom.) In the mid-1190s the first national customs system was introduced. These developments suggest that royal revenues reached new high levels during Richard's and John's reign. By 1213–14 John had accumulated some 200,000 marks. But these large accumulations were soon spent. These were years of war, of the Third Crusade and of the defence of the Angevin Empire. John's final failure in 1214 ushered in a long period of relative peace. Not until 1294 would the English taxpayer once again find himself paying for a major European war.

In the meantime, however, there were two other significant thirteenth-century innovations—the development of taxation of the clergy, and the establishment of a customs system. Since 1199 the Church had been made subject to an income tax imposed by the pope. Initially intended to finance crusades, it was later used for a variety of 'good causes'—as defined by the pope. Thus in 1217 Honorius III ordered bishops and prelates to help out the boy-king Henry III. From then on the Church was frequently required to subsidize the king, particularly if he had taken the cross, as Henry III did in 1250 and Edward I did in 1287. In 1291, for example, Edward received no less than 100,000 marks out of the proceeds of a papal crusading tax. By the mid-thirteenth century it had already become clear that the English Church was prepared to give financial aid to the king—though, naturally, assemblies of clergy haggled over the amount and took the opportunity of their meeting to discuss other matters which they felt needed remedying. Hardly surprising then that Henry III should go one step further in 1254 and ask for a clerical grant without first seeking papal consent. This precedent was followed in 1269, and then on three occasions by Edward I (1279–80), 1283, and 1290) in the years before 1294.

The customs duty in Richard's and John's reigns had been a war measure; it lapsed when John sought a truce with Philip Augustus in 1206. The importance of the duty on wool exports established in 1275 was that it became a permanent addition to the Crown's peacetime revenue. Its yield varied according to the fortunes of the wool trade but at the rate agreed in 1275, half a mark (6s. 8d.) per sack, it brought in between £8,000 and £13,000 per annum in the years before 1294. These new measures, papal taxation of the English Church and the customs duty on wool, were both related to the presence of Italian mercantile and banking houses in England. On the one hand, it was the ubiquitous Italian businessman that enabled the thirteenth-century Papacy to operate as an international finance corporation. On the other, credit finance came to play an increasingly large part in government. Edward I's debt to the Ricciardi of Lucca for the years from 1272 to 1294 totalled nearly £400,000; 48 per cent of this debt was repaid out of the customs receipt from a trade in which the Italians were increasingly involved. Kings, of course, had borrowed before. In the 1250s, Henry III owed the Ricciardi over £50,000; in the 1150s, Henry II used loans from a Flemish businessman, William Cade, to finance the making of the Angevin Empire. What was significant in the late thirteenth century was both the scale of the operations and the linkage between credit and customs. Compared with the sums obtainable from these new sources, the amounts to be derived from traditional levies, scutages, tallages, and feudal aids, were hardly worth the trouble of collecting and they gradually fell into disuse.

The customs system of 1275 had been granted in Parliament after discussion between the king's advisers and the merchants. Characteristic of all these taxes was that someone else's consent was required: either the pope's, or the merchants', or the clergy's, or the country's. By contrast land, lordship, and jurisdiction were revenue-producing rights which did not require meetings of influential men to approve their exploitation—indeed all influential men enjoyed similar rights (though on a smaller scale) and presumably took them for granted—so long as they were not abused. Whereas 85 per cent of Henry I's recorded revenue came from land, lordship, and jurisdiction, they provided less than 40 per cent of Edward I's. The higher the proportion of Crown revenue that came from taxation, the greater was the need for political mechanisms that enabled that consent to be obtained. This is the process known as the growth of representative institutions; in the case of the tax on movables it is the growth of Parliament.

During the long years of freedom from foreign war after 1214 the tax on movables remained an occasional resource of the Crown. War was occasional and other acceptable justifications for the tax were rare, so consent was only occasionally forthcoming—certainly not as often as Henry III would have liked. But the growing potential of the tax was revealed by the last of the seven levies collected between 1208 and 1293: the assessed yield of the

1/15 of 1290 was over £116,000. How was consent to this extraordinary tax obtained? The king's advisers would have had to make a case. Presumably, they pointed to the expenses of his recent stay in Gascony (1286–9) and of his future crusade; they may well have pointed out that in the interests of Christian piety he was sacrificing a lucrative source of revenue in deciding to expel the Jews—although by 1290 the Jewish community had been squeezed so hard by royal financial demands that it had little more to give. But to whom did they make the case? They made it to the men who represented 'the community of the realm' and, in the first instance, these were the magnates—the sorts of influential men who always had attended major political assemblies, whether Anglo-Saxon, Norman, or Angevin. The assembly of 1290, 'Parliament' as it was now called, met from April to July and in its first ten weeks it got through a great deal of business, including some important legislation. In mid-July another group of men arrived, knights of the shire. Less than a week later Parliament was dissolved. Why had the knights been so belatedly summoned to attend? Because the magnates were reluctant to approve the tax. They agreed to it but 'only insofar as they were entitled to'. Yet they had not been similarly reluctant to deal with other kinds of parliamentary business, judicial, political, legislative. In other words the magnates still adequately represented 'the community of the realm' in most fields—but not when taxation was on the agenda. From the late twelfth century onwards, kings had grown accustomed to bargaining with individual shire communities, so it was an obvious step to require these local communities to choose men to speak for them on some of those occasions when the king wanted to summon an assembly to represent the community of the whole realm. Assemblies of magnates were being reinforced in this way from the 1250s onwards and gradually the knights, yeomen, and burgesses who represented shires and boroughs—the Commons—were being accorded a more prominent role. As the proceedings of the Parliament of 1290 make clear it was above all else the king's need for taxation which stimulated this development.

Was the process also the result of social change? Was there a thirteenth-century 'rise of the gentry' which meant that traditional political institutions had to be reshaped? Did the gentry now count for more in the localities so that if kings wanted their needs widely understood and their taxes efficiently collected they had to offer them a place in the main political forum of the realm? These are difficult questions, so difficult indeed to answer in the affirmative that some historians have argued that, on the contrary, the thirteenth century was a period of crisis for the knightly class. One of the problems is a familiar one: the growing volume of evidence. We know much more about the thirteenth-century gentry than we do about their predecessors. But did Simon de Montfort and his friends court the gentry more assiduously in the period 1258–65 than John and the rebel barons had done in 1212–15? Magna Carta contains clauses which appeal to wider social groups than the barons, but so too does Henry I's Coronation Charter. To whom was Edward the Confessor appealing when, in 1051, he decided not to collect the *heregeld*? Neither in the twelfth century nor in Anglo-Saxon times did society consist only of barons and peasants. The sort of men who got themselves chosen to be knights of the shire in the late thirteenth century were exactly the sort of men who always had attended the great political assemblies. True, they had come then in the retinues of the magnates, but it was in their retinues that sensible magnates found their best advisers—and presumably they had listened to them. The knights of the late thirteenth century were not coming to these meetings for the first time; they were simply coming under another guise. It may be that the evidence of political change—the more elaborate representative institutions of the thirteenth century, the larger share of taxation in crown revenue—still has to be set within a framework of underlying social continuity.

Law and Justice

From the reign of Henry II onwards, royal judges began to hold local sessions (assizes) so frequently that it becomes possible to speak of the application over almost the entire country of a common body of customary law, the 'common law', the custom of the king's court as described in treatises such as 'Glanvill' and 'Bracton'. The previous system had been one in which, generally speaking, local courts had applied local custom. Kings, of course, had long been held to be responsible for law and order; in particular they were expected to deal with serious offences, the pleas of the Crown, but until a regular, centrally-directed machinery of justice was established, their activity in this field could only be sporadic. They intervened when influential people were involved and they launched occasional drives against theft, especially cattle-rustling. In this respect, the Anglo-Saxon system of justice survived the Norman Conquest. The change came in

1166 with the Assize of Clarendon, reinforced in 1176 by the Assize of Northampton. These assizes introduced regular measures for the trial by royal judges of those suspected of serious crimes. At first Henry II's judges were simply men whom the king trusted—they might be earls, barons, bishops, abbots, or counsellors from the royal household, exactly the sort of people whom earlier kings had sent out on specific commissions of justice or inquiry—the biggest and most famous of such inquiries being the Domesday survey. For men such as these, holding courts of law was just one of the many tasks, administrative, diplomatic, and military, which they carried out on the king's behalf. But the introduction of frequent circuits meant an ever-increasing burden of judicial work and by the end of the twelfth century we can identify a group of men, most of them laymen, who specialized in legal business, in effect professional judges. There were, of course, lower courts dealing with less serious offences, but the 'professional' courts increasingly came to dominate the field. For one thing the lower courts had no authority to innovate, whereas the king could, and did, create new offences. For example the crime of conspiracy was 'invented' in 1279 when Edward I ordered the itinerant judges to inquire into confederacies to defeat the ends of justice. Since the king's courts dealt not only with crime but also with disputes concerning property they were clearly felt to be performing a useful service. Magna Carta criticized many aspects of royal government, but not this one. Indeed it asked that the king's judges should visit each shire four times a year, more frequently than was in practice possible.

The judges were men learned in the law; being learned, they naturally responded to shifts in attitudes and ideas prevailing within educated opinion. One such shift was in the direction of a self-consciously rational approach to intellectual problems—an approach typified by Abelard's dictum: 'By doubting we come to inquiry, by inquiring we come to perceive the truth.' When applied to the law, this was a dictum which could have far-reaching implications. For example, if the guilt or innocence of a suspect could not readily be determined, it had for centuries been customary to send him to the ordeal, usually the ordeal of hot iron or the ordeal of water. This system worked well enough while men believed in it—it relied on the same psychological insight as the modern lie-detector—but was highly vulnerable to doubt. If an innocent man came to doubt the ordeal's efficacy as the means whereby God would prove his innocence then he was all the more likely to fail the ordeal. Once raised, these doubts could not be stilled. At first they seemed shocking—as when voiced by William Rufus—but eventually they became conventional. Finally, in 1215 Pope Innocent III forbade the participation of priests in the ordeal and, in England at least, this meant that the system came to an abrupt end. After an initial period of confusion, trial by ordeal was replaced by trial by jury: this was a method which had already been used with some success in settling disputes about possession of land. In 1179 Henry II had ordered that, in a case concerning property rights, the defendant might opt for trial by jury rather than trial by battle—the method which had been introduced into England by the Normans and the efficacy of which, like the ordeal, was vulnerable to doubt. But this rule when applied to criminal justice meant that there was a trial only when the accused opted for one. Obviously he came under great pressure. By a statute of 1275 he was condemned to a 'prisone forte et dure' until he did opt for trial. In consequence, many men died in prison, but because they had not been convicted, their property was not forfeited to the Crown. For this reason some chose to die rather than risk trial. Not until the eighteenth century was this right to choose taken away.

At first, and particularly in property litigation, juries had been called upon to settle straightforward questions to which they might reasonably be expected to know the answer. But problems arose when more complicated cases came before them and when trial by jury replaced the ordeal. For, unlike God, a jury was not omniscient. So efforts were made to cut through the complexities of any given dispute in order to isolate a specific question which the jury could fairly be expected to decide. But to do this well required specialized knowledge and skill; in other words it needed professional lawyers. And so, in the course of the thirteenth century, a legal profession developed, with its own schools, its own literature, and its own language (law French).

Despite all these changes, in many fundamental respects Anglo-Saxon attitudes towards justice continued to flourish. In the Anglo-Saxon and Anglo-Norman periods, serious offences had been dealt with under a procedure which ended with the guilty party being required to pay compensation to the victim or his family. The new machinery of justice established by the Angevins tended to impose punishment without compensation. In many cases, homicide, wounding, and rape for example, this was felt to be intolerable, so despite the impression given by writers such as 'Glanvill' and 'Bracton' who would have us believe that the new principles had effectively displaced the old,

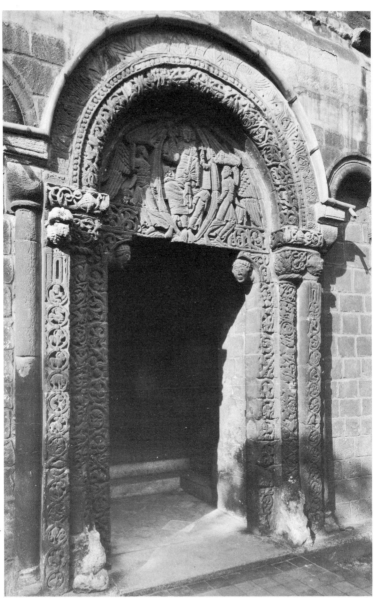

Ely Cathedral: south door. A fine example of twelfth-century sculpture. The tympanum has Christ in an aureole supported by angels. The door surround, composed of arabesques, foliage scrolls, birds, and beasts, may well be evidence of a strong English decorative tradition.

it seems that in reality the old procedures survived; they were adapted and grafted on to the new. What this meant was that those who could afford it escaped punishment but paid compensation to the victim or his kin, while those who could not, suffered the consequences.

Church and Religion

Domesday Book suggests that the village priest was usually reckoned to be a member of the peasant community. His church belonged to the local lord. If an estate were divided then the profits of the church which went with that estate might also have to be divided. In many ways, the village priest shared the lifestyle of the ordinary villager. He was very unlikely to be celibate; indeed, he was probably married and may well have inherited his position from his father. Given this basic situation, one can only admire the temerity of those eleventh-century reformers who aimed to abolish both lay control of the Church and the family life of the clergy. Under papal stimulus, the campaign for reform reached England in 1076. In subsequent decades, it was gradually stepped up and in the long run it even had a kind of success. By the late thirteenth century, married clergy were exceptional. On the other hand, plenty of them—including some of the most powerful—continued to have mistresses. Ranulf Flambard of Durham and Roger of Salisbury had their counterparts almost two hundred years later in Walter Langton of Coventry, who was accused of strangling his mistress's husband, and Robert Burnell, Edward I's chancellor, whom the king twice tried to have translated from Bath and Wells to Canterbury. As far as lay patronage and family connection were concerned, these two aspects of church life were hardly touched. 'The Lord deprived bishops of sons, but the devil gave them nephews.'

Yet even the limited success of the campaign against clerical marriage is remarkable—given how ineffective decrees on this subject had been in the seven hundred years from the fourth century onwards. It may well be linked with the general improvement in education in the twelfth and thirteenth centuries. If society at large became more literate then the clergy could more readily be recruited from the laity; they did not have to remain what they had come close to being, a hereditary caste. The more people went to school, the more they learned to know, and some of them to respect, the ancient law of the Church. Certainly there is reason to believe that in thirteenth-century

England a higher proportion of the population was celibate than had been in the eleventh century. Quite simply, there were far more people who had taken vows of chastity. Everywhere in Europe monasticism flourished and England was no exception. In 1066 there were some fifty religious houses in England and perhaps 1,000 monks and nuns. By 1216 there were approximately 700 houses and some 13,000 monks, nuns, canons, and canonesses. A century later, the total was nearer 900 houses and 17,500 members of the religious orders. Seen in the context of an overall tripling of the population these are impressive figures. Even so they fail to make plain the extent to which religious life had become diversified and enriched. In the eleventh century, all the houses were Benedictine in type. By the mid-thirteenth century not only were there several hundred Benedictine houses, there were also a number of new orders from which a man or woman could choose—regular canons, Cistercians, Gilbertines (the one peculiarly English order), Templars, Hospitallers, Carthusians, Dominicans, Franciscans, Carmelites, and Austin friars. Within this framework, almost every conceivable variety of religious life, rural, urban, contemplative, ascetic, active, was now catered for. What is more, most of those who entered the religious life now did so because they chose to. Whereas the old Benedictine houses had recruited their monks largely from the children given by their aristocratic parents to be brought up in the cloister (oblates), from the mid-twelfth century onwards those who entered both the new and the old orders were adults. The Cistercians, who established the new pattern, prohibited entry for anyone under the age of sixteen and insisted upon a year's noviciate. Conscripts had been replaced by volunteers.

During the course of the twelfth century, the English Church established the diocesan and parochial organization under which it was to live for centuries. The last new dioceses to be created were Ely (in 1108) and Carlisle (1133). Dioceses were divided into archdeaconries, and archdeaconries into rural deaneries. In the Norman period, as before, new parishes were created almost at will—the will of the local lord; but thereafter it became much harder. The territorial organization of the Church became, as it were, frozen in its twelfth-century state. This was certainly not because demographic and economic expansion was now levelling off. On the contrary, new settlements continued to be founded and the old ones continued to grow. What was happening was that the development of canon law and of papal jurisdiction was tending to protect innumerable vested interests. The rise of the lawyer, itself the result of change in one sphere of

Thirteenth-century tallage roll. The Jews in England depended on royal protection – and had to pay for it. Presumably a bored government clerk was responsible for this seemingly anti-Semitic drawing of Isaac fil' Jurnet of Norwich and some of his associates which decorates this tallage roll, an exchequer document recording Jewish payments to the Crown.

life, made it harder to change things in others. Where this created a real pastoral problem was in the towns. Bishops wrestled with the problem but much of their effort was frustrated by the proprietary interests of patrons, churchmen as well as laymen. The thirteenth century found a solution, but it needed a radical departure, a new form of religious life, to make it possible. This new form was provided by the mendicant orders, the friars—mobile missionaries whose international organization cut clean through diocesan and parochial boundaries. The first friars to come to England were the Dominicans. They arrived in 1221 and headed for Oxford. Three years later, the Franciscans arrived; their earliest friaries were in Canterbury, London, and Oxford. The Carmelites and Austin friars arrived in the 1240s. By 1300 the friars had founded some 150 houses in England.

The coming of the friars, like the growth of canon law, is a movement which reflects one of the basic circumstances of the English Church. Although its growing material wealth was firmly rooted in English soil, in its spiritual, intellectual, and corporate life as a Church it was simply a part of Latin Christendom. This was particularly true of the period from the late eleventh century onwards. Even though the Anglo-Saxon Church had always been open to Continental influences, the fact that, after 1066, it became French in its speech and emphatically Latin in its learning tended to accentuate this receptiveness. Still more important was the Gregorian reform movement and the associated development of canon law and papal jurisdiction over the entire Latin Church. The reformers' demand for *libertas ecclesiae*, the privileged freedom of the Church, undeniably had some dramatic consequences; but in the end it turned out to be unobtainable. While liberty was linked with privilege and the continued possession of great corporate wealth, kings and other secular patrons could not afford to renounce some of their crucial powers, in particular the power to appoint, even though by the thirteenth century they were having to work through the legal machinery of the Roman curia in order to obtain their ends. The fact was that the spiritual weapons at the Church's disposal, excommunication and interdict, were ultimately insufficient to deter the secular power. They tended, moreover, to become blunted through over-use. In areas which really mattered to the lay world, not just patronage but also war, tournaments, and business practice, the heroic days of the Gregorian reform gradually, in the course of the twelfth and thirteenth centuries, gave way to a period of accommodation. But where the reformers did succeed was in translating the theory of papal headship of the Church into the fact of a centralized system of government. To a quite remarkable extent, the clergy learned to do what the pope told them to do. Thus when Pope Innocent III, in pursuit of his quarrel with King John, laid an interdict on England, the clergy obeyed. For six years, from 1208 to 1214, the church doors were closed and the laity were locked out; they were denied the sacrament of the altar, solemnization of marriages, burial in consecrated ground. Even when the pope, beginning in 1199, ordered the taxation of the Church, the clergy grumbled but paid up. From 1228 onwards we can trace a continuous series of resident collectors in England; they bore the title of *nuncio* and almost all of them were Italians. Here too there was accommodation. It seemed realistic to win the king of England's approval and so, by 1300, it was the king who received the lion's share of the proceeds.

Throughout this period, Catholic Christianity remained the unchallenged religion of the country. It was taken for granted. When the churches were closed for six years there was hardly a murmur of public protest—but neither was there an upsurge of interest in alternative religions. In the twelfth and thirteenth centuries, heresy was no more of a threat to the English Church than it had been in the eleventh: in this respect England was different from many parts of Europe. Throughout this period there were a few non-Christians—Jews—in the country, but their position was always precarious, at times painfully so, and in 1290 they were expelled. Most Christians rejoiced.

Economy

The basic outline of the English economy in 1086 emerges very clearly from the repetitive, laconic phrases of Domesday Book. This was a fundamentally agrarian economy. Over 90 per cent of the people lived in the country and earned their daily bread and ale from the resources of the land. The land was already well settled—some 13,000 settlements are named—and much cultivated. As much as 80 per cent of the arable acreage of 1914 had been under the plough in 1086. Pasture, woodland, and fen were also exploited. Most men were farmers and fishers. Neither trade nor industry could offer a major alternative source of employment. Domesday statistics—though they have to be used as cautiously as any other statistics—can help to fill out the picture. People called *villani* comprised the most numerous class (41 per cent of the total recorded population). Their land holdings came to about 45 per cent of all the land. The next largest number (32 per cent) were the people known as 'bordars' or 'cottars'; they held only 5 per cent of the land. Thus, although there were enormous individual variations, it is clear that we are dealing with two distinct classes: those who had a substantial stake in the village fields and those who possessed hardly more than a cottage and its garden. In addition there were the 14 per cent of the total who were described either as 'free men' or 'sokemen'. Since they held a fifth of the land they seem to belong, economically speaking, to the same class as the *villani*. Finally there were the slaves, 9 per cent of the recorded population, who held no land.

At the other end of the social scale were the king and a tiny group of powerful men, all of them *rentiers* who lived in style on the revenues of their great estates. Less than two hundred laymen and roughly one hundred major churches (bishoprics, abbeys, and priories) held between them about three-quarters of the assessed value of the whole country. These men—in legal terminology they were known as the king's tenants-in-chief— had tenants of their own. A wealthy baron like William de Warenne, for example, had granted out holdings worth about £540 out of an estate valued at over £1,150. Some of these subtenants were men described as knights and their tenancies as knights' fees. (Although many of the knights were no richer than

A page from Domesday Book for Yorkshire. Domesday Book (so called because it was thought of as being as authoritative as the Last Judgement on Doomsday) was compiled in 1086–7 after William I had ordered a detailed inquiry 'to find out what and how much each landholder held in land and livestock, and what it was worth'. No other eleventh-century survey remotely approaches its thoroughness.

the richest *villani* the fact remains that they lived in closer association with their lords and therefore belonged to a different social group.) The rest of a tenant-in-chief's estates—usually between a half and three-quarters of them—were kept 'in demesne', and it was from these demesne lands that a lord drew the bulk of his income and food. A monastic house, with a fixed centre, needed regular supplies of foodstuffs, but other great landlords, who were more peripatetic, would probably be more interested in money. Most demesnes therefore were leased—'farmed' was the technical term—in return for a money rent. Most of the lessees came from exactly the same range of social ranks as did the holders of knights' fees; together they constituted a landowning 'middle class', a gentry.

What happened to the English economy in the two hundred years after 1086? Even over so long a period as this it can be argued that, in many fundamental respects, there was little change. England was no more urbanized in 1286 than in 1086. True, there were more and larger towns but then there were more people altogether. There were undoubtedly striking improvements in ship design—a continuing feature of northern Europe from the eighth century onwards. In this period it meant, above all, the development of the 'cog', a large, tubby bulk-carrier with a stern-post rudder and a deep draught. This meant economies of scale in the maritime trade which had long linked the east coast with the Scandinavian world and the west with the Atlantic coast of France. Presumably the volume of trade in wool, cloth, timber, salted fish, and wine was increasing and merchants' profits may well have been increasing too. Even so there was no English commercial revolution, no development of banks and credit facilities of the kind that can be claimed for thirteenth-century Italy. One consequence of this relative backwardness was that in the thirteenth century an increasingly high proportion of England's foreign trade came to be in Italian hands. Their reserves of liquid capital enabled Italian companies to offer attractive terms. They could not only buy an abbey's entire wool clip for the current year; they could also buy it for years in advance. By lending large sums to Henry III and Edward I, they obtained royal patronage and protection. In a very real sense late thirteenth-century England was being treated as a partially developed economy. Much of its import-export business was handled by foreigners (Gascons and Flemings as well as Italians). Its main exports were raw materials—wool and grain—rather than manufactured goods. There had been, in other words, no industrial revolution.

Throughout this period the major industries remained the same ones: cloth, building, mining and metalworking, salt production, and sea fishing. Moreover, despite the claims sometimes made for the cloth fulling-mill, there were no significant advances in industrial technology. Nor was there anything to compare with the highly-capitalized development of the Flemish cloth industry in the twelfth and thirteenth centuries. On the other hand growing Flemish demand for English wool did help to preserve the favourable balance of trade which, throughout this period, ensured an inflow of bullion sufficient to maintain the one coin, the silver penny, at a consistently fine standard. (Whereas in more rapidly developing and more highly monetized regions, people used a much debased coinage to perform the economic function of small change. In this sense too the English economy saw comparatively little change.)

Above all there was no agricultural revolution. Despite the fact that thirteenth-century experts on estate management, men such as Walter of Henley or Henry of Eastry, approached their job in a rational and scientific manner, the technical limitations under which they worked meant that no significant increase in yields was possible, neither from sheep in terms of weight of fleece, nor from seed in terms of yield of grain. Though the use of the horse as a draught animal was spreading, this was of marginal

Royal building. Dover Castle was described by Matthew Paris as 'the key of England'. In the 1180s Henry II, who built the great keep and inner bailey, spent some £7,000 on Dover, far more than on any other contemporary English castle. The Crown's spending on building, however, extended well beyond the immediate needs of defence.

Royal patron, architect, and workmen are all portrayed in a
thirteenth-century drawing of the building of the abbey of St.
Albans (from Matthew Paris's *Vitae Offarum*).

importance. The main problems lay not in ploughing, but in
sowing, reaping, and maintaining soil fertility. Sowing and
reaping by hand was wasteful and slow. Marl and most other
types of fertilizer were either expensive or unobtainable. Only
animal dung was generally available and it was widely and
systematically used. But the high costs of feeding flocks and
herds through the winter meant that there were upper limits to
the amount of dung that could be produced. And unless there
were basic improvements in primary production—as there were
not—improvements at the second stage of production, for
example the introduction of windmills around 1200, could only
be of marginal economic importance. Thus in many respects
England remained a stagnant economy. It can indeed be argued
that, by comparison with some of its neighbours, especially
Flanders and Italy, England was less advanced in the thirteenth
century than it had been in the eleventh.

But having said all this, it must be made clear that in one vital
respect there had been considerable change. By the late thirteenth century there were far more people living in England than
there had been in 1086—notwithstanding the fact that men and
women were familiar with *coitus interruptus* as a method of birth

control. Exactly how many people there were, it is impossible to say. Estimating population at the time of the Domesday survey is an extremely difficult task. Most historians would put it at between one and a quarter and two and a quarter millions. Estimating the late thirteenth-century population is even more hazardous. Some historians would go as high as seven millions; others would put it much lower, perhaps five millions. But almost all agree that the population more than doubled and most would accept that it probably trebled. The hypothesis of slow growth from the eleventh (or perhaps indeed from the tenth) century, followed by an acceleration from the end of the twelfth century onwards seems to be a plausible one. But not only did rates of growth vary (probably) over time; they also varied (certainly) in space. Thus the population of the North Riding of Yorkshire probably increased some twelvefold in the two hundred years after 1086; elsewhere, and particularly in those areas which were already relatively densely settled by the time of the Domesday survey, that is along the south coast and in some parts of East Anglia, the growth rate was very much smaller, though it was particularly high in the silt belt around the Wash.

What were the economic consequences of this increase of population? They can best be summed up by the phrase, 'expansion without growth'. Thus the immediate consequence was the physical expansion of settlement and cultivation. The expansion of settlement was a fairly straightforward matter. Indeed, there are plenty of signs of what the citizen of the modern world is inclined to call progress. Towns flourished. Their main function was to act as local markets. Where we know the occupations of their inhabitants, the predominance of the victualling trades and of craftsmen-shopkeepers in leather, metal, and textiles is striking. Even for the big towns—and by European standards England contained only one genuinely big town, London, assessed in 1334 at four times the wealth of its nearest rival, Bristol—long-distance and luxury trade remained less important. An increasing density of rural population meant that towns increased both in size and in number. Between 1100 and 1300, some 140 new towns were planted and, if it is not just a trick of the evidence, it would seem that the decades between 1170 and 1250 saw the greatest number, Portsmouth, Leeds, Liverpool, Chelmsford, Salisbury, for example. Mostly they were founded by local lords who expected to make a profit out of the money rents and tolls they planned to collect. Some were sited where they could take advantage of the expansion of maritime commerce, as larger ships meant that coastal ports such as

Boston, King's Lynn, and Hull (all new foundations) did better than up-river ports such as Lincoln, Norwich, and York.

In the countryside, too, the hand of the planner is sometimes visible, particularly in the regular-form villages which were laid out in those northern areas which had been laid waste by the Normans. Elsewhere, in already densely-settled East Anglia for example, villages sometimes moved to new sites straggling along the edge of common land, presumably in order to free good arable land from the 'waste' of being built upon.

But finding room to live was one thing; growing enough food to live on quite another. In general the expansion of farmland took place not so much through the establishment of new settlements as through piecemeal increase around existing centres. Huge acreages of forest, fen, marsh, and upland were cleared, drained, and farmed. Some of this was on potentially good soil—the silt belt around the Wash is the classic example—but much of it, like the clearings in the Sussex Weald, would always remain poor. This is 'the journey to the margin'—men moved out to the margins of cultivation and farmed land that was indeed marginal: it produced returns which were barely worth the labour expended. So pressing was the demand for food, bread above all, that even other 'necessities'—fuel and building timber—were having to give way.

Naturally attempts were made to farm the existing arable more intensively. In the thirteenth century the three-field, instead of the two-field, system came to be more widely adopted. This meant that a third rather than a half of the land was left fallow each year. But more intensive land use required a correspondingly more intensive application of fertilizers if soil quality were to be maintained. Unfortunately, the expansion of arable was sometimes at the expense of both pasture and woodland. The effect of this on livestock numbers could hardly have permitted increased manure production and may have actually led to a decrease in droppings. This in turn could have led to soil exhaustion and lower, rather than higher, yields. Whether or not yields did decline towards the end of the thirteenth century, one thing that does seem clear is that, if the physical limit of cultivation were reached and population still continued to grow, then one of two things would have to happen. Either more food would be imported or the average standard of living would have to fall. There is no evidence that grain imports rose. If anything the trend was probably in the opposite direction. English grain dealers took their merchandise in bulk-carrying ships to regions such as Flanders, Gascony, and Norway, that is, to places where industrialization or specialization had reached a higher pitch than in England and where regional economies were geared to the import of basic foodstuffs in return for cloth, wine, and forest products. Moreover the abundant estate records of thirteenth-century England make it clear that the average size of tenant holdings was shrinking. In this period more people means less land per head.

Despite this gloomy picture many thirteenth-century villagers may have been better off than their predecessors at the time of Domesday Book. They were relatively free from the devastation caused by war. None of them was a slave. Slavery is a feature of economies characterized by labour shortage; as population, and therefore the supply of labour, rose so slavery declined. True, many of them were serfs (or villeins)—perhaps as much as half the total population—whereas the *villani* and cottagers of Domesday Book (three-quarters of the listed population) were free. But although the *villani* and cottagers were free inasmuch as they were not slaves, it is clear that they were not very free—thus the existence of the much smaller Domesday class (only 14 per cent of those listed) called precisely 'free men'. What made life difficult for the *villani* and cottagers was that their lords were free too—free and powerful. They were free to manipulate custom in order to impose as many burdens as they could, and in a period of relative labour shortage this is likely to have meant a heavy regime of labour services: at times like this lords would not be content to pay wages at levels set by the market. Only as supply rose would lords increasingly turn to the alternative of wage labour. In the twelfth century, many tenants found their obligations converted from labour service to payment of a money rent. At this point, the development of the legalistic outlook becomes important. In the decades either side of the year 1200, the king's judges formulated rules to determine who had the right to have their disputes heard in the royal courts and who had not. They decided that those who had the right were 'free', while those who had not were 'servile'. The effect of this classification of society into two distinct categories was to enserf half the population: to make them legally unfree. But what the lawyers took with one hand they gave with the other. The more everything came to be defined and written down, the more customary tenures tended to become 'frozen' in that state in which they were written down. It became less easy to manipulate custom; more effectively than before custom tended to protect the status quo. In this sense, even unfree tenants in the thirteenth century were less vulnerable to the arbitrary exactions

Sheep farming and weaving in the twelfth century.
(From the Eadwine Psalter, Canterbury)

of individual lords than many free tenants of the eleventh century had been. Thirteenth-century lords who tried to manipulate custom often found themselves involved in long legal battles with well-organized village communities.

But although customary law may have offered a poor tenant some protection from his lord's demands, it could do nothing to protect him from the grim realities of economic change. In the years either side of 1200, half the villagers of England may have been enserfed, but this mattered little compared with the fact that poor villagers became still poorer. Those who really suffered towards the end of the thirteenth century were not servile tenants as such, but those tenants, whether free or servile, who were poor and those who had no land at all. We know something about tenants. Mortality rates on the Winchester manors suggest that from 1250 onwards the poorer tenants were becoming increasingly 'harvest-sensitive'—a euphemistic phrase meaning that, with each bad harvest, more of them died, either of starvation or of the diseases attendant upon malnutrition. Study of the West Midlands manor of Halesowen suggest that poor tenants there—the successors of the cottagers of Domesday—had a life expectancy some ten years less than the better-off tenants, the successors of the Domesday *villani*. What happened to the landless we can only guess; the nature of the evidence is such that they rarely find themselves mentioned in thirteenth-century records. Labourers on great estates customarily received not only cash but also an allowance of grain sufficient to sustain a family. But what about those landless labourers who became 'surplus to the economy'? Presumably they also became 'harvest-sensitive'.

But the economic clouds which brought misery for the poor were nicely lined with silver for the rich. The growth of population meant an increasing demand for food. Prices rose, particularly around 1200 and in the late thirteenth century. On the other hand, a plentiful supply of labour meant that money wage rates, both for piece-work and for day-work, remained stable throughout the century. Real wages, in other words, fell. In these circumstances, wealthy landowners could do very well. Selling their surplus produce on the market brought increasing profits. Markets proliferated. Between 1198 and 1483 some 2,400 grants of market were made by the Crown and of these over half came in the period before 1275. Equally a rising demand for tenancies meant growing rent-rolls. To take just one example, the bishop of Ely's net income rose from £920 in 1171–2 to £2,550 in 1298. But this does not quite mean that all the fortunate possessor of a great estate had to do was sit back and let the laws of supply and demand do their work for him. In the twelfth century, as before, most of the manors belonging to a wealthy tenant-in-chief were in fact held by his tenants, either as knights' fees or leased out at fixed rents to 'farmers'. At a time of stability or gradual expansion, this made good sense; from the lord's point of view it kept his administrative costs down to a minimum. The stability of the system is indicated by the fact that long-term leases for a life or for several lives were common, and that these long-term grants tended to turn into hereditary tenures.

But the steep rise in prices around 1200 created severe problems for the lord living on fixed rents. If he, rather than his tenants, were to take advantage of the market economy, then he had to switch to direct management of his manors. To abandon an age-old system was not easy and many lords encountered fierce resistance from their tenants, but gradually it was done. The most famous description of the process can be read in Jocelin of Brakelond's account of the business-like life of Abbot Samson of Bury St. Edmunds (abbot 1182–1211). The landlord took his estates into his own hands, appointed bailiffs and reeves to run them and sell the surplus on the open market. Under this new regime, the lord's expenses and profits were going to vary from year to year. This would have made it very easy for his officials to cheat him unless a close check were kept on their activities. So a detailed record of the manorial year was drawn up and then sent, together with similar returns from the other manors, to be checked by auditors who represented the central administration of a great estate. (The survival of masses of these accounts means that we know a great deal about some aspects of the thirteenth-century English rural economy.) The auditors had a policy-making as well as a fraud-detecting role. They fixed targets for each manor, the levels of production of grain and livestock which had to be reached. They took investment decisions, whether to build new barns, whether to buy fertilizers, and so on. Inspired by these concerns a whole new literature was born, treatises on agriculture and estate management, of which Walter of Henley's *Husbandry* is the most famous. All these changes presupposed the existence of widespread practical literacy: without this it would not have been possible to carry through the managerial revolution—for that is what it was—of the early thirteenth century.

The whole point of the new system was to maximize the lord's profits, and to do so in as rational a way as possible. It seems unlikely that this was an approach which was going to concern itself with the problems facing the poor, the lame ducks of the economic system, nearly all of whom were born lame. At a manorial level there are innumerable cases of resistance to a lord's demands, both passive resistance and direct, sometimes legal, action. In the towns, too, there is increasing evidence of a struggle between rich and poor. By the 1290s England was a country choked with people, a traditional economy unable to cope with the strains of population pressure, even perhaps a land on the brink of class warfare.

RALPH A. GRIFFITHS

4. The Later Middle Ages

(1290–1485)

To those who lived at the time, and to many historians since, the fourteenth and fifteenth centuries seemed a dangerous, turbulent, and decadent age. England's civil and foreign wars—especially those in Scotland, France, and the Low Countries—lasted longer, extended further afield, cost more, and involved larger numbers of men than any it had fought since the Viking Age. Within the British Isles, Welshmen were distrusted by the English, despite Edward I's conquests; uprisings culminating in Owain Glyndŵr's rebellion (from 1400) seemed to justify this distrust and recall prophecies that foretold of the expulsion of the English from Wales. Celtic prejudice against Englishmen flourished with all the bitterness and resentment of which the defeated or oppressed were capable: 'The tyranny and cruelty of the English', claimed a Scot in 1442, 'are notorious throughout the world, as manifestly appears in their usurpations against the French, Scots, Welsh, Irish and neighbouring lands.' Famine, disease, and (from 1348) plague drastically reduced England's population by the early fifteenth century, perhaps by as much as a half, and this severely disrupted English society. Towards the end of the fifteenth century, French statesmen were noting with disapproval Englishmen's habit of deposing and murdering their kings and the children of kings (as happened in 1327, 1399, 1461, 1471, 1483, and 1485) with a regularity unmatched anywhere else in Western Europe. Spiritual uncertainty and the spread of heresy led the choleric Chancellor of Oxford University, Dr Thomas Gascoigne, to conclude that the English Church of his day was decayed, and its bishops and clergy failing in their duty. One popular poet, writing about 1389, thought that this seemingly decadent age was all too appropriately reflected in the extravagant and indecent fashion for padded shoulders, tightly-drawn waistbands, close-fitting hose, and long pointed shoes.

There are, of course, dangers in taking contemporaries at their own estimation, particularly if they lived at times of special tension or turmoil. It is now accepted that wars can have a creative side, in this case giving Englishmen a sharper sense of national identity; that famine and disease need not utterly prostrate a society, or economic contraction necessarily mean economic depression; that the growth of heresy and criticism of religious institutions may spur men to greater personal devotion; that, as with the evolution of Parliament, political crises have constructive features; and, finally, that literary and artistic accomplishments are rarely extinguished by civil commotion or social ferment. From the vantage point of the late twentieth century, the later Middle Ages now appear as an age of turbulence and complexity, sure enough, but also as an age of vitality, ambition, and, above all, fascination.

England at War, 1290–1390

The king and his court, with the royal family and household at its centre, were the focus and fulcrum of English government and politics. Central to both was the relationship between the king and his influential subjects: the barons or magnates first and foremost, but also country knights and esquires who often aspired to join the baronial ranks, wealthy merchants, and the bishops and talented clerks—all of whom sought patronage, position, and promotion from the Crown. A successful king was one who established a harmonious relationship with all or most of these influential subjects, for only then could political stability, effective government, and domestic peace be assured. This was no simple or easy task. The growing emphasis on the king's sovereign authority in his kingdom, reinforced by the principle (from 1216) that the Crown should pass to the eldest son of the dead monarch and by the extension of royal administration in the hands of a network of king's clerks and servants, was bound to be at the expense of the feudal, regional power of the great landowners. Yet that very principle of hereditary monarchy, while it reduced the likelihood of royal kinsmen squabbling over the Crown, made it more likely that unsuitable kings (by their youth, character, or incapacity) would sometimes wear it. Above all, the persistent warfare of the fourteenth and fifteenth centuries imposed heavier obligations on England's kings. From Edward I's reign onwards, there was no decade when Englishmen were not at war, whether overseas or in the British Isles. Every generation of Englishmen in the later Middle Ages knew the demands, strains, and consequences of war—and more intensely than their forebears.

After the civil war of Henry III's reign, a successful effort was made to reconcile England and restore domestic peace whereby the king and his subjects could re-establish a stable relationship that gave due regard to the rights and aspirations of both. The new monarch, Edward I (1272–1307), showed himself to be capable, constructive, and efficient in his government, and also determined to emphasize his position as sovereign. But his unrelenting insistence on asserting his sovereignty in all the territories of the British Isles, even those beyond the borders of his realm, began the era of perpetual war.

In Wales, he overwhelmed Gwynedd, the most vigorous and independent of the surviving native lordships, and with Llywe-lyn ap Gruffydd's death in 1282 the conquest of Wales was successfully completed after two hundred years of intermittent warfare. The Crown thereby expanded its territories in North and West Wales to form a principality that covered half the country; in 1301 this was conferred on the king's eldest son as the first English-born Prince of Wales. It was a notable achievement, if a costly one. Material damage had to be made good; an imaginative plan for future security included a dozen new and half-a-dozen reconstructed fortresses, most of them comple-

Harlech Castle (Gwynedd), one of a series of massive fortresses constructed by Edward I between 1277 and 1301 to subdue and control North Wales. He spent over £75,000 in all, £9,500 on Harlech in the period 1283–90.

mented by new walled boroughs peopled by loyal immigrants; and a permanent administration was devised for the conquered lands. This administration (announced in the statute of Rhuddlan, 1284) began as a military regime but soon established peace and stability by a judicious combination of English innovation and Welsh practice. Firmness, tempered by fairness and conciliation, was the hallmark of relations between the new governors and the Welsh population, and rebellions in 1287, 1294–5, and 1316 were not widespread or dangerous threats. Yet the costs of conquest were prodigious. Soldiers and sailors, architects, craftsmen, and labourers were recruited in every English county and beyond to serve in Wales. At least £75,000 was spent on castle-building between 1277 and 1301 alone (when a skilled mason earned less than 2s. a week), whilst the suppression of the 1294–5 revolt cost about £55,000. Fortunately, royal government in Wales proved eminently successful: by the mid-fourteenth century it was producing a profit for the royal exchequer and the Welsh gentry prospered in co-operation with an alien regime.

No sooner had Llywelyn been eliminated than Edward I turned to the lords of the Welsh march (or borderland)—mostly English magnates—to establish his sovereign rights over them and their subjects too; and he brought the Welsh Church and bishops more directly under his control. The whole enterprise of Edwardian conquest showed an imagination and determination and a grasp of strategy that went far beyond the military campaigns. But the feelings of bitterness among the conquered, who were ruled in Church and State by an alien hierarchy, could not easily be removed. If English domination were to become oppressive, if the economic benefits of stable rule dried up, or if relations between native and immigrant deteriorated, serious problems would be created for the English state, and colonial rule would be threatened.

Edward I was equally intent on exerting his superior lordship over Scotland. This was an exceptionally ambitious undertaking because Scotland, unlike Wales, had its own monarch (of the house of Canmore) and Scotsmen's sense of independence was fierce, especially in the remoter Highlands. But, as with Wales, an opportunity to assert England's overlordship had arisen in Edward's reign in 1286 on the death of King Alexander III and of his granddaughter and heiress four years later. Edward accepted the invitation of the Scottish 'guardians of the realm' to settle the succession question, and he took advantage of this 'Great Cause' (1291–2) to secure recognition of himself as 'lord superior' of Scotland. Scottish resistance and Edward's efforts to make his

A typical Welshman, as seen from Westminster towards the end
of the thirteenth century; long hair, plain homespun cloak, one shoe –
and his invaluable longbow.

claim a reality began a barren period of mutual hostility between
the two countries that lasted well into the sixteenth century. The
Scots sought French aid (1295) and papal support, and they
generated a vigorous patriotism in defence of their political
independence under the leadership of William Wallace (exe-

cuted 1305) and Robert Bruce (King Robert I, 1306–29). A score of English invasions in the half-century after 1296 succeeded in establishing an uneasy military and administrative presence in the Lowlands, but it was difficult to sustain in poor and hostile country and had to be financed largely from England. Nor did the English command the northern seas or subdue and control the north and west of Scotland. Thus, the English had none of the advantages—or success—that attended their ventures in Wales, and even in battle (notably at Bannockburn, 1314) their cavalry forces suffered humiliating defeat at the hands of more mobile Scotsmen. The treaty of Northampton (1328), which recognized King Robert and surrendered the English claim to overlordship, was quickly disowned by Edward III when he took personal charge of the government in 1330. Anglo-Scottish relations thereafter were a sad catalogue of invasion, border raids, unstable English occupation of southern shires, Franco-Scottish agreements that hardened into the 'Auld Alliaunce'—even the capture of King David II at Neville's Cross (1346). Scotland proved a persistent and expensive irritation after English claims and ambitions were thwarted by determined and united resistance by the Scots.

After Bannockburn, Robert I tried to forestall further English operations in Scotland by exploiting the situation in Ireland. During 1315–18 his brother, Edward Bruce, secured the support of Anglo-Irish magnates and Gaelic chiefs, and in 1316 he was declared High King of Ireland. Soon afterwards, Robert himself visited Ireland and this may have been designed to stimulate a 'pan-Celtic' movement against Edward II of England (1307–27). This Scottish intervention was a severe shock to the English government and revealed the weakness of its regime in Dublin. No English king visited Ireland between 1210 and 1394—not even Edward I, conqueror of the Welsh and 'hammer of the Scots'. Instead, Edward I ruthlessly stripped the country of its resources of men, money, and supplies, especially for his wars and castle-building in Wales and Scotland. Harsh exploitation and absentee rule led in time to administrative abuse and the decay of order, of which the Anglo-Irish magnates and Gaelic chiefs took full advantage. The king's officials presided over an increasingly feeble and neglected administration, whilst a Gaelic political and cultural revival had taken root in the thirteenth century. This contributed to the success of Edward Bruce, during whose ascendancy Ireland, said a contemporary, 'became one trembling wave of commotion'. The English lordship never recovered and henceforward was unable to impose its authority

The Oak Coronation Chair, made for Edward I to encase the Stone of Scone
which the king seized in 1297, symbolizes the claims of English kings to
superiority over Scotland.

throughout the island. Instead of being a financial resource,
Ireland became a financial liability, with a revenue after 1318 that
was a third of what it had been under Edward I and therefore

quite inadequate to sustain English rule. Periodic expeditions led by minor figures could do little to revive the king's authority and the area under direct rule consequently contracted to the 'pale' around Dublin. It was a confession of failure when the government resorted to racial and cultural separation, even persecution, by a series of enactments culminating in the statute of Kilkenny (1366). The 'lord of Ireland' had a perfunctory lordship in the later Middle Ages that was costly, lawless, hostile to English rule, and open to exploitation by the Scots, the French, and even by Welsh rebels.

The recognition of overlordship which English monarchs demanded of the Welsh, Scots, and Irish was denied to the French king in Gascony, where these same English kings, as dukes of Aquitaine, had been feudal vassals of the Crown of France since 1204. Gascony lay at the heart of Anglo-French relations both before and during the so-called Hundred Years War (1337–1453): it replaced Normandy and Anjou as the main bone of contention. At Edward I's accession, this prosperous, wine-producing province was England's only remaining French territory, and the political link with England was reinforced by a flourishing export trade in non-sweet wine which was complemented by the transport of English cloth and corn by sea to Bordeaux and Bayonne: in 1306–7 the duchy's revenue was about £17,000 and well worth fighting for. Friction with the French king over Gascony's frontier and the rights of Gascons was gradually subsumed in the larger issues of nationhood and sovereignty posed by an assertive, self-conscious French state bent on tightening its control over its provinces and vassals (including the English duke of Aquitaine). For their part, Edward I and his successors were reluctant to see French royal rights emphasized or given any practical meaning in Gascony. The result was a series of incidents, peace conferences, 'brush-fire' wars in which French armies penetrated Gascony and the duchy was periodically confiscated, and English expeditions— even a visit by Edward I himself (1286–9).

Relations between England and France might have continued to fester in this fashion had it not been for two other factors. The English government resented the Franco-Scottish alliance (from 1295) and was angered by the refuge offered by the French (1334) to the Scottish King David II after Edward III had invaded Scotland. Even more contentious were the consequences of the approaching extinction of the senior male line of the French royal house of Capet. The deaths, in rapid succession, of four French kings between 1314 and 1328, requiring the swearing of homage for Gascony on each occasion, were irritating enough, but the demise of the last Capet in 1328 raised the question of the succession to the French throne itself. At that point, the new English king, Edward III (1327–77), was in no position to stake his own claim through his French mother, Isabelle, but in 1337, when the Gascon situation had deteriorated further, he did so. His action may have been primarily tactical, to embarrass the new Valois monarch, Philip VI, though for an English king to become king of France would have the undeniable merit of resolving at a stroke the difficult Gascon issue: the political stability and economic prosperity of Gascony would be assured. Thus, when a French fleet was sighted off the Norman coast *en route* (so the English believed) for Scotland in 1337, war began— and would last for more than a century.

England's war aims were neither constant nor consistently pursued. Especially in the fourteenth century, its war diplomacy was primarily dictated by a series of immediate problems, notably of how to maintain independent rule in Gascony and how to deter Scottish attacks across the northern border in support of the French. Even after Edward III claimed the French Crown in 1337, he was prepared to ransom John II, the French king captured at the battle of Poitiers (1356), and to abandon his claim in the treaty of Brétigny (1360) in return for practical concessions. Nevertheless, dynastic ties, commercial and stra-

A ball game, mid-fourteenth century, from a realistic misericord in Gloucester Cathedral. Two youths, with tight leggings and pointed shoes, kick and handle a large ball in a game akin to rugby or soccer. Such popular games often led to injury and riots, and from the fourteenth century kings tried to divert sporting energies to more useful archery.

tegic considerations, even differing attitudes to the Papacy, which was installed at Avignon from 1308 to 1378, combined to extend the Anglo-French conflict to the Low Countries, to Castile and Portugal, as well as to Scotland, Ireland, and even Wales. To begin with, the wars (for this was a disjointed series of conflicts rather than one war) were fought by sieges in northern France in 1338–40; then there was more intensive campaigning by pincer movements through the French provinces of Brittany, Gascony, and Normandy in 1341–7 (resulting in the English victory at Crécy and the capture of Calais). This was followed by bold marches or *chevauchées* by Edward III's eldest son, Edward the Black Prince, from Gascony in 1355–6 (culminating in the great victory at Poitiers) and by the king himself in 1359 to Rheims, the traditional coronation seat of French kings. The renewal of war in Castile (1367) inaugurated a period of more modest and fitful campaigning in Portugal, Flanders, and France itself, with both sides gradually exhausting themselves.

The advantage in the war lay initially with England, the more united and better organized of the two kingdoms. Its prosperity, based especially on wool production, and its experience of warfare in Wales and Scotland, were invaluable foundations for larger-scale operations on mainland Europe. The existence of highly independent French provinces dictated English strategy. Edward III's campaigns in the Low Countries in 1338–40 relied on the support of the cloth-manufacturing cities of Flanders which, though subject to the French king, had vital commercial links with England. In the 1340s a succession dispute in Brittany enabled English forces to intervene there and even to garrison certain castles; while Gascony, though far to the south, afforded direct access to central France.

The wars within the British Isles gave the English government a unique opportunity to develop novel methods of raising substantial forces. Supplementing and gradually replacing the traditional feudal array, the newer paid, contracted armies, recruited by indentured captains, were smaller, better disciplined, and more dependable and flexible than the loosely organized and ponderous French forces. English men-at-arms and archers, proficient in the use of the longbow and employing defensive tactics in battle, had a decisive advantage which brought resounding victories against all the odds in the early decades of the war (most notably at Crécy and Poitiers). The war at sea was a more minor affair, with naval tactics showing little novelty or imagination. It was usually beyond the capability of fourteenth-century commanders to stage a naval engagement and the battle of Sluys (which the English won in 1340) was incidental to Edward III's expedition to Flanders. The English never kept a fleet permanently in being, but the Valois, learning the expertise of their Castilian allies, later constructed dockyards at Rouen which in time gave them an edge at sea (witness their victory off La Rochelle in 1372).

English investment in the French war was immense and unprecedented. Expeditions were organized with impressive regularity and were occasionally very large (over 10,000 men in 1346–7, for instance). The financial outlay was prodigious and tolerated so long as the war was successful; but as the margin of England's military advantage narrowed after 1369, so the government resorted to newer and more desperate expedients, including poll taxes. Shipping for defence and expeditions could not be supplied solely by the traditional obligation of the southern Cinque Ports, and hundreds of merchant vessels (735 for the siege of Calais in 1347, for example) were impressed and withdrawn from normal commercial operations. Coastal defence against French and Castilian raiders, who grew bolder after 1369, was organized by the maritime shires of the south and east, supported by others inland—but even this could not prevent the sacking of Winchelsea (1360), Rye (1377), and other ports. The costs of war were indeed high. It is true that conquered French estates were enjoyed by many a fortunate soldier, and ransoms were profitable during the victorious years (King John II's ransom alone was fixed at £500,000). But the lives and occupations of thousands of Englishmen, Welshmen, and Irishmen were disrupted by war service; supplies of food, materials, and equipment were diverted to operations that were entirely destructive; and the wool and wine trades were severely hampered. What is remarkable is that England was able to engage in these enterprises overseas for decades without serious political or social strains at home, and at the same time to defend the Scottish border, keep the Welsh calm, and avoid Irish uprisings. This achievement owed much to the inspiration, example, and leadership of Edward III and the Black Prince, both of whom embodied the chivalric virtues vaunted by the nobility and admired by society at large. To Jean Froissart, the Hainaulter who knew them both and kept a record of the most inspiring chivalric deeds of his age, the king was 'gallant and noble [whose] like had not been seen since the days of King Arthur'. His son appeared as 'this most gallant man and chivalrous prince' who, at his death in 1376, a year before Edward III himself died, 'was deeply mourned for his noble qualities'. King Edward

Sea-fight, probably off Calais in 1416, between the earl of Warwick (see his banner *left*) and a French ship. Grappling at close quarters, bows and arrows, lances, and hurling stones from the crow's nest were the primitive naval tactics of the age. (From a *Pageant* of the earls of Warwick c.1485–90)

presided over a regime in England that was less harsh than Edward I's and far more capable than Edward II's.

These wars were a catalyst of social change, constitutional development, and political conflict in England which would otherwise have occurred more slowly. Moreover, along with the rest of Europe, England in the fourteenth century experienced population and economic fluctuations that increased tension and uncertainty. The result was a series of crises which underlined how delicately balanced was the relationship between the king and his subjects (especially his magnates, who regarded themselves as representing the entire 'community of the realm') and how crucial to a personal monarchy was the king himself. Able and determined—even far-sighted—Edward I and his advisers may have been, but the king's obstinate and autocratic nature seriously strained relations with his influential subjects. Between 1290 and 1297, the propertied classes, the merchants, and especially the clergy were subjected to extraordinarily heavy and novel demands for taxes (four times as frequently as in the first half of Edward's reign) for the king's enterprises in France and the British Isles. There was resistance and a property tax of 1297 produced only a fraction (£35,000) of what had been anticipated. Further, armies had been summoned by the king for prolonged service outside the realm. Edward's attempts to silence resistance shocked the clergy and embittered the merchants. The leading magnates, including Welsh marcher lords who resented Edward's invasion of their cherished franchises, reacted by resuming their time-honoured role as self-appointed spokesmen of the realm, and they presented grievances to the king in 1297 and again in 1300. They deployed Magna Carta as their banner against taxation without the payers' consent, and against oppressive and unprecedented exactions. Yet, when Edward died in the arms of his attendants at Burgh-by-Sands on 7 July 1307, just as he was about to cross the Solway Firth on his sixth expedition to Scotland, the problems of wartime remained. He bequeathed to his son and successor, Edward II (1307–27), an expensive war in the north that was nowhere near a victorious conclusion, and political unrest in England compounded by a dwindling of trust between monarch and subject. These two preoccupations—political stability and war—dominated public affairs during the following 200 years and had a profound effect on the kingdom's social and political cohesion and on its economic prosperity. The new king would need exceptional tact if a further crisis of authority were to be avoided.

Tact was not Edward II's outstanding quality. Starved of affection during childhood, ignored by his father in adolescence, and confronted by unsolved problems at his accession, Edward II sought advice, friendship, even affection, from ambitious favourites such as Peter Gavaston and Hugh Despenser who were unworthy of the king's trust and whose influence was resented by many magnates. These facts, together with the determination of the magnates (led by Thomas, earl of Lancaster) to extract from Edward concessions and reforms which Edward I had been unwilling to confirm, turned the formidable difficulties of ruling a kingdom that was facing setbacks in Scotland, Ireland, Wales, and France, into a struggle for political reform and personal advancement. An extended and more specific coronation oath (1308) bound the new king more firmly to observe English law and custom, and ordinances drawn up by the magnates in 1311 sought to limit the king's freedom of action; these ordinances were announced in Parliament in order to gain wide support and approval. Edward II had all the stubbornness of his father (though without his ability) and Gavaston's murder (1312) converted this quality into an unshakeable resolve not to be dominated by his friend's murderers. Meanwhile, the burdens of war and defence on the king's subjects were scarcely less heavy than they had been during Edward I's conquests, and this at a time of severe social distress and poverty caused by a succession of disastrous harvests and livestock diseases during 1315–22. Civil war (1321–2) and the king's deposition (1326–7) were the fateful outcome of the failure of king and governed to co-operate to mutual benefit. Edward denounced the ordinances

A knight preparing for the lists, which were a preparation for war and a chivalric sport. Sir Geoffrey de Luttrell is being armed by his wife and daughter.

in 1322, again in a Parliament (at York), and after the defeat of his opponents at Boroughbridge in 1322, he executed Lancaster. By 1326, Edward's deposition in favour of his namesake son and heir seemed the only alternative to a mean, oppressive, and unsuccessful regime that engendered civil strife. This awesome step, engineered with Queen Isabelle's connivance, the acquiescence of Prince Edward, and with substantial magnate and other support, demonstrated in a Parliament, was unprecedented: since the Norman Conquest, no English king had been deposed from his throne. In 1327, therefore, every effort was made to conceal the unconcealable and justify the unjustifiable. Browbeaten, tearful, and half-fainting, the wretched king was forced to assent to his own abdication, and a meeting of Parliament was used to spread the responsibility as widely as possible. Although the accession of Edward's son ensured that the hereditary principle remained intact, the inviolability of anointed kingship had been breached.

Although only nineteen in 1327, Edward III was already a parent and far more capable than his father and more sensitive than he to the attitudes and aspirations of his magnates—indeed, he shared them, particularly in warfare and in accepting the chivalric obligations of an aristocratic society. At the same time, the new king's grandiose and popular plans in France raised issues similar to those posed by Edward I's enterprises in the British Isles and Gascony. Should these plans ultimately prove unsuccessful, the implications for England might well be similar to those that had surfaced in Edward II's reign. The outbreak of prolonged war in 1337 meant increased taxation at a level even higher than that of Edward I's last years, and Edward III showed the same ruthlessness towards merchants, bankers, and landowners as Edward I had done. Moreover, the absences of the king on campaign, in the thick of the fighting which he and his magnates relished, posed serious questions for a sophisticated administration normally under the personal direction of the king. Edward's ordinances (issued at Walton-on-Thames, 1338) for the government of England from abroad caused friction between the king and his advisers in northern France on the one hand, and those councillors remaining in England on the other. Some even feared that, if the war were successful, England might take second place in King Edward's mind to his realm of France. Thus, in 1339–43 another crisis arose in which magnates, merchants, and the Commons in Parliament (now the forum in which royal demands for taxation were made) protested to the king. Edward was induced to act more circumspectly and

King Edward III, eldest son of Edward II and Isabelle of France; succeeded in 1327; married Philippa of Hainault in 1328. The gilt copper effigy in Westminster Abbey was carved ten years after his death (1377).

considerately towards his magnates, clergy, and subjects generally. The eventual reconciliation, and the re-establishment of the trust in the king that had proved so elusive since the 1290s, was possible because Edward III was a sensible and pragmatic monarch, with a self-confidence that did not extend to arrogance.

He appointed ministers acceptable to his magnates, he pandered to the self-importance of Parliament, and he developed a remarkable *rapport* with his subjects which sustained his rule in England and his ambitions in France for a quarter of a century. Further crisis was avoided, despite England's involvement in its most major war yet.

There was an enormous contrast with the situation in the 1370s and 1380s. For the generation of Englishmen alive then, the frustrations of the resumed war in France (from 1369) and of debilitating skirmishes in Ireland and on the Scottish border were unsettling; and renewed taxation, after a decade when England had enjoyed the profits of war and a respite from taxes, was resented. Raids on south-coast ports were frequent, uncertain naval control of the Channel imperilled trade and upset the merchants, and expensive *chevauchées* in France were occasionally spectacular but rarely profitable. Yet the abrupt reversal of English policy in 1375, involving a humiliating truce with France and payments to the mistrusted pope, only served to affront and exasperate Englishmen. Moreover, after the death (1369) of Queen Philippa, a paragon among queens, Edward III lapsed gently into a senility that sapped his strength and impaired his judgement. The Black Prince, too, began to suffer from the effects of his wartime exertions; in fact, he predeceased his father in June 1376. Yet the financial, manpower, and other burdens on England's population were not eased. Questions were raised, especially by the Commons in Parliament, about the honesty as well as the competence of the king's advisers and officials. Strengthened by a rising tide of anticlericalism in an age when the reputation of the Papacy and the Church was severely tarnished, the outcry had swept Edward III's clerical ministers from power in 1371 and others were accused of corruption, even treason. Another political crisis had arisen. In the 'Good Parliament' of 1376, the longest and most dramatic assembly yet held, the allegedly corrupt and incapable ministers—even the old king's influential mistress, Alice Perrers—were accused by the Commons and tried before the Lords in a novel and highly effective procedure (impeachment) which henceforward enabled persons in high places to be held publicly to account for their public actions.

The crisis entered a new phase when King Edward himself died in June 1377. He was succeeded by the Black Prince's only surviving son and heir, Richard II (1377–99), who was ten years of age. England was faced with the prospect of only the second royal minority since 1066 and the first since 1216. On the latter occasion there had followed a period of political turbulence centring on the young Henry III; a similar situation developed after 1377 and played its part in precipitating the Peasants' Revolt (1381) in eastern and south-eastern England. A series of poll taxes was imposed during 1377–80 to finance the war. These taxes were at a rate higher than was usual and the tax of 1379 was popularly known as 'the evil subsidy'. They sparked off violence in East

Main roads in medieval England and Wales

Anglia against the tax-collectors and the justices who tried to force compliance on the population. But what turned these irritations into widespread rebellion was the prolonged dislocation of unsuccessful war, the impact of recurrent plagues, and the anticlerical temper of the times. Hopes of remedy placed by the rebels in the young King Richard proved to be vain, though he showed considerable courage in facing the rebels in London during the summer of 1381.

Richard was still only fourteen, and the aristocratic rivalries in the ruling circle continued, not least among the king's uncles. This and the lack of further military success in France damaged the reputation of the council that governed England in Richard's name and even affected the king's own standing in the eyes of his subjects. Richard, too, was proving a self-willed monarch whose sense of insecurity led him to depend on unworthy favourites reminiscent of Edward II's confidants. As he grew older, he naturally wanted to expand his entourage and his household beyond what had been appropriate for a child. Among his friends and associates were some who were new to the ranks of the aristocracy, and all were generously patronized by the king at the expense of those (including his uncle Gloucester) who did not attract Richard's favour. In 1386 Parliament and a number of magnates attacked Richard's closest associates and even threatened the king himself. With all the stubbornness of the Plantagenets, Richard refused to yield. This led to further indictments or appeals of his advisers by five leading 'appellant' lords (the duke of Gloucester, and the earls of Warwick, Arundel, Nottingham, and Derby, the king's cousin), and a skirmish took place at Radcot Bridge in December 1387 when the king's closest friend, the earl of Oxford, was routed. At the momentous 'Merciless Parliament' (1388), the king was forced to submit to aristocratic correction which, if it had been sustained, would have significantly altered the character of the English monarchy. Once again, the pressures of war, the tensions of personal rule, and the ambitions of England's magnates had produced a most serious political and constitutional crisis. The institution of hereditary monarchy emerged largely unscathed after a century and more of such crises, but criticism of the king's advisers had reached a new level of effectiveness and broader sections of opinion had exerted a significant influence on events. These were the political and personal dimensions of more deep-seated changes that were transforming England's social and economic life in the later Middle Ages.

Wealth, Population, and Social Change

England's wealth in the later Middle Ages was its land, the exploitation of which engaged most Englishmen: growing corn, producing dairy goods, and tending livestock. England's most important industry, textiles, was indirectly based on the land, producing the finest wool in Europe from often very large sheep flocks: St. Peter's Abbey, Gloucester, owned over 10,000 sheep by 1300, when the total number in England is thought to have been in the region of fifteen to eighteen millions. The wealthiest regions were the lowlands and gently rolling hill-country of the

A Kentish peasant, c.1390, forced to carry barefoot a sack of hay and straw publicly from Wingham to the archbishop's palace six miles away at Canterbury. Tenants in the late fourteenth century tried to avoid such humiliating labour services to their lords. (From the Register of Archbishop William Courtenay (1381–96), fo.337ᵛ)

midland and southern shires, with extensions into the borderland and southern littoral of Wales. Other industries were less significant in creating wealth and employing labour, but Cornish tin-mining was internationally famous and the tin was exported to the Continent. Lead, iron, and coal mining was quite modest, though the coastal traffic in coal from the Tyne Valley and the neighbourhood of Swansea reflected its growing domestic and industrial use. As for financial and commercial services, the economy gained little from what became, in modern times, one of the nation's prime sources of wealth. Few English merchants—the de la Poles of Hull were an exception—could compete with the international bankers of Italy, with their branches in London, despite the fact that Edward I and Edward III were slow to honour their war debts to these Italian companies. England's mercantile marine was generally outclassed, except in coastal waters, by foreign shipping; but the Gascon wine-run and woollen shipments to the Low Countries did fall increasingly into the hands of English merchants and into the holds of English vessels. The thousand and more markets and fairs dotted about the English and Welsh countryside—more numerous by 1350 than in the past—served mainly their local community within a radius of a score or so miles. Most of these small towns and villages—Monmouth, Worcester, and Stratford among them—were integrated with their rural hinterland, whose well-to-do inhabitants frequently played a part in town life, joining the guilds, buying or renting town residences, and filling urban offices. A small number of towns, including some ports, were larger and had broader commercial horizons: Shrewsbury's traders travelled regularly to London by the fifteenth century, and merchants from the capital and Calais (after 1347) visited the Welsh borderland in search of fine wool. Bristol, with its vital link with Bordeaux, was rapidly becoming the entrepôt of late medieval Severnside; whilst York, Coventry, and especially London were centres of international trade.

From this wealth sprang the prosperity of individuals, institutions, and the Crown. The greatest landowners were the lay magnates (small in number, like 'skyscrapers on a plain'), bishops, monasteries, and other religious institutions. In 1300 these still benefited handsomely from a market boom created by the expanding population of the previous century. Prices were buoyant and landed incomes substantial: after the earl of Gloucester died at Bannockburn (1314), his estates were estimated to be worth just over £6,000 a year, whilst those of Christ Church Priory, Canterbury, produced in 1331 a gross annual income of more than £2,540. Landowners therefore exploited their estates directly and took a personal interest in their efficient management. They insisted on their rights as far as possible, squeezing higher rents out of tenants and carefully recording in manor courts the obligations attached to holdings. Such landed wealth was the foundation of the political, administrative, and social influence of the aristocracy, many of whom had estates in several counties as well as Wales and Ireland: Humphrey, earl of Hereford and Essex, for instance, inherited property in Essex, Middlesex, Huntingdonshire, Hertfordshire, and Buckinghamshire, and also in Brecon, Hay, Huntington, and Caldicot in the Welsh march. Land was equally the basis of the gentry's fortunes, albeit on a more local, shire level; whilst it gave ecclesiastical landowners an earthly authority that complemented their hold on men's minds and souls. This wealth could support pretensions and ambitions on a more national stage, as in the case of Thomas, earl of Lancaster, the richest earl in the England of his day.

The peasantry in 1300 were living in a world where land was

A 'lost village' among 1,300 and more in the Midlands and eastern England. Middle Ditchford (Gloucestershire) was probably abandoned in the mid-fifteenth century because of declining population and the conversion of its streets, lanes, and open fields (still well marked, with ridge-and-furrow cultivation in foreground) to pastoral farming.

scarce and opportunities for economic advancement were limited by the tight controls of the landowners. Prices were high—the price of wheat after 1270 was consistently higher than it had been earlier in the century—and there was little cash to spare after food, clothing, and equipment had been bought. Wages in an over-stocked labour market were low and reduced the purchasing power of skilled and unskilled alike: a carpenter earned 3*d.* a day (without food) and a labourer 1*d.* or 1½*d.* Grumbles, complaints, and spasms of violence were directed at landowners and their officials, and rent strikes and refusals to perform customary labour services were not uncommon.

The merchants of 1300, most notably the exporters of wool and importers of wine, thrived in an expanding market from the Baltic to Spain, Portugal, and, especially after the opening of the sea-route from the Mediterranean, to northern Italy. During 1304–11 wool exports averaged annually 39,500 sacks (each containing at least 250 fleeces) and only 30–40 per cent of these cargoes was shipped by foreigners. The rising antipathy towards alien merchants in English trade reflects the self-confidence and assertiveness of native (or denizen) merchants. Edward I legislated (1280s) in their interest, notably to facilitate the recovery of debts at law, which was essential to the expansion of trade. But when war came, merchants were among the first to resist heavy taxation, especially the *maltolt* (or 'evil tax') of 1294, and the impressment of their ships.

The king was the largest landowner of all, even before Edward I acquired a principality in Wales and the estates of the house of Lancaster merged with the Crown's in 1399. The growth of national taxation under Edward I and his successors enabled the Crown to tap the wealth of private landowners and merchants, too. Not even the peasantry escaped, as was well appreciated by those who sang the popular lament, 'Song of the Husbandman', in Edward I's reign. Then, in 1327, all who had goods worth at least 10*s.* a year were required to pay 1*s.* 8*d.* in tax, and doubtless the less well-off had the burden passed on to them indirectly. The preoccupation with war made the king heavily dependent on the wealth and forbearance of his subjects. If that wealth ceased to grow, or if the prosperity of individuals and institutions were punctured, then the king's extraordinary commitments might eventually be beyond his means and his subjects' tolerance wear dangerously thin.

By the mid-fourteenth century the prosperous period of 'high farming' was almost over. Prices were falling, making cultivation for a market less profitable. Wages were rising, more so for

The country house of a wealthy late medieval gentleman. Great Chalfield Manor (Wiltshire), built c.1470–80 by Thomas Tropenell, an ambitious lawyer who served the Hungerford family and prospered under Lancastrian and Yorkist kings, had a great hall and great chamber for his family and domestic offices and quarters for his servants.

agricultural labourers than for craftsmen, and there was no advantage in employing women, who were paid the same as men—indeed, in bear-baiting they were paid more! The principal reason why large-scale farming was losing some of its attraction was that the population boom came to an end and went, full throttle, into reverse. As the pool of available labour shrank, wages rose; as the population declined so did the demand for food and supplies, and prices followed suit.

England's population reached its peak, perhaps over four millions, about the end of the thirteenth century. At that time, there was insufficient cultivable land to ensure that all peasant families had an adequate livelihood. A high population coupled with low living standards inevitably meant poverty, famine, and disease, and a mortality that crept upwards and brought the demographic boom to a halt. The plight of those living at or below the poverty-line was made worse by a series of natural

disasters related to over-exploitation of the land and exceptionally bad weather in the opening decades of the fourteenth
century. Poor harvests were calamitous for a society without
adequate storage facilities: there was less to eat and no cash to
buy what now cost much more. The harvests of the years 1315,
1316, 1320, and 1321 were exceptionally bad; cattle and sheep
murrains were especially prevalent in 1319 and 1321, and on the
estates of Ramsey Abbey (Cambs.) recovery took twenty years;
and in 1324–6 parts of England had severe floods which drowned
thousands of sheep in Kent. Famine and disease spread, and on
Halesowen Manor (Worcs.) 15 per cent of males died in 1315–17.
Agricultural dislocation was widespread, grain prices soared
(from 5s. 7¼d. to 26s. 8d. per quarter in Halesowen during
1315–16), and wool exports collapsed. However, it was a temporary calamity and England gradually recovered during the 1320s;
but the vulnerability of the poor in particular had been starkly
demonstrated.

Longer lasting and more profound were the consequences of
plague. The first attack, known since the late sixteenth century as
the Black Death but to contemporaries as 'the great mortality',
occurred in southern England in 1348; by the end of 1349 it had
spread north to central Scotland. Geoffrey le Baker, a contemporary Oxfordshire cleric, described its progress from the ports,
where it arrived in rat-infested ships, and men's helplessness in
diagnosing its cause and dealing with its effects.

And at first it carried off almost all the inhabitants of the seaports in Dorset, and
then those living inland and from there it raged so dreadfully through Devon and
Somerset as far as Bristol and then men of Gloucester refused those of Bristol
entrance to their country, everyone thinking that the breath of those who lived
amongst people who died of plague was infectious. But at last it attacked
Gloucester, yea and Oxford and London, and finally the whole of England so
violently that scarcely one in ten of either sex was left alive. As the graveyards did
not suffice, fields were chosen for the burial of the dead . . . A countless number
of common people and a host of monks and nuns and clerics as well, known to
God alone, passed away. It was the young and strong that the plague chiefly
attacked . . . This great pestilence, which began at Bristol on [15 August] and in
London about [29 September], raged for a whole year in England so terribly that it
cleared many country villages entirely of every human being.

While this great calamity was devastating England, the Scots rejoicing thought
that they would obtain all they wished against the English . . . But sorrow
following on the heels of joy, the sword of the anger of God departing from the
English drove the Scots to frenzy . . . In the following year it ravaged the Welsh as
well as the English; and at last, setting sail, so to speak, for Ireland, it laid low the
English living there in great numbers, but scarcely touched at all the pure Irish
who lived amongst the mountains and on higher ground, until the year of Christ
1357, when it unexpectedly and terribly destroyed them also everywhere.

At a stroke, the Black Death reduced England's population by about a third. By 1350, Newcastle upon Tyne was in desperate financial straits 'on account of the deadly pestilence as by various other adversities in these times of war', and Carlisle was 'wasted and more than usually depressed as well by the mortal pestilence lately prevalent in those parts as by frequent attacks' (by the Scots). Seaford (Sussex) was reported even in 1356 as 'so desolated by plague and the chances of war that men living there are so few and poor that they cannot pay their taxes or defend the town'. Tusmore (Oxon.) was another victim of the plague: by 1358 permission was given to turn its fields into a park because every villein was dead and the village no longer had any taxpayers. Nevertheless, the Black Death's effects were not immediately or permanently catastrophic. The behaviour of a Welshman living in Ruthin was not uncommon: he 'left his land during the pestilence on account of poverty', but by 1354 he had returned 'and was admitted by the lord's favour to hold the same land by the service due from the same'. In any case, in a well-populated country, dead tenants could be replaced and landowners' incomes over the next twenty years were cut by no more than 10 per cent. It was the recurrence of plague over the following century—particularly the attacks of 1360–2, 1369, and 1375—which had lasting effects, even if these outbreaks were more local and urban. The population steadily declined to about 2½ millions—or even less—by the mid-fifteenth century.

For those who survived an ugly death, life may not have been as wretched in the late fourteenth and fifteenth centuries as it undoubtedly was before. For many peasants, this became an age of opportunity, ambition, and affluence: Chaucer was able to portray his pilgrims in the *Canterbury Tales* with good-humoured optimism, not in an atmosphere of gloom and despondency. The peasant in a smaller labour market was often able to shake off the disabilities of centuries, force rents down, and insist on a better wage for his hire; and with the collapse in prices, his standard of living rose. The more successful and ambitious peasants leased new property, invested spare cash by lending to their fellows and, especially in the south and east, built substantial stone houses for the first time in peasant history.

Landowners, on the other hand, were facing severe difficulties. Market production in wheat, wool, and other commodities was less profitable, the cultivated area of England contracted, and agricultural investment was curtailed. Wages and other costs climbed and it seemed advisable to abandon 'high farming' techniques in favour of leasing plots to enterprising peasants. Entire communities were deserted—the 'lost villages' of England—and many of these were abandoned as a result of the twin afflictions of demographic crisis and prolonged war: among the English regions with the highest number of 'lost villages' are Northumberland, close to the Scottish border, and the Isle of Wight, the goal of enemy marauders. Only in the last decades of the fifteenth century—from the 1460s in East Anglia—did England's population begin to rise at all significantly, and it is likely that the level of 1300 was not reached again until the seventeenth century.

England's economy had contracted markedly in the later fourteenth century, but it was not universally depressed. After men came to terms with the psychological shock of the plague visitations, society adjusted remarkably well, though not without turmoil. Landowners had the most painful adjustment to make and they reacted in several ways, not all of which were calculated to preserve domestic peace. Some, including the more conservatively-minded ecclesiastical landlords such as the abbot of St. Albans, resorted to high-handed measures, even oppression and extortion, to preserve their hold on their remaining tenants. Some exploited their estates ruthlessly in order to conserve their incomes, and the harsh attitudes of magnate families such as the Mortimers, with extensive estates in Wales, may have helped cause the Glyndŵr rebellion (1400). Others, such as the dukes of Buckingham later in the fifteenth century, adopted more efficient methods of management to improve the profitability of their estates. Yet others saw the enclosure of fields and commons for pasture and cultivation as less costly and an alternative means of buttressing unsteady rent-rolls; enclosure gathered speed especially in the north and west in the later fifteenth century. Large and small, the landowners as a group acted 'to curb the malice of servants, who were idle, and not willing to serve after the pestilence, without excessive wages'. Edward III's ordinance (1349) to restore pre-plague wage levels and discourage mobility among an emancipated labour force was quickly turned into a parliamentary statute (1351). Moreover, the well-placed magnate or gentleman had supplementary sources of wealth available to him: royal patronage in the form of grants of land, money, and office (as the Beaufort relatives of King Henry VI well knew); family inheritance, which enabled Richard, duke of York (d. 1460) to become the richest magnate of his age; and fortunate marriage with a well-endowed heiress or a wealthy widow. Others prospered in the king's service, not least in war. Henry V's spectacular victories enabled the capture of ransomable prisoners and the acquisition of estates in northern France, and as late as 1448 the duke of Buckingham was expecting more than £530 a year from the French county of Perche. Some invested the profits of service and war in the mid-fifteenth century in the grandest manner, building imposing and elegant castles: witness Sir John Fastolf's at Caister (Norfolk), or the Herberts' huge fortress-palace at Raglan (Gwent), or Sir Ralph Botiller's castle at Sudeley, Gloucestershire. Such means and resources as these facilitated the emergence of aristocratic lines that were every whit as powerful as those of earlier centuries and often with entrenched regional positions like those of the Nevilles and Percies in the north and the Staffords and Mortimers in the west.

Similar adjustments were taking place in English towns and trade. Wool-growing remained the main pastoral occupation, but the pattern of its industry was transformed during the fourteenth century. Partly as a result of the war and its disruption of Flemish industry, and partly as a result of changes in English taste and demand, cloth manufacture absorbed growing quantities of wool previously exported; a number of the wool ports, such as Boston and Lynn in eastern England, began to decline. Leading cloth-manufacturing centres such as Stamford and Lincoln were overtaken by a host of newer ones sited in villages and towns near fast-flowing streams and rivers that ran the fulling-mills. York found itself upstaged by Leeds, Halifax, and Bradford; further south, East Anglia, the west country, and even Wales developed a flourishing cloth industry, with Bristol as the main outlet in the west. London was in a class of its own: the only medieval English town with a population probably in excess of 50,000 in the late fourteenth century. It was an entrepôt for the kingdom, a terminal of the Baltic, North Sea, and Mediterranean trades; it attracted immigrants from the home counties and East Anglia, and especially from the East Midlands; and its suburbs were creeping up-river towards Westminster. No less than in the countryside, these changes unsettled life in a number of towns, whose burgess oligarchies strove to maintain their control in a changing world. The landowners of England thus strove to counter the economic crisis, but it was often at the price of straining relations with an increasingly assertive peasantry and established urban communities.

The cumulative effect of economic, social, political, and military strains in fourteenth-century England is seen most graphically in the Peasants' Revolt (1381). It was exceptional in

John Ball, the priestly demagogue who inspired the rebellious peasants in 1381, preaching to the rebel host led by Wat Tyler (*left foreground*); banners proclaim the rebels' loyalty to King Richard II.

its intensity, length, and broad appeal, but not in its fundamental character which was revealed in other conspiracies and insurrections in the years that followed. Widespread violence was sparked off in 1381 by yet another poll tax, this one at 1s. a head, three times the rate of 1377 and 1379. People responded with evasion, violence towards the collectors and the justices who investigated, and ultimately, in June 1381, with rebellion. Agricultural workers from eastern and south-eastern England were joined by townsmen and Londoners; the grain- and wool-growing countryside of East Anglia had felt the full impact of the contraction and dislocation of the economy and the social contradictions of an increasingly outmoded feudal society. Moreover, the rebels were disillusioned by the political mismanagement of the 1370s and the recent dismal record in France, and they feared enemy raids on the coast. Although heretics played no major role in the rebellion, radical criticism of the doctrines and organization of the English Church predisposed many to denounce an establishment that seemed to be failing in its duty.

Pressure on the government and an appeal to the new king ('With King Richard and the true-hearted commons' was the rebels' watch-word) held out the best hope for remedy of grievances, and the populace of London offered a pool of potential sympathizers. The rebels accordingly converged on London from Essex and Kent (where Wat Tyler and a clerical demagogue, John Ball, emerged as leaders). They threw prisons open, sacked the homes of the king's ministers, ransacked the Tower, and tried to frighten Richard II into making far-reaching concessions which, if implemented, would have broken the remaining bonds of serfdom and revolutionized landholding in Church and State. But the rebellion was poorly planned and organized and more in the nature of a spontaneous outburst of frustration. By 15 June the rebels had dispersed to their homes.

Still at War, 1390–1490

In 1389, when Richard II was twenty-two years old, he declared: 'I am of full age to govern my house, and my household, and also my realm. For it seems unjust to me that the condition which I am now in should be worse than the condition of the least of my kingdom.' The events of 1386–8, when the appellant lords sought to dictate the choice of the king's friends and ministers and to regulate his political actions, had poisoned relations between the unforgiving king and his critics. Among these were some of the most powerful magnates in the realm, with estates in central and southern England that together rivalled in size the remoter franchises of the Crown in Wales, Cheshire, and Cornwall. After 1389, however, Richard cautiously asserted himself as king of England, and with intelligence and courage he tried to deal with the consequences of his predecessors' ambitions and policies during the previous century. In a period of comparative political calm, Richard carefully constructed a party of loyalists, based on his household and the distant franchises, particularly Cheshire and North Wales. The earl of Arundel's forfeited lordships gave him an enhanced royal power in the Welsh march, where aristocratic lordships were at their most independent. The large and expensive expedition to Ireland in 1394–5, the first by an English king since 1210, was successful in revitalizing English rule and bringing Gaelic and Anglo-Irish lords to heel by a skilful mixture of firmness and conciliation; Richard may even have had the final and long-delayed conquest of the island in mind. This venture certainly strengthened his power in yet another royal lordship and demonstrated what his household organization and resources could achieve, albeit temporarily. Towards Scotland, following the English defeat at Otterburn (1388), Richard took the more traditional paths of encouraging dissident Scottish magnates and planning military campaigns; but in the 1390s he came to appreciate the benefits of peace. A treaty with France in 1396 and Richard's marriage to Isabelle of Valois halted an even more debilitating war; if the cessation of hostilities had run its intended course (to 1426), it would have provided the longest period of peace in the entire Hundred Years War. At home, the king was able to concentrate on restoring royal government which had been so seriously damaged by the personal and political weaknesses of the 1370s and 1380s. To this end, ceremony and visual symbolism were creatively used as royal propaganda.

Richard was imaginative, shrewd, and masterful. Other of his attributes were less desirable in a king. His upbringing and adolescent experiences bred an insecurity that led to over-confidence, a lack of proportion, and arbitrariness. Wilfully extravagant towards his friends, he could be capricious, secretive, and harsh towards his enemies, and in 1397–8 he exiled the earl of Warwick, executed Arundel, murdered Gloucester, and then exiled Derby and Nottingham too. Ruthlessly deploying the monarch's personal powers ('He threw down whomsoever violated the Royal Prerogative' was part of the inscription he composed for his own tomb), Richard's last two years have been justly termed tyrannous. The pope was induced to threaten excommunication against any who 'attempts anything prejudicial against the right of our Crown, our regality or our liberty, or maliciously defames our person', while Richard's treaty with France promised French aid against his own subjects should the need arise. His second visit to Ireland in May 1399 presented Henry Bolingbroke, earl of Derby and now duke of Hereford and Lancaster, with the opportunity to return to England, retrieve his position, and recover the duchy of Lancaster estates of his father that had recently been seized by Richard. The king's methods had outrun English law and custom—and the tolerance of his greater subjects. But his deposition later in the year (29 September) ended the most coherent attempt yet to lift the burden of war from Englishmen's shoulders.

The dethronement of Richard II was a momentous decision. Despite the precedent of 1327, the situation in 1399 was different in one important respect. It was the first time since Richard the Lionheart's death that an English king had ended his reign

King Richard II, only surviving son of Edward, Prince of Wales and Joan of Kent; married (i) 1382 Anne of Bohemia, (ii) 1396 Isabelle of Valois; succeeded in 1377; deposed in 1399 and probably murdered. The portrait was possibly painted at Richard's court c.1390.

without leaving a son and heir, and the realm now faced the possibility of a disputed succession. Custom since 1216 had vested the succession in the senior male line, even though that might mean a child-king (as in the case of Henry III and Richard II himself). But there was as yet no acknowledged rule of succession should the senior male line fail. In 1399 the choice by blood lay between the seven-year-old earl of March, descended through his grandmother from Edward III's second son, Lionel, and Henry Bolingbroke, the thirty-three-year-old son of King Edward's third son, John. Bolingbroke seized the Crown after being assured of support from the Percy family whom Richard had alienated. But in the extraordinary circumstances created by Richard II's dethronement and imprisonment, neither March nor Bolingbroke had obviously the stronger claim. No amount of distortion, concealment, and argument on Bolingbroke's part could disguise what was a *coup d'état*. Hence, as in the twelfth century, an element of dynastic instability was injected into English politics which contributed to domestic turmoil, and encouraged foreign intrigue and intervention in the following century.

England, meanwhile, could not escape the consequences of its earlier attempted subjugation of the 'Celtic' peoples in the British Isles. After the failure of Richard II's imaginative policies, a more stable relationship was needed to ensure security for the realm now that further conquest and colonization were patently beyond its resources. In practice, English kings abandoned all serious intention of implementing their claims to overlordship in Scotland and much of Ireland. In the fifteenth century, they were on the defensive against the Scots, partly because of the renewal of war in France and partly because of England's internal difficulties in Henry IV's reign (1399–1413) and after 1450; the Scots even sent substantial reinforcements to aid the French in 1419. For a brief time (1406–24), the captivity in England of King James I deterred major hostilities across the border, but thereafter the Scots became more daring, hoping to recover Roxburgh Castle and also Berwick, which they achieved in 1460–1. Raids, sea skirmishes, and piracy, together with ineffective truces, combined to produce a state of interminable 'cold war'. Only after the end of the Hundred Years War (1453) and the establishment of the Yorkist regime in England (1461) was there a really purposeful search for a more stable relationship. An Anglo-Scottish treaty was sealed in 1475, and a 'perpetual peace' in 1502, despite misgivings in France and the occasional English campaign in Scotland, such as Richard, duke of Gloucester's seizure of Berwick in 1482. This marked a significant shift in relations between the two countries, although border society continued to thrive on raids and disorder was a way of life.

The equilibrium reached in relations with Ireland was less satisfactory for England than for the Gaelic population and the Anglo-Irish nobility. Richard II's bold assertion of royal authority had failed, and was not repeated in the Middle Ages. The king's lordship of Ireland, though heavily subsidized from England, was consistently weak: the Gaels enjoyed independence and comparative prosperity, and the Anglo-Irish cherished their own power and came to terms with their Gaelic counterparts. The English government's main concern was security ('Ireland is a buttress and a post under England', declared a contemporary in the 1430s), and only when this was threatened during the Welsh rebellion (1400–9) and in the 1450s was more interest shown in Irish affairs. Internal political fragmentation and separation from England were the result. The greater Anglo-Irish magnates were the only source of power on which the government could rely to preserve some semblance of its authority: most Englishmen were reluctant even to go to Ireland, effective rule from Dublin was impossible, and the resources for conquest simply did not exist. The real rulers of fifteenth-century Ireland were magnates such as the earls of Ormond and Kildare; even if the government had wanted to dislodge them, it could not. An equilibrium in Anglo-Irish relations was reached, but at the cost of surrendering effective English control.

In Wales, the heritage of complete conquest brought its own problems, notably a resentment which, in the unsettled economic climate of the late fourteenth century, was focused on the Anglicized boroughs and directed against officials in Church and State who were mostly from the English border shires or even further afield. This resentment was channelled into rebellion by Owain Glyndŵr from 1400 and after this unpleasant experience most Englishmen regarded Wales with suspicion and fear. One contemporary urged:

> Beware of Wales, Christ Jesus must us keep,
> That it make not our child's child to weep,
> Nor us also, if so it go this way
> By unwariness; since that many a day
> Men have been afraid of there rebellion. . . .

Wales, then, posed a security problem and one much closer to hand. It not only provided a landfall for enemies from overseas (as at the height of Glyndŵr's rebellion and repeatedly during the Wars of the Roses), but was a land marred by misgovernment

and disorder. Henry V showed firmness tempered by conciliation in dealing with Welshmen immediately after the rebellion
collapsed, and marcher lords were ordered to attend to their
lordships. But later on, neither the Crown nor the marcher lords
were capable of sustaining vigorous rule, and the Welsh
squirearchy, brothers-in-arms of the English gentry, showed less
and less responsibility. Yet these Welsh squires were needed by
the Crown and the marcher lords to govern Wales, for the Crown
became immersed in civil war and by the fifteenth century the
smaller number of lords were deterred from living in their
lordships by falling incomes and Welsh hostility. The country,
which by 1449 'daily abundeth and increaseth in misgover-
nance', consequently presented a problem of order—and therefore of security—for much of the century. Successive English
regimes, from Henry VI to Henry VII, sought to keep the Welsh
peaceful, improve the quality of government, and control the
local squirearchy, for only then could the threat to the border
shires and to the stability of the kingdom be lifted. In the first half
of the century, the aim was to tighten up the existing machinery
of law enforcement, relying on royal officers and marcher lords to
fulfil their responsibilities. More radical and constructive solu-
tions were eventually adopted, especially by Edward IV, who
settled his son, the Prince of Wales, at Ludlow in the 1470s with a
supervisory power in the principality of Wales, the marcher
lordships, and the English border shires. This was a bold act of
devolution that gave future princes responsibility throughout
Wales.

The territorial power of the English magnates (the barons,
viscounts, earls, marquesses, and dukes in ascending order of
status) was crucial to the peace of the realm and the success of
royal government. They became in the fifteenth century a
strictly-defined and hereditary social group that was practically
synonymous with the parliamentary peerage sitting in the House
of Lords. The monarch could create peers (as Henry VI and
Edward IV readily did) and could elevate existing ones to higher
rank, while the king's patronage was essential to maintain
magnate wealth and influence. Monarchs who did not appreciate
this risked serious conflict with their magnates (as Richard II and
Richard III discovered to their cost). Though few in number—at
most sixty families, and perhaps half that figure after decades of
civil war—they were vital not only because of the independent
lordships which some of them held in the Welsh march and the
dominance of the Nevilles and Percies in the north, but also
because of their social and political control of the English

King Henry V, eldest surviving son of Henry IV and Mary Bohun; married 1420 Katherine of Valois; succeeded 1413; died on campaign in France. One of a series of royal portraits from the time of Henry VIII.

provinces. They were a more effective buttress of the Crown than its own bureaucracy or civil service. This was especially true in a century when three dynasties seized the Crown by force and had formidable military commitments at home and overseas to which the magnates made a notable contribution. The humiliation of defeat in France and the loss of English territories there was directly felt by the magnates and was something which Edward IV and Henry VII later strove to avoid.

These magnates had an identity of interest with the gentry of England—the 6,000 to 9,000 gentlemen, esquires, and knights who sought the 'good lordship' of the magnates and provided 'faithful service' in return. The magnates gave fees, land, and offices, and the gentry advice, support, and military aid: in 1454 the duke of Buckingham gave his badge to 2,000 of his retainers. Towns and townsmen were part of this relationship of mutual interest and service which historians have unflatteringly dubbed 'bastard feudalism'. The behaviour of the magnates and the gentry and townsmen in two distinct Houses of Parliament—the Lords and Commons—was another aspect of this interlocking relationship.

The co-operation of the magnates and their clients was especially vital to the usurping dynasties of the fifteenth century. The Lancastrians were well placed becaused Henry IV inherited the network of interests created by his father, John of Gaunt. At £12,000 a year, Gaunt was the richest magnate in late medieval England and his extensive estates and patronage were now at the disposal of his descendants as kings of England (1399–1461). The Yorkists (1461–85), as heirs of the earl of March, the alternative candidate in 1399, were less well endowed, except in the Welsh march. Their failure to enlist the support of most magnates was a serious weakness in a dynasty which survived for just twenty-four years. Henry VII, who inherited the estates, territorial influence, and patronage not only of Lancaster and York, but also of Neville, Beaufort, and other casualties of civil war, established the firmest control of all over the English magnates and gentry.

The first usurper, Henry IV, had the advantage of displacing a king who had alienated many and whose noble sympathizers were discredited. Henry's drive, perseverance, and powers of conciliation—not to say his generosity—and his Lancastrian connections enabled him to overcome the most daunting combination of enemies that any English king had faced. Richard II's die-hard supporters were foiled in their plot to assassinate Henry and his sons at Windsor Castle, and these rebels were apprehended and killed at Cirencester (December 1399). The danger from such 'Ricardians' led to Richard's own mysterious death in Pontefract Castle soon afterwards. The Percy earls of Northumberland and Worcester, virtual kingmakers in 1399, were so disenchanted by 1403 with the king's aim to win over all shades of opinion that they plotted several risings. Northumberland's son Hotspur, while marching to join the Welsh rebels, was defeated and killed near Shrewsbury. A Percy alliance with Archbishop Scrope of York raised the north of England, but Henry again acted quickly and in 1405 executed the prelate. Northumberland's last strike, with Scottish aid, collapsed at Bramham Moor, where the earl was slain (1408).

The Welsh rebellion had deeper roots in the soil of a colonial society. The distress experienced by a plague-ridden people, oppression by alien landowners bent on maintaining their incomes, a tendency to close the doors to opportunity against aspiring Welshmen, even resentment at Richard II's removal, combined to throw the country into revolt (1400). The variety of rebel motives and the divisions in Welsh society meant that this was no purely national, patriotic rising. Yet it was the most serious threat that Henry IV had to face and the most expensive to suppress. From his estates in north-east Wales, Owain Glyndŵr laid waste castles and Anglicized towns. He and his guerrilla forces exploited the mountainous terrain to harass and exhaust the enemy and then disappear 'among rocks and caves'. Their success can be measured by the length of the rebellion, the absence of decisive battles, and the fruitlessness of royal expeditions. Glyndŵr could occasionally muster 8,000 men, and he sought aid from France (1403) and fellow 'Celts' in Scotland and Ireland (1401). In 'parliaments' in 1404 and 1405, he produced grand schemes for an independent Wales, with its own ecclesiastical organization and universities (aims which were not finally realized for another four centuries), and his alliance with the Percies was intended as a prelude to the dismemberment of Henry IV's realm.

The English, led by the king and his eldest son, Prince Henry, conducted several Welsh campaigns (1400–5), whose strategy was akin to that adopted in France—with pincer movements, destructive *chevauchées*, and co-ordinated supply by land and sea. The burden fell most heavily and frequently on the border shires and the West Midlands, which time and again were ordered to array men for service in Wales. These armies were substantial ones—4,000 strong—especially when one recalls that the armies sent to France rarely exceeded 5,000–6,000 men. But service in Wales was nothing like as popular as service in the lusher fields of France; there was difficulty in raising enough cash to pay the soldiers and garrisons, and in September 1403 Henry IV was told that 'you will not find a single gentleman who will stop in your said country'.

Generally secure in the north and west, Owain had his own

problems of manpower, supply, and money, and the failure of his march on Worcester in 1405 caused his star to wane. He lost his Scottish ally when James I fell into English hands (1406), and an Anglo-French truce was arranged in 1407.

By 1408, the greatest dangers for Henry IV had passed: by perseverance, decisiveness, and a readiness to live in the saddle, as he pursued his enemies across England and Wales and to Edinburgh beyond, Henry overcame them all. By conciliation, he obtained Parliament's support without surrendering any significant part of his royal powers, and his four sons, Henry, Thomas, John, and Humphrey, were a maturing asset. Only two further threats to the dynasty occurred after his death in 1413. When the anticlericalism of certain courtiers turned to heresy the following year, Henry V did not hesitate to condemn even his old friend, Sir John Oldcastle. The last revolt before 1450 to be justified by the usurpation of 1399—that in favour of the earl of March in 1415—was suppressed just before King Hal left for France. Henry IV could claim considerable success in establishing his dynasty on firm foundations. International acceptance was won by alliances in Germany, Scandinavia, Brittany, and Burgundian Flanders.

Henry V inherited a realm that was sufficiently peaceful, loyal, and united for him to campaign extensively in France (from 1415) and to spend half of the next seven years abroad. With experience of war and government as Prince of Wales, he proved a capable, fearless, and authoritarian monarch who abandoned the careful ways of his father. Even during his absences in France, his kingship was firm and energetic, enabling him to wage a war that was as much a popular enterprise as Edward III's early campaigns had been. His reign was the climax of Lancastrian England.

Henry prepared for war by conciliating surviving Ricardians and renewing foreign alliances. The condition of France, with an insane king and quarrelsome nobles, encouraged his dreams of conquest. By 1415 he felt able to demand full sovereignty over territories beyond Edward III's vision and even to revive Edward's claim to the French Crown. Henry's ambitions coincided with his subjects' expectations. Large armies were raised under the leadership of enthusiastic magnates and knights; the realm voted taxation frequently and on a generous scale, and the king was able to explain his aims publicly so as to attract support. He even built a navy to dominate the Channel. This enthusiasm hardly faded at all before his death, though the parliamentary Commons expressed (1420) the same unease about the con-

English military enterprises in western Europe in the later middle ages

sequences for England of a final conquest of France as had their forebears to Edward III.

Henry V's strategy was Edward's—to ally with French nobles to exploit their divisions and press his own dynastic claim. Throughout the war, Burgundy's support was essential to

English success. Quite soon, however, the invader's aims broadened into conquest and colonization on an unprecedented scale. The 1415 expedition tested the water and the victory at Agincourt strikingly vindicated traditional English tactics. In 1417–20, therefore, Henry set about conquering Normandy which, along with adjacent provinces, was the main theatre of war during and after Henry's reign. The treaty of Troyes (1420) with Charles VI made him regent of France and heir to the Valois throne in place of the Dauphin. This extraordinary treaty dictated Anglo-French relations for more than a generation. Though Henry V never became king of France (he predeceased Charles VI in 1422), his baby son, Henry VI of England and, to the Anglophiles, Henry II of France, inherited the dual monarchy. It would require unremitting effort to maintain it.

Henry V and John, duke of Bedford, his brother and successor as military commander in France, pushed the Norman frontier east and south during 1417–29 and they defeated the French successively at Agincourt (1415), Cravant (1423), and Verneuil (1424). This was the high point of English power in France. Under Bedford, a 'constructive balance of firmness and conciliation' sought to make both the conquered lands and further campaigns (southwards in Anjou and Maine) pay for themselves. But the French resurgence inspired by Joan of Arc and the coronation of Charles VII at Rheims (1429) foiled this plan, and the English advance was halted after the defeat at Patay. Thereafter, the Normans grew restless under their foreign governors, England's Breton and Burgundian allies began to waver, and the English Parliament had to find yet more cash for the war in northern France where garrison and field armies were an increasingly heavy burden. The English were in a military as well as a financial trap—and without the genius of Henry V to direct them.

During the 1430s the search for peace became more urgent, particularly in England. The Congress of Arras (1435) and discussions at Gravelines (1439) were unproductive, largely because English opinion remained divided as to the desirability of peace and the wisdom of significant concessions. But the recovery in Charles VII's fortunes, the mounting cost of English expeditions to defend Lancastrian France, Bedford's death in 1435, and especially the defection of Burgundy were decisive factors. The government freed the duke of Orléans (a captive in England since Agincourt) to promote peace among his fellow French princes (1440), though he did not have much success. In 1445 Henry VI married the French queen's niece, Margaret of

Anjou, but even that only produced a truce, and a proposed meeting of kings never took place. Eventually, Henry VI promised to surrender hard-won territory in the county of Maine as an earnest of his personal desire for peace. His failure to win the support of his subjects for this move—especially those magnates and gentry who had lands in France and had borne the brunt of the fighting—led to the exasperated French attacking Normandy in 1449. Their onslaught, supported by artillery, was so spectacularly successful that the English were defeated at Rouen and Formigny, and quickly cleared from the duchy by the end of August 1450. '. . . never had so great a country been conquered in so short a space of time, with such small loss to the populace and soldiery, and with so little killing of people or destruction and damage to the countryside,' reported a French chronicler.

Gascony, which had seen few major engagements under Henry V and Henry VI, was invaded by the triumphant French armies, and after their victory at Castillon on 17 July 1453, the English territories in the south-west were entirely lost. This was the most shattering blow of all: Gascony had been English since the twelfth century, and the long-established wine and cloth trades with south-west France were seriously disrupted. Of Henry V's 'empire', only Calais now remained. The defeated and disillusioned soldiers who returned to England regarded the discredited Lancastrian government as responsible for their plight and for the surrender of what Henry V had won. At home, Henry VI faced the consequence of defeat.

Within three weeks of Castillon, Henry VI suffered a mental and physical collapse which lasted for seventeen months and from which he may never have fully recovered. The loss of his French kingdom (and Henry was the only English king to be crowned in France) may have been responsible for his breakdown, though by 1453 other aspects of his rule gave cause for grave concern. Those in whom Henry confided, notably the dukes of Suffolk (murdered 1450) and Somerset (killed in battle at St. Albans, 1455), proved unworthy of his trust and were widely hated. Those denied his favour—including Richard, duke of York and the Neville earls of Salisbury and Warwick—were bitter and resentful, and their efforts to improve their fortunes were blocked by the king and his court. Henry's government was close to bankruptcy, and its authority in the provinces and in Wales and Ireland was becoming paralysed. In the summer of 1450, there occurred the first popular revolt since 1381, led by the obscure but talented John Cade, who seized London for a few

King Henry VI, only son of Henry V and Katherine of Valois; succeeded 1422; married 1445 Margaret of Anjou; deposed 1461 and restored 1470–1; probably murdered. An early portrait (c.1518–23), possibly from a contemporary likeness.

days and denounced the king's ministers. The king's personal responsibility for England's plight was inevitably great.

Henry VI was a well-intentioned man with laudable aspirations in education and religion; he sought peace with France and wished to reward his friends and servants. But no medieval king could rule by good intentions alone. Besides, Henry was extravagant, over-indulgent, and did not have the qualities of a shrewd and balanced judge of men and policies. He was intelligent and well educated, but he was the least experienced of kings and never shook off the youthful dependence on others which had been the inevitable hallmark of his long minority (1422–36). Many of his problems were admittedly unavoidable. The dual monarchy created by his father made heavier and more complex demands than those placed on a mainly military conqueror such as Edward III or Henry V. His minority was a period of magnate rule which created vested interests that were not easily surrendered when the king came of age—particularly by his uncle, Humphrey, duke of Gloucester, and his great-uncle, Henry Beaufort, cardinal-bishop of Winchester. Moreover, after Gloucester's death in 1447, Henry was the only surviving descendant of Henry IV in the senior male line, a fact which led him to distrust the duke of York, the heir of that earl of March who had been passed over in 1399. There was, then, ample reason for disenchantment with late Lancastrian rule, and in Richard of York there was a potential leader of the discontented.

Despite the king's illness, the birth of a son to his abrasive queen in October 1453 strengthened the Lancastrian dynasty, but it hardly improved the immediate prospect for the realm or for Richard of York. As England's premier duke and Henry's cousin, York was twice appointed protector of the realm during the king's incapacity (1454–5, 1455–6). But as such he aroused the queen's fierce hostility which erupted in the battles of Blore Heath and Ludford Bridge (September–October 1459), and in the subsequent Parliament at Coventry which victimized York, the Nevilles, and their supporters. This alienation of powerful men by a regime with a disastrous record at home and abroad led York to claim the Crown in October 1460. After his death at Wakefield soon after, his son Edward took it for himself on 4 March 1461, with the aid of the earl of Warwick. The period of dynastic war that is popularly known as the Wars of the Roses was now well under way amid conditions that had been ripening during the 1450s.

The new Yorkist monarch, Edward IV, suffered from a cardinal disadvantage: the deposed king, his queen, and his son were still at large. They thus provided a focus for their adherents and their Scots and French sympathizers, who were only too eager to embarrass a weak English regime. After Henry's capture in the north (1465), Edward felt more secure, though even then the former king was kept a prisoner in the Tower of London and his queen and son received shelter in Scotland and then in France. More serious still was Edward's failure to gain broad support from the English magnates and their clients. Furthermore, in the late 1460s he gradually alienated his powerful 'kingmaker', the earl of Warwick, who (like Northumberland after 1399) came to resent Edward's growing independence. Edward was also deserted by his feckless brother, George, duke of Clarence. These various elements combined to plot rebellion (1469) and, with encouragement from Louis XI of France, came to an uneasy agreement in July 1470 with the exiled Lancastrian Queen Margaret. Warwick, Clarence, Lancastrians, and dissident Yorkists returned to England and sent Edward IV fleeing to his ally, the duke of Burgundy. They promptly restored (or 'readopted') Henry VI, the first English king to have two separate reigns (1470–1). When Henry's Parliament assembled in November 1470, the chancellor was appealing beyond Westminster to the country at large when he took as the text of his opening sermon, 'Return O backsliding children, saith the Lord'.

But the deposed Edward, like Henry VI before him, was at liberty and he was able to raise a force with Burgundian help. Moreover, Henry's restored regime was undermined by a series of conflicting loyalties and mutually exclusive interests. Thus, when Edward returned to England in March 1471, he was able to defeat and kill Warwick at Barnet before marching west to vanquish at Tewkesbury the Lancastrian queen and prince, who had only just returned from France. At last Edward IV was dynastically secure: Queen Margaret was captured after Tewkesbury, her son was slain in the battle, and on the very night Edward returned triumphantly to London (21 May) Henry VI died in the Tower, most probably murdered. The main Lancastrian royal line was extinct. The Yorkist dissidents were either cowed or dead, and Clarence, though for a time reconciled with his brother, was subsequently executed for further indiscretions in 1478.

The relative political security which Edward enjoyed in the 1470s allowed him to attempt a period of constructive rule. He tried to repair England's reputation abroad by alliances with Brittany, Burgundy, and Scotland, and also by retracing the steps of previous kings to France. His expedition of 1475 was a near-disaster when his Breton and Burgundian allies proved fickle, but in the treaty of Picquigny Louis XI provided him with a handsome financial inducement to retire to England. Edward's

King Richard III, third son of Richard, duke of York and Cecily Neville; married Anne Neville in 1472; usurped the throne 1483 and was killed at Bosworth. An early portrait (c.1512–20), possibly from a contemporary likeness.

attempts to reorganize the government's financial administration were on lines suggested during the Lancastrian period. If he pleased Parliament by declaring his readiness to rule without special taxes, his desire to reward friends and attract political supporters meant that he could embark on no consistent programme of increasing his revenues. He curried favour with merchants and Londoners, participating in trade on his own account and maintaining good relations with Flanders and the Hanse League of German ports. Above all, the stability of his later years owed much to the continuity of service of several able and loyal officers of state.

Why, then, did the Wars of the Roses not come to an end and why did not posterity come to know of a Tudor dynasty only among the squirearchy of North Wales? The Yorkists fell victim in 1483–5 to two of the most common hazards to afflict a personal monarchy: a minority and a ruthlessly ambitious royal kinsman. When Edward IV died on 9 April 1483, his son and heir, Edward, was twelve. His minority need not have been long, and in any case England had weathered previous minorities without undue difficulty. But the degeneration of political behaviour since the 1450s, especially the often arbitrary, ruthless, and illegal actions of Edward IV, Warwick, and Clarence, made Edward V's accession particularly perilous. The Yorkist brothers, Edward, Clarence, and Gloucester, seem to have been unable to outgrow aristocratic attitudes to embrace the obligations of kingship in the short time their dynasty was on the throne. Edward relied on a circle of magnates, most of them linked with his own or his wife's Woodville family, to extend his authority in the kingdom: Gloucester in the north, the Woodvilles in Wales, and Lord Hastings in the Midlands. It worked well enough while Edward lived, but in 1483 the dangers of relying on an exclusive faction surfaced. Mistrust, particularly between Gloucester and the Woodvilles, undermined the ruling circle, and those outside it—not least the long-established Percies in the north and the duke of Buckingham in Wales and the West Midlands—saw their opportunity.

In these circumstances, the character and ambition of the sole remaining Yorkist brother, the thirty-year-old Richard of Gloucester, led him to contemplate seizing his young nephew's Crown for himself. He usurped the throne on 26 June, imprisoned (and probably murdered) Edward V and his brother, 'The Princes in the Tower', and executed the queen's brother and Lord Hastings. His only concession to customary rules of inheritance of the Crown was his unprincipled declaration that

Edward IV and his sons were bastards; he ignored the children of Clarence. Richard III's actions and methods led to a revival of dynastic warfare. In October 1483, the duke of Buckingham, who was descended from Edward III's fifth son, Thomas, rebelled. More successful was the landing from France in August 1485 of Henry Tudor, though his claim to the throne through his mother, representing the illegitimate Beaufort line of Edward III's son, John, was tenuous. Nevertheless, at Bosworth Field on 25 August 1485 he vanquished and slew King Richard III. By then, Richard's own royal line seemed bankrupt: his wife and his only son were already dead.

A number of factors enabled Henry VII to keep his Crown after Bosworth. Alone among the usurpers of the fifteenth century, he was fortunate to have slain his childless predecessor in battle. The support which he received from the disillusioned Yorkists was crucial, especially that of Edward IV's queen. Also England's magnates were war-weary: their ranks were depleted, and in some cases their territorial power was either weakened or destroyed. As a result, attempts to dethrone Henry were poorly supported in England and the Yorkist pretenders (such as Lambert Simnel in 1487) failed to carry conviction. The actual fighting during 1455–85 may have amounted to only fifteen months, and the size of the armies involved may not have been very large; but the significance of a battle need bear no relation to the numbers engaged or the casualties sustained. The Wars of the Roses came close to destroying the hereditary basis of the English monarchy and Henry Tudor's seizure of the Crown hardly strengthened it. Henry posed as the representative and inheritor of both Lancaster and York, but in reality he became king, and determined to remain king, by his own efforts.

Henry VII presented himself as the unifier of England after 1485, and the gold medal struck to commemorate his marriage in 1486 portrays the king, representing the house of Lancaster, and his Yorkist queen, Elizabeth.

Towards a Nation

English kings enjoyed a mastery in their kingdom which French monarchs might have envied, and the Crown embodied the unity of England. Its wearer was not as other men. The coronation ceremony stressed his semi-spiritual quality, which seemed proven by the alleged power of the royal touch to cure the skin disease scrofula. Richard II insisted that those who approached him should bend the knee, and 'Majesty' became the common address in the fifteenth century.

The tentacles of royal administration—enabling decisions, grants of taxation, and legal pronouncements to be implemented—stretched to the extremities of the British Isles in every direction but the north and west. The franchises of the bishop of Durham and the earl of Chester stood outside the shire system of England and had a special independence. But there was no question of their being beyond the reach of the king's government: the bishops of Durham were almost always the king's choice and, like Anthony Bek (d. 1311) and Thomas Langley (d. 1437), often royal councillors; whilst after 1301 the earl of Chester was also Prince of Wales and the king's eldest son, and for most of the later Middle Ages the king administered Cheshire because there was no adult earl.

The king's administration was a co-operative affair. In each county the sheriffs and the newer justices of the peace functioned best with the aid of the nobility and local gentry, whose interests in turn were securely tied to the monarch, the greatest single source of wealth and patronage in the realm. Parliament, with its commons' representatives from counties and towns between Carlisle and Cornwall, Shrewsbury and Suffolk, came to play an essential part in late medieval government. By Edward I's reign, war and domestic upheaval had fortified the king's need to consult his subjects ('the community of the realm', as contemporaries termed them) and to seek their advice in reaching and implementing decisions affecting the realm at large. It also seemed wise, from time to time, to include local representatives as well as lay and ecclesiastical lords in a central assembly that was Parliament. The wish to tap the wealth of townsmen and smaller landowners as well as the nobility; the need for material aid and expressions of support in war and political crises; and the advisability of having the weight of a representative assembly behind controversial or novel changes in the law or in economic and social arrangements—all these factors combined to give Parliament a frequency (it met on average once a year during 1327–1437), distinctive functions, and established procedures, and to give the commons' representatives a permanent role in it from 1337 onwards. This institution, unique among the parliaments of medieval Europe, discussed both important matters of business and minor matters raised by individuals. It won a monopoly of taxing Englishmen; it was the highest court in the land; and it made new law and modified existing law through legislation. Even the commons' representatives won privileges for themselves, not least free speech and freedom from arrest during parliamentary sittings. It remained essentially an instrument of government at the king's disposal, but it could sometimes criticize his policies and ministers (as in the 1370s and 1380s and the 1440s), though almost never the king himself. When the practical needs that had brought Parliament into existence and encouraged its development disappeared, it met far less often: only once in every three years on average between 1453 (the end of the Hundred Years War) and 1509.

The commons' representatives had to be informed, courted, and persuaded before they returned home to their constituents, considerable numbers of whom desired information about affairs. It was, after all, they who paid taxes, served in war and defence, and who were asked for their co-operation and obedience. The government was, therefore, well advised to weigh carefully the news it transmitted to the realm and the opinions it hoped the king's subjects would adopt. Well-developed methods of communication and propaganda were used to this end. The preambles of official proclamations could popularize a policy and justify a practice: Edward IV's proclamation against Margaret, queen of the deposed Henry VI, made much of the memory of Archbishop Scrope of York, who had been executed by Henry's grandfather and had since taken on the aura of a martyr. This was skilful propaganda to sustain opposition to the Lancastrian dynasty, for proclamations were sent to every shire for public reading and display. Songs and ballads reached wide audiences too, and some that were officially inspired stressed the glories of Agincourt out of all proportion. Sermons were no less effective in moulding opinion and mobilizing support: in 1443 Henry VI requested that good, stirring preachers be sent through every diocese to reinforce from the pulpit royal appeals for money for yet another French campaign. Coronations, royal progresses, and the formal entries of kings and queens into York, Bristol, and Gloucester (as well as London) were occasions for lavish displays of official propaganda, harnessing mythology, Christianity, and patriotism. In 1417, Henry V was portrayed for all to see at his reception by London as a soldier of Christ returning from crusade against the French. If any citizen harboured lingering doubts about the justice of his invasion of France, this was calculated to remove them.

The circulation of letters to inform, persuade, and justify was as near as the pre-printing age came to publication; such letters soon found their way into popular chronicles. In this way, Henry V reported to his subjects the progress of his French campaigns. Even fashionable writers of the day became official propagandists. In the fifteenth century, authors rarely produced their work unsolicitedly. Thomas Hoccleve was a humble government bureaucrat who was paid by Henry V to produce laudatory verses about Agincourt and the English siege of Rouen (1419). John Lydgate was patronized by Henry VI and his court over a long period, implanting in the popular mind all the jingoism that could be wrung out of the successful defence of Calais against Burgundian attack in 1436.

The king, his court, and his ministers—the principal exploiters of these channels of communication—resided most often at Westminster, London, or Windsor. The shrine of English monarchy was Westminster Abbey, and Parliament usually met at Westminster (all thirty-one Parliaments did so between 1339 and 1371, and none met elsewhere after 1459). The departments of government gradually settled into permanent offices at Westminster or, to a lesser extent, London, which was the largest and wealthiest city in the land. In the later Middle Ages, it became the undisputed capital of the kingdom in every sphere except the ecclesiastical (where Canterbury remained the seat of the primate of All England). Along with Westminster and the growing riverside suburb in between, London became the administrative, commercial, cultural, and social focus for the kingdom. Government increased in extent, sophistication, and tempo in the later Middle Ages, particularly in wartime: regular taxes had to be collected and managed, frequent meetings of Parliament were held, the customs service was developed, the practicalities of war and defence had to be organized, and law and order throughout the kingdom was supervised there. Concentrated, co-ordinated, and sedentary government was the result. York lost its claims as a rival centre when the persistent war with Scotland in the first third of the fourteenth century was overtaken by the much greater preoccupation with France. Moreover, the absence of Edward III and Henry V on campaign abroad emphasized the trend towards a fixed, centralized governmental headquarters that could operate without the participation of the king himself. The crisis of 1339–41 brought home to Edward III that he could no longer take the machine of government with him, as Edward I and his predecessors had done. By 1340 the exchequer had returned to Westminster, which it never left again. The bureaucracy of the king's chancery, exchequer, and law courts expanded in the capital and, as a group of ambitious small landowners, in the neighbouring counties. Magnates, bishops, and abbots acquired inns or houses in or near the city, and the surnames of London's inhabitants and the language they spoke suggest that many humbler folk were migrating to the capital from every part of the kingdom—and from Wales and Ireland too.

The English character of the Church in England was its second most significant and enduring quality in the later Middle Ages. Its first was the Catholic faith and doctrine which it shared with other Latin churches. But it was widely accepted that this universal Church, headed by the pope in Rome as spiritual father, was a family of individual churches, each with its own character and autonomy. The Englishness of the Church in England became more pronounced in the later Middle Ages as the ecclesiastical dimension of English nationhood. This owed something to the English language and the separate experience of the English people, and a good deal to English law and custom, the framework within which Englishmen (including the clergy) lived and which the king swore to uphold in his coronation oath. Moreover, the Church of England, including its buildings, had been established, encouraged, and patronized by English kings, noblemen, gentry, and townsmen, giving them a personal and family interest in individual churches and their priests. The bishops were great landowners—the bishop of Winchester had an annual income of £3,900 in the mid-fifteenth century—who sat in Parliament and were among the king's councillors. They, and lesser dignitaries too, were usually promoted because they were trusted by, and useful to, the Crown and could be rewarded in the Church without cost to the exchequer. There were, then, good practical reasons why Englishmen should control the English Church and mould its character and personnel. This seemed the more urgent during the French wars. In 1307 and regularly thereafter, the pope's role in the organization and administration of the English Church, even in the appointment of bishops, was bitterly opposed. After all, most popes in the fourteenth century were French-born, and during 1308–78 they lived at Avignon, where they were in danger of becoming lap-dogs of the French (or so it was widely believed). By contrast,

The pre-reformation dioceses of England and Wales (thirteenth century)

only one pope had been an Englishman (in the mid-twelfth century) and none had ever visited England—and would not do so until 1982.

The trend towards an Anglicized Church can be illustrated in several ways. Church law, based on the codes of the early Fathers and replenished by papal legislation, was received and generally applied in the Church courts of England, and the pope's ultimate jurisdiction in ecclesiastical matters was acknowledged. But in practice, Church law was limited by royal authority, particularly when clerks accused of crimes tried to claim 'benefit of clergy'. From Edward I's day, the pope's ability to tax the English clergy was severely curtailed and most papal taxes found their way into the king's coffers instead of fuelling the enemy's war effort (as many believed). More serious still were the limitations on the pope's power to appoint bishops and other important members of the English Church from the mid-fourteenth century onwards, and during the Great Schism (1378–1417, when there were two, sometimes three, popes simultaneously claiming Christendom's allegiance), the pope whom England supported was in no position to resist. The anti-papal statutes of Provisors (1351, reissued 1390) and *Praemunire* (1353, extended 1393) were used by English kings to impose a compromise on the pope whereby the initiative in appointments rested with the king. As a result, very few foreigners were appointed in the English Church by the fifteenth century unless, as with Henry VII's nomination of three Italian bishops, they had the government's specific approval.

Few clergymen in England protested at this state of affairs. The bishops did not do so because of the men they were and the way in which they were appointed. The Church did not do so corporately because it feared papal taxation. The clergy did not do so because English kings were the protectors of the faith against heretics and a buttress against anticlerical attack. In 1433, even an abbot of St. Albans could declare that 'the king knows no superior to himself within the realm'.

Predominantly English in character were two expressions of religious fervour outside the institutional church of late medieval England: the devotional fashion was strictly orthodox in theology, whereas the Lollard movement inspired by John Wycliffe was heretical. The fourteenth century saw a burgeoning interest in mystical and devotional writings, most of them in English from the latter part of the century and appealing to a growing literate public. Such people took for granted the teachings and practices of the Church but preferred a personal, intuitive devotion focused on the sufferings and death of Christ, the Virgin Mary, and the Lives of Saints, collected in the *Golden Legend*. The writers were frequently solitary figures commending the contemplative life to their readers. By far the most popular devotional works were by Richard Rolle, a Yorkshire hermit, and, later, by the recluse, Dame Juliane of Norwich. The *Book of Margery Kempe*, the spiritual autobiography of the wife of a Lynn burgess, exemplified the virtues which lay men and women sought, and the revelations, visions, and ecstasies by which they came to possess them. Laymen such as Henry, duke of Lancaster (who in 1354 wrote a devotional work of his own in French), and devout women such as Lady Margaret Beaufort, mother of Henry VII, turned to this intense spiritual life as a reaction to the arid theological discussions of scholars, though they did not stray into the unorthodoxy of Lollardy whose spiritual roots were not dissimilar.

Lollardy (probably a name derived from *lollaer*, a mumbler—of prayers) was the only significant heretical movement to sweep through medieval England, and Wycliffe was the only university intellectual in the history of medieval heresy to inspire a popular heretical movement against the Church. It was a largely indigenous English scheme of thought that laid great store by books and reading. Though Wycliffe is unlikely to have written in England, he inspired a series of English polemical works and also the first complete translation of the Bible by 1396. To begin with, he appealed to the anticlerical temper of his times and gained reputation and support among noblemen, courtiers, and scholars for his criticism of the Church's wealth and the unworthiness of too many of its clergy. But his increasingly radical theological ideas, placing overwhelming confidence in Holy Scripture, led to his condemnation and withdrawal from Oxford. The sympathy which he had received from influential men ebbed away when confronted with the strict orthodoxy of Henry IV (who added burning in 1401 to the armoury of the persecutors of heresy) and almost disappeared when Lollardy became tinged with rebellion in Sir John Oldcastle's rising. Deprived of its intellectual spring and its powerful protectors, Lollardy became a disjointed, unorganized but obstinate movement of craftsmen, artisans, and poor priests in the Welsh borderland and industrial towns of the Midlands. Their beliefs became more and more disparate and eccentric, but their basic hostility to ecclesiastical authority, their devotion to the Scriptures, and their belief in an English Bible prefigured the Reformation and were to be central convictions in later English Protestantism.

The spread of literacy and the increased use of the English language were twin developments of the late fourteenth and fifteenth centuries. They were symptomatic of Englishmen's growing awareness of public affairs, and reflect feelings of patriotism and nationhood.

It is easier to be persuaded of all this than to prove it in detail. There are no contemporary estimates of how rapidly and how far literacy spread; nor is it possible for us to quantify it with the

Exeter Cathedral, early fourteenth century. The nave, looking east, is the longest unbroken vista of Gothic vaulting in the world (over 300 ft.). The solid pillars and exuberant vaulting create a symmetrical avenue of what appear as towering palm trees. Completed by 1360, mainly by Bishop Grandisson, and financed by the wealth of the English Church before the Black Death.

data provided by largely innumerate contemporaries. A rough index of its growth becomes available if the statutes of 1351 and 1499 defining the legal privilege of 'benefit of clergy' (then the literate class) are compared. In 1351 it was stated that all laymen who could read should be accorded 'benefit of clergy'. One hundred and fifty years later, the situation had so changed that a distinction was drawn between mere lay scholars and clerks in holy orders, and only to the latter was 'benefit of clergy' now to be extended. Maybe the literate class had expanded to the point where 'clerical' was a meaningless adjective to apply to it, though the statute of 1499 attributed the need for change to abuse rather than to the expansion itself.

An equally generalized indication is provided by comparing the two popular risings of the later Middle Ages—the Peasants' Revolt (1381) and John Cade's rebellion (1450). In 1381 the complaints of the peasantry from Kent and Essex were (as far as we know) presented to Richard II orally, and all communications with the king during the revolt appear to have been by word of mouth; at the Tower of London, Richard had to ask that the rebels' grievances, hitherto roared at him by the insurgents outside, be put in writing for him to consider. Compare this with 1450, when the demands of Cade's followers, also drawn from Kent and the south-east, were submitted at the outset in written form of which several versions were produced and circulated. They are long documents, with a coherent and comprehensive argument, expressed in English, sometimes of a colloquial kind. The business of publishing manuscripts was extending its range at this very time. John Shirley (d. 1456) is known to have run his business from four rented shops near St. Paul's Cathedral and to have produced, for sale or loan, 'little ballads, complaints and roundels'. Twenty years later, customs accounts document the importation of large quantities of manuscript books through London—over 1,300 in 1480–1 alone.

One may cautiously introduce some figures to indicate that late medieval literacy was not confined to the noble, clerical, or governmental classes. As was probably the case with Cade's rebels, some artisans and craftsmen could now read and write. Eleven out of twenty-eight witnesses in a legal suit of 1373 described themselves as *literatus* (or capable of understanding Latin and therefore, one presumes, English too); and a mid-fifteenth-century will provided a similar proportion of 'literates' among witnesses who included merchants, husbandmen, tailors, and mariners. There were doubtless others whom, literate or not, one would never dream of employing as witnesses, but we are undeniably moving towards Sir Thomas More's enthusiastic estimate at the beginning of the sixteenth century that more than 50 per cent of Englishmen were literate.

If we cannot accept such figures with complete confidence, we can at least observe literate men—rarely women—at work in a variety of occupations. They filled some of the highest political offices in the land hitherto reserved for clerics: from 1381, laymen frequently became Treasurer of England, an office for which a command of reading and writing—if not of figures—was an essential qualification. Literate laymen were employed as clerks in government service, a niche which the poet Thomas Hoccleve occupied for over thirty-five years. It is also clear that by 1380 tradesmen were keeping written bills; soon afterwards country yeomen were writing—certainly reading—private letters, and even peasants who served as reeve of their manor were functioning in an administrative environment whose business was increasingly transacted on paper and parchment. By Edward IV's time, the rules and regulations of some craft guilds were insisting on a recognized standard of literacy for their apprentices.

The reading habits of at least well-to-do laymen reflect the same thing. Reading chronicles was very popular, and not only in London; the surviving manuscripts alone run into hundreds and show signs of being produced in increasing numbers as the fifteenth century wore on—most of them in English. Merchants and others took to owning 'common-place books', those personal, diminutive libraries of poems, prophecies, chronicles, and even recipes, through which they browsed at leisure. They possessed books and carefully disposed of them—particularly the religious and devotional ones—in their wills.

This literate world was increasingly an English world. The facility to speak and understand French (and therefore to read and write it) was in marked decline before the end of the fourteenth century; even for official and formal business in government and private organizations, English was becoming at least as common. Discussions in Parliament were taking place in English by the middle decades of the century, and the first written record of this dates from 1362. Although only a rough and ready guide, it is worth noting that the earliest known property deed drawn up in English is dated 1376, the earliest will 1387. The proceedings of the convocation of Canterbury were conducted in English quite often by the 1370s, and Henry IV spoke to Parliament in English in 1399 and had his words carefully recorded. The reasons for this quiet revolution are complex, but among them may be numbered the patriotism generated by the long French war; the popularity of Lollardy, which set great store by English books and sermons; the lead given by the Crown and the nobility; and, of course, the greater participation of the English-speaking subject in the affairs of the realm, not least in Parliament. The triumph of the written language was assured.

Before that happened, one major problem had to be faced: that of regional dialects. Only then could the full potential of English as a written and spoken tongue be realized. It must be admitted that in this first century or so of popular, literate English, quaint Cornish, wilfully foreign Welsh, and such unintelligibilities as the Yorkshire dialect could not be fully absorbed into a common idiom; but much headway was made. The spreading tentacles of government helped, developing and extending the use of a written language for official communication throughout the realm during the first half of the fifteenth century. A further factor was the emergence in the fourteenth century of London as the settled capital of the kingdom, with York as a subsidiary administrative centre and Bristol as the second commercial metropolis, each evolving a dialect that inevitably became comprehensible to the others and gradually fused in a stand-ardized English. This dialect was predominantly midland English, which triumphed at the expense of a city-bound tongue; and for this reason it was the more easily adopted in rural shires. That the victor was a midland dialect was in large part due to the substantial migration of midlanders and easterners to London in the fourteenth and fifteenth centuries. Lollardy was partly responsible too, for it was especially vigorous in the Midlands and west country, and most of its written works were in varying forms of the midland tongue. By capturing London, this midland dialect in speech and writing captured the kingdom.

Geoffrey Chaucer had serious misgivings as to whether his writings would be understood across England—and he wrote for a limited, charmed circle.

> And for there is so great diversity
> In English and in writing of our tongue
> So pray I God that none miswrite thee,
> Nor thee mismetre for default of tongue.
> And read whereso thou be, or else sung
> That thou be understood, God I beseech.

In a legal case of 1426, it was stated that words were pronounced differently in different parts of England 'and one is just as good as the other'. Half a century later, William Caxton could be more optimistic that his printed editions of several hundreds would, with care, be quite comprehensible from one shire to another. He realized that 'common English that is spoken in one shire varieth from another'; but by using 'English not over rude, nor curious, but in such terms as shall be understood by God's grace', he anticipated little difficulty. The greater ease of understanding, in both speech and writing, that had developed meanwhile was crucial to the effectiveness of communication, the common expression of opinion, and the forging of a sense of nationhood.

English had become 'the language, not of a conquered, but of a conquering people'. The self-confidence of its writers reached the heights of genius in Chaucer, and it attracted patronage from the wealthiest and most influential in the realm—from kings, noblemen, gentlemen, and townsmen. English prose in the fourteenth and fifteenth centuries was far outshone in quality and popularity by English verse in all its forms: lyric and romance, comedy and tragedy, allegory and drama. Much of this poetry fell squarely in the northern European tradition, and the literary revival of the north-west and the Midlands in the fourteenth century was mainly of alliterative, unrhymed verse. But it was sponsored by local gentry and magnates such as the Bohuns (earls of Hereford) and the Mortimers (earls of March), and could produce works of considerable imaginative power in *Sir Gawain and the Green Knight* and *Piers Plowman*. In the same region, ritual Christian drama in the English Miracle Play Cycles was developed during the fourteenth century and achieved great popularity in northern towns such as York, Beverley, Wakefield, and Chester, where the plays were organized and performed by the town guilds.

At the same time, in the south and east, a newer mode of verse was appearing which owed more to current fashions of style and content in French and early Renaissance Italian writing. Through the pen of Chaucer, and to a lesser extent his friend John Gower, it created masterpieces of English literature. These were unequalled in their richness of thought and vocabulary, their imagination and depth of human understanding, and in their sheer artistry. *Troilus and Criseyde*, written about 1380–5, and especially the immensely ambitious and complex panorama of *The Canterbury Tales* (written 1386–1400 but never completed), decisively extended English literary accomplishment. They displayed a wisdom, worldliness, and inventiveness, and a mastery of contemporary English idiom in all its variety, which earn Chaucer his place as the greatest English medieval writer.

Gower, a Kentishman, was patronized by Richard II and, later, by Henry Bolingbroke. Chaucer, who came of London merchant stock, grew up in aristocratic and royal circles, and he was one of the most lionized and richly rewarded poets of any age. This reflects both the extraordinary quality of his writing, and also the recognition which influential contemporaries were prepared to give to the English language which he enriched. If Chaucer's disciples, Hoccleve and Lydgate, seem second-rate in comparison with their master, at least the royal, court, and city patronage which these authors received assured a bright future for what was essentially the English literary school of the capital.

The same sources of wealth and taste were placed at the disposal of England's architects and builders. Developing their ideas from the predominant Gothic style of much of Europe, of which the pointed arch is the symbol and most characteristic feature, they created architectural styles which have a good claim to be regarded as distinctively English. Since the nineteenth century, these have been termed Decorated (more accurately free-flowing and curvilinear) and Perpendicular (or rather vertical and rectilinear), and they are best identified in the window and arch design of England's cathedrals, larger parish churches, and colleges. In so far as any new architectural development can be explained with precision, it is thought that renewed diplomatic and crusader contacts with the Muslim and Mongol worlds of Egypt and Persia towards the end of the thirteenth century transmitted knowledge of Eastern building styles and techniques to the far West. The delicate tracery and luxuriant naturalistic motifs which are a feature of the new Decorated style appear on the three surviving Eleanor Crosses that Edward I erected in the 1290s to mark the stages in the journey of his wife's body from Lincoln to its burial at Westminster. Eastern influences have also been observed in the hexagonal north porch and doorway of St. Mary Redcliffe, Bristol, dating from early in the fourteenth century. After only half a century (1285–1335) of these extravagant complexities, which were unparalleled in Gothic Europe and have been hailed as 'the most brilliant display of sheer inventiveness in the whole history of English medieval architecture', a reaction set in. This reaction produced the most English style of all, the Perpendicular. In an age when England was at war, this was rarely imitated on the European mainland. Its simpler, cleaner lines and larger, lighter spaces may have appeared first in the royal chapel of St. Stephen, Westminster (destroyed 1834), or in the city cathedral of St. Paul (burned 1666). Either way, it quickly spread to the west country, through courtly influence focused on Edward II's shrine at Gloucester. It can still be admired on the grand scale in the choir of Gloucester

A perpendicular parish church. St. John's Church, Yeovil (Somerset), was rebuilt by its rector 1362–82 in the simple, lighter and elegant style that was common, especially in the west country.

Cathedral, dating from the mid-1330s, as well as in the later naves of Canterbury (from 1379) and Winchester (from 1394). Decoration was now concentrated English-style in roof vaulting, culminating in the fan vaults of Hereford's chapter house (now destroyed) and the cloisters at Gloucester, which were built after 1351.

Yet Perpendicular building is found most frequently and at its best in the greater parish churches of England such as Cirencester, Coventry, and Hull. Not even plague and warfare, which may have inhibited large-scale projects for a while in the fifteenth century, could deter clothiers and landowners in East Anglia and the west country from lavishing their wealth on these monuments to English taste and skill. Perpendicular architecture experienced an exuberant resurgence in the latter part of the fifteenth century in some of the most famous of English buildings, most of them sponsored by the Crown—Eton College, St. George's Chapel, Windsor (from 1474), King's College Chapel, Cambridge, and Henry VII's Chapel in Westminster Abbey. It was incontestably 'the Indian Summer of English medieval architecture'.

Incomparably English were the Perpendicular towers of late medieval parish churches, ranging from the sturdy St. Giles Church, Wrexham, to the soaring shaft of St. Botolph's, Boston, and the elegance of Taunton, St. Stephen's, Bristol, and St. John's, Cardiff. So, too, were the carved timber roofs of the fourteenth and fifteenth centuries, beginning with the timber vault planned for the chapter house at York after 1291, and the replacement of the tower of Ely Cathedral, which collapsed in 1322, by a timber vault and lantern tower. This roof work culminated in the great hammer-beam oak roof of Westminster Hall (1394–1400), commissioned by Richard II and judged to be 'the greatest single work of art of the whole of the European middle ages'. Masons, carpenters, and architects were patronized by kings, courtiers, noblemen, and others from the thirteenth century onwards, and not simply for religious building; they also worked on royal and private castles and manor houses. Although forming a profession largely based in London and connected with the office of king's works, these craftsmen were assigned duties throughout England and Wales. They placed their expertise and experience at the disposal of noblemen and bishops and thereby created a national style to suit national tastes.

Englishmen's sense of nationhood and their awareness of their own Englishness are not easily gauged. But they sometimes compared themselves—and were compared by others—to peoples of different race, language, country, or cultural and political tradition. In the later Middle Ages, Englishmen confronted, frequently violently, other peoples both in the British Isles and in mainland Europe. These confrontations were a forcing-house of nationhood and self-conscious Englishness. Such experiences gave rise to a number of emotions, which made English people aware of their nature, unity, and common traditions and history.

So long as England was ruled by Norman dukes or Angevin counts, and Anglo-Norman barons held estates on both sides of the Channel and others did so in both England and Scotland, it was impossible for the ruling élite to think of itself as exclusively English. But this became possible once Normandy and Anjou were overrun by the French and formally surrendered to them in 1259, for the cross-Channel nobility had then to decide where its prime allegiance lay. It became more likely, too, with the growing self-consciousness of the Scottish kingdom, particularly when Edward I's wars made land-holding across the border a thing of the past. Thereafter, the separateness of England was identified with its encircling seas. In the mid-1430s a pamphleteer advised:

> Keep then the seas about in special;
> Which of England is the round wall,
> As though England were likened to a city
> And the wall environ were the sea . . .

English kings from Edward I were more truly English in upbringing and outlook than any since King Harold. Indeed, Henry VI in his thirty-nine-year reign never visited Scotland or Ireland; he only once set foot in Wales—a day at Monmouth—and never again went to France after his coronation visit at the age of nine.

As to foreigners, the dominance of Flemings and then Italians in England's overseas trade in the thirteenth century fostered resentment of their commercial success. In Henry VII's reign Englishmen were said to 'have an antipathy to foreigners, and imagine that they never come into their island but to make themselves master of it and to usurp their goods . . . '. After all, natives of a country at war with England might, like the alien priories attached to French monasteries, send money to an enemy, or, like the servants of Henry IV's queen, the duchess of Brittany, act as spies for France. Not for nothing did the king's clerks scratch 'Do not show to aliens!' on state papers at the outset of the Hundred Years War.

England's wars, waged successfully by humble bowmen as well as knights and noblemen, created among all ranks a self-confidence that warmed English hearts. A well-informed observer said in 1373 that 'the English are so filled with their own greatness and have won so many big victories that they have come to believe they cannot lose. In battle, they are the most confident nation in the world.' Pride in their victories seemed unbounded, and individual kings embodied the achievements. Under Edward III, 'the realm of England has been nobly amended, honoured and enriched to a degree never seen in the time of any other king', whilst Henry V's reputation among his subjects reached even greater heights. Englishmen's belief in their superiority—a short step from pride and self-confidence—remained unshaken even in the mid-fifteenth century, by which time England's fortunes seemed far less golden. The wild Gaels were treated as 'mere Irish' and the Flemings in 1436 with undisguised scorn:

> Remember now, ye Flemings, upon your own shame;
> When ye laid siege to Calais, ye were right still to blame;
> For more of reputation, be Englishmen than ye,
> And come of more gentle blood, of old antiquity.

An Italian visitor around 1500, when England's overseas 'empire' was all but lost, could still report that 'the English are great lovers of themselves and of everything belonging to them. They think that there are no other men than themselves, and no other world but England; and when they see a handsome foreigner they say that "he looks like an Englishman", and that "it is a great pity that he should not be an Englishman".' Feelings of superiority easily turned to disdain or even hate. After decades of war with the French, Francophobia was common and matched only by the Anglophobia of the French, who came to regard the English as 'a race of people accursed'. At no time was this distaste for things French stronger than during the reign of Henry V. He may have claimed the French Crown, but in England he discouraged the use of the French language in government and literate society. The London brewers took their cue from their admired king, and when they wrote their ordinances in English they noted that 'our mother tongue, to wit, the English tongue, hath in modern days begun to be honourably enlarged and adorned . . . and our most excellent lord, King Henry V, hath procured the common idiom . . . to be commended by the exercise of writing'.

Tales of a British past and practical feelings of insecurity had combined with the vigour and ambition of English kings down to Edward I—perhaps Edward III—to take the English into Scotland, Wales, and Ireland. Their success in absorbing these territories was limited; and try as they might to Anglicize the Welsh and Irish in culture, language, and habit, the English with their dependent dominions were denied political nationhood in the later Middle Ages. The English delegation to the Church's Council at Constance (1414–17) declared:

whether a nation be understood as a people marked off from others by blood relationship and habit of unity, or by peculiarities of language (the most sure and positive sign and essence of a nation in divine and human law) . . . or whether a nation be understood, as it should be, as a territory equal to that of the French nation, England is a real nation . . .

But they spoilt their political case by adding that Scotland, Wales, and Ireland were part of the English nation.

FURTHER READING

1. ROMAN BRITAIN

BEFORE THE ROMAN CONQUEST

Richard Bradley, *The Prehistoric Settlement of Britain* (London, 1978), particularly readable.

Barry Cunliffe, *Iron Age Communities in Britain* (2nd edn. London, 1978), general account of the centuries immediately before the Roman Conquest.

John Brailsford, *Early Celtic Masterpieces from Britain in the British Museum* (London, 1975).

GENERAL SURVEYS

Sheppard Frere, *Britannia: a History of Roman Britain* (2nd edn. London, 1974), a standard work.

Peter Salway, *Roman Britain (Oxford History of England,* vol. 1a) (Oxford, 1981), large-scale general history, with essays on major themes.

Malcolm Todd, *Roman Britain 55 BC–AD 400: the Province beyond Ocean (Fontana History of England)* (London, 1981), perceptive and up-to-date narrative.

John Wacher, *Roman Britain* (London, 1978)

Peter A. Clayton (ed.), *A Companion to Roman Britain* (Oxford, 1980), exceptionally well-illustrated essays.

Roger J. A. Wilson, *A Guide to the Roman Remains in Britain* (2nd edn. London, 1980), recommended to those wishing to visit the accessible material remains of the period.

Ordnance Survey, *Map of Roman Britain* (4th edn. Southampton, 1978), 2 sheets, scale 1:625,000, and gazetteer.

Philip Dixon, *Barbarian Europe (The Making of the Past)* (Oxford, 1976), excellent, well-illustrated background reading, helping to place the end of Roman Britain in its European context.

SPECIAL ASPECTS

Anthony Birley, *The People of Roman Britain* (London, 1979), illuminating study based on the people known by name in Roman Britain.

A. L. F. Rivet and Colin Smith, *The Place-Names of Roman Britain* (London, 1979), major work of reference: gazetteer, accompanied by linguistic and geographical analysis.

P. A. Holder, *The Roman Army in Britain* (London, 1982), welcome first modern account.

David J. Breeze, *The Northern Frontiers of Roman Britain* (London, 1982), current thought, well presented.

Peter Marsden, *Roman London* (London, 1980).

J. M. C. Toynbee, *Art in Britain under the Romans* (Oxford, 1964), enormously learned, wide-ranging, and clear.

Charles Thomas, *Christianity in Britain to AD 500* (London, 1981), thought-provoking re-examination.

2. THE ANGLO-SAXON PERIOD

GENERAL HISTORY

F. M. Stenton, *Anglo-Saxon England* (3rd edn. Oxford, 1971), the standard history.

J. Campbell (ed.), *The Anglo-Saxons* (Oxford, 1982), an outstandingly good recent book, with many new ideas and splendid illustrations.

P. Hunter Blair, *An introduction to Anglo-Saxon England* (Cambridge, 1956), summarizes the main events and themes.

ORIGINAL SOURCES

The Anglo-Saxon Chronicle, trans. G. N. Garmonsway (London, 1953); the late Anglo-Saxon vernacular chronicle, providing contemporary comment from Alfred's reign onwards.

Bede, *Ecclesiastical History of the English People*, trans. L. Sherley-Price (rev. edn. Harmondsworth, 1968), a brilliant and vivid narrative account written in the early eighth century, the most important single source for earlier Anglo-Saxon history.

ARCHAEOLOGY, ART, AND LITERATURE

R. L. Bruce-Mitford, *The Sutton Hoo Ship Burial: a Handbook* (3rd edn. London, 1979), a well-illustrated account of the most important archaeological discovery from the Anglo-Saxon period.

The Earliest English Poems, trans. M. Alexander (2nd edn. Harmondsworth, 1977), translations of the more important Anglo-Saxon poems, including *The Battle of Maldon* and selections from *Beowulf*.

H. M. and Joan Taylor, *Anglo-Saxon Architecture*, i–iii (Cambridge, 1965–78), a comprehensive account of the surviving Anglo-Saxon churches.

D. Talbot Rice, *English Art 871–1100* (Oxford, 1952), a well-illustrated general account.

D. M. Wilson (ed.), *The archeology of Anglo-Saxon England* (Cambridge, 1976), chapters by several authors on the various kinds of physical evidence for the period.

THE MERCIAN SUPREMACY

A. Dornier (ed.), *Mercian Studies* (Leicester, 1977), a collection of essays relating to the Mercian region, especially during the eighth century.

LATE ANGLO-SAXON KINGSHIP AND GOVERNMENT

F. Barlow, *Edward the Confessor* (London, 1970), the standard biography.

D. Hill (ed.), *Ethelred the Unready: papers from the Millenary Conference* (Oxford, 1978), a recent collection of important and original studies on the late tenth and early eleventh centuries.

THE CHURCH

H. Mayr-Harting, *The coming of Christianity to Anglo-Saxon England* (London, 1972), the best general account of the conversions.

P. Hunter Blair, *The world of Bede* (London, 1970), religion and learning in eighth-century Northumbria.

M. Deanesly, *The pre-Conquest church in England* (London, 1961), a general survey of ecclesiastical institutions.

SCOTLAND AND WALES: GENERAL HISTORY
A. A. M. Duncan, *Scotland: the making of the kingdom* (Edinburgh, 1975).
W. Davies, *Wales in the early Middle Ages* (Leicester, 1982).

3. THE EARLY MIDDLE AGES

GENERAL
M. T. Clanchy, *England and its Rulers 1066–1272* (Glasgow, 1983), a thought-provoking combination of political and cultural history.
G. W. S. Barrow, *Feudal Britain 1066–1314* (London, 1956), especially good on Scotland and Wales.
F. Barlow, *The Feudal Kingdom of England 1042–1216* (3rd edn. London, 1972), an excellent outline.
D. M. Stenton, *English Society in the Early Middle Ages 1066–1307* (2nd edn. Harmondsworth, 1952), a brief social survey.

STUDIES OF SOME MAJOR POLITICAL THEMES
H. R. Loyn, *The Norman Conquest* (3rd edn. London, 1982), a brief and balanced survey of a standard problem.
J. Le Patourel, *The Norman Empire* (Oxford, 1976), magisterial. The starting-point for all future studies of this subject.
J. C. Holt, *Magna Carta* (Cambridge, 1965), indispensable for the political and social context of the charter.
G. O. Sayles, *The King's Parliament of England* (London, 1975), a distillation of 40 years of research and argument by Richardson and Sayles.

ROYAL BIOGRAPHIES
D. C. Douglas, *William the Conqueror* (London, 1964), a splendidly traditional biography.
R. H. C. Davis, *King Stephen* (London, 1967), lively and stimulating. What could be better?
W. L. Warren, *Henry II* (London, 1973), somehow contrives to be both massive and readable.
J. Gillingham, *Richard the Lionheart* (London, 1978), emphasizes the importance of the Angevin dominions in France.
W. L. Warren, *King John* (Harmondsworth, 1961), seeks to rescue John from the damning verdict of thirteenth-century chroniclers.

OTHER BIOGRAPHIES
C. R. Cheney, *Hubert Walter* (London, 1967), a lucid account of the career of the most powerful churchman of the age.
S. Painter, *William Marshal* (Baltimore, 1933), the story of a tournament knight who becomes regent of England.

CHURCH
F. Barlow, *The English Church 1066–1154* (London, 1979), a lively analysis of a radical and tumultuous age.
D. Knowles, *The Monastic Order in England 940–1216* (2nd edn. Cambridge, 1963), a scholarly history of monasticism by a scholar monk.
——*The Religious Orders in England*, vol. 1 (Cambridge, 1962), important for the coming of the friars.

SCOTLAND

G. W. S. Barrow, *Kingship and Unity. Scotland 1000–1316* (London, 1981), an invaluable brief survey.

WALES

D. Walker, *The Norman Conquerors* (Swansea, 1977);

A. C. Reeves, *The Marcher Lords* (Swansea, 1983): succinct thematic volumes in *A New History of Wales* series.

ECONOMY

J. L. Bolton, *The Medieval English Economy 1150–1500* (London, 1980), the most helpful general introduction.

F. Miller and J. Hatcher, *Medieval England: Rural Society and Economic Change 1086–1348* (London, 1978), a judicious survey of the rural economy.

S. Reynolds, *An Introduction to the History of English Medieval Towns* (2nd edn. Oxford, 1982), the thinking man's introduction to English urban history.

G. A. Williams, *Medieval London: from Commune to Capital* (London, 1963), a vivid and detailed account of thirteenth and early fourteenth-century London.

LANGUAGE AND LITERACY

M. T. Clanchy, *From Memory to Written Record: England 1066–1307* (London, 1979), a fascinating analysis of the development of literacy and the literate mentality.

ART

T. S. R. Boase, *English Art 1100–1216* (Oxford, 1953);

P. Brieger, *English Art 1216–1307* (Oxford, 1957): two classic surveys of art and architecture.

4. THE LATER MIDDLE AGES

GENERAL SURVEYS

F. R. H. DuBoulay, *An Age of Ambition* (London, 1970), a stimulating look at themes (e.g. class, marriage, sex) often neglected.

S. B. Chrimes, C. D. Ross, and R. A. Griffiths (eds.), *Fifteenth-century England, 1399–1509: Studies in Politics and Society* (Manchester, 1972), up-to-date essays on central topics.

J. R. Lander, *Conflict and Stability in Fifteenth-century England* (3rd edn. London, 1977), an overall (if gloomy) view of the century.

M. Prestwich, *The Three Edwards* (London, 1980), clear and succinct.

PARTICULAR THEMES

A. R. Bridbury, *Economic Growth: England in the Later Middle Ages* (London, 1962).

K. B. McFarlane, *The Nobility of Later Medieval England* (Oxford, 1973), essays by a master-historian.

R. H. Hilton, *The English Peasantry in the Later Middle Ages* (Oxford, 1975).

C. Platt, *The English Medieval Town* (London, 1976), a pleasant, illustrated book.

J. Bellamy, *Crime and Public Order in England in the Later Middle Ages* (London, 1973).

R. G. Davies and J. H. Denton (eds.), *The English Parliament in the Middle Ages* (Manchester, 1981), nicely integrated essays.

J. C. Dickinson, *An Ecclesiastical History of England: the Later Middle Ages* (London, 1979).

K. B. McFarlane, *John Wycliffe and the Beginnings of English Nonconformity* (London, 1952).

J. Evans, *English Art, 1307–1461* (Oxford, 1949).

G. Mathew, *The Court of Richard II* (London, 1968), attractively written and illustrated.

S. Medcalf (ed.), *The Context of English Literature: The Later Middle Ages* (London, 1981), a rare attempt to integrate cultural and social history.

J. Brown (ed.), *Scottish Society in the Fifteenth Century* (London, 1977), essays on central topics.

G. Williams, *Owen Glendower* (Oxford, 1966).

J. F. Lydon, *Ireland in the Later Middle Ages* (Dublin, 1973).

C. D. Ross, *The Wars of the Roses* (London, 1976), wise and well illustrated.

A. E. Goodman, *The Wars of the Roses* (London, 1981), good on military matters.

RECENT ROYAL AND POLITICAL STUDIES

E. L. G. Stones, *Edward I* (Oxford, 1968).

R. Barber, *Edward, Prince of Wales and Aquitaine* (London, 1978).

J. A. Tuck, *Richard II and the English Nobility* (London, 1973).

J. L. Kirby, *Henry IV of England* (London, 1970).

K. B. McFarlane, *Lancastrian Kings and Lollard Knights* (Oxford, 1972), two major themes explored with insight.

M. W. Labarge, *Henry V* (London, 1975).

R. A. Griffiths, *The Reign of King Henry VI* (London, 1981), more than a biography of the king.

C. D. Ross, *Edward IV* (London, 1974).

——*Richard III* (London, 1981).

CHRONOLOGY

* Entries in *italics* denote events belonging to the history of the Roman Empire.

55–54 BC	Expeditions of Caesar
49 BC	*Caesar defeats Pompey: effective end of Roman Republic**
	Julio-Claudian Emperors (27 BC–AD 69)
34–26 BC	Projected expeditions of Augustus
	Britain between the invasions: period of political and economic change
by 12 BC	*Permanent Roman bases on Rhine*
AD 40	Expedition of Gaius cancelled
	Claudius (41–54)
by 43	Death of Cunobelinus
43	Claudian invasion
by 47	Conquest of south and east of England completed
49	Foundation of Colchester
c.50	Foundation of London
51–2	Defeat and capture of Caratacus
	Nero (54–68)
61	Revolt of Boudica
69	*'Year of the Four Emperors'*
	Flavian Emperors (69–96)
70–84	Conquest of Wales and north completed
	Conquest of Scotland
	Trajan (98–117)
c.100	Scotland temporarily lost: frontier on Tyne–Solway line
	Hadrian (117–38)
122	Hadrian in Britain: the Wall begun
	Antonine Emperors (138–92)
	Antoninus Pius (138–61)
140–3	Antonine advance into Scotland: by 143 Antonine Wall begun
c.158	Serious trouble in the north
? c.160	Temporary reoccupation of Antonine Wall
	Marcus Aurelius (161–80); major wars on the Danube
? c.163	Hadrian's Wall restored
193	Clodius Albinus proclaimed in Britain
	Severan Emperors (193–235)
196–213	Britain divided into two provinces
208–11	Campaigns of Septimius Severus and Caracalla in Scotland
235–70	*Imperial crisis: civil wars and invasions in East and West*
260–73	*'Gallic Empire'*
270s	Renewed growth in Britain
	Diocletian (284–305)
	'The Tetrarchy'

287–96	Carausius and Allectus
296	Britain recovered by Constantius
after 296	Britain becomes a civil diocese of four provinces
	House of Constantius (305–63)
306	Campaign of Constantius I in Scotland; Constantine the Great proclaimed at York
324	*Constantine sole emperor; foundation of Constantinople*
340–69	Period of severe stress: internal troubles, harassment by barbarians
350	*Magnentius proclaimed in Gaul*
353	*Constantius II sole emperor*
353	Purge by Paul the Chain
	House of Valentinian (364–92)
367–9	'Barbarian Conspiracy', recovery and restoration of Britain by the elder Theodosius
	House of Theodosius (379–455)
	Theodosius the Great (379–95)
383	Magnus Maximus proclaimed in Britain; victory over Picts
	Honorius (395–423)
398–400	Victories over Picts, Scots, Saxons
400–2	Possible troop withdrawals by Stilicho
402–3	*Western imperial court withdrawn from Milan to Ravenna*
406	Britain revolts from Honorius: two emperors proclaimed
407	Constantine III proclaimed in Britain
	Constantine III rules from Arles (407–11)
409	Britain revolts from Constantine III: end of Roman rule in Britain
410	Emperor Honorius withdraws Roman forces from Britain
429	St. Germanus visits Britain
c.450	The *adventus Saxonum*: Hengest and Horsa settle in Kent (traditional date)
455	Hengest rebels against Vortigern (traditional date)
477	Saxon settlement of Sussex (traditional date)
495	Saxon settlement of Wessex (traditional date)
c.500	Battle of *Mons Badonicus*
560	Æthelberht, later over-king, becomes king in Kent
577	The West Saxons capture Gloucester, Cirencester, and Bath
597	St. Augustine's mission arrives in Kent
616	Raedwald of East Anglia, as over-king, makes Edwin king of Northumbria
c.624	Death of Raedwald, and his probable burial in the Sutton Hoo barrow
627	Conversion of Edwin and the Northumbrian court
633	Battle of Heavenfield; Oswald of Northumbria becomes over-king
635	Conversion of King Cynegils of Wessex
642	Oswald is killed at Oswestry by King Penda of Mercia
655	Penda is defeated and killed at the *Winwaed* by Oswy of Northumbria, who becomes over-king
664	Synod of Whitby
669	Arrival of Archbishop Theodore
672	Synod of Hertford; battle of the Trent, marking the beginnings of the rise of Mercia
685–8	Expansion of Wessex under Caedwalla to include Kent, Surrey and Sussex
716	Æthelbald becomes king of Mercia

731	Bede completes his *Ecclesiastical History*
746–7	First Council of Clofesho
757	Death of Æthelbald; Offa becomes king of Mercia
786	Legatine Council held under Offa
793–5	Danish raids on Lindisfarne, Jarrow, and Iona
796	Death of Offa
825	Egbert of Wessex defeats Mercia and annexes Kent, Essex, Surrey, and Sussex
835	Big Danish raid on Kent
865	The Danish 'Great Army' lands
867	Northumbria falls to the Danes
870	East Anglia falls to the Danes; murder of St. Edmund
871	The Danes attack Wessex; Alfred becomes king
874	Mercia falls to the Danes
878	(March) The Danes drive Alfred into the Somerset marshes
	(May) Alfred defeats the Danes at Edington; Guthrum is baptized
899	Death of Alfred; Edward 'the Elder' becomes king of Wessex
910–20	Edward and Æthelflaed reconquer most of the Danelaw
919	Norse kingdom of York is founded by Raegnald
924	Death of Edward; Athelstan becomes king
937	Athelstan defeats the Norse, Scots, and Strathclyde Welsh at Brunanburh
939	Death of Athelstan; Edmund becomes king
940	Dunstan begins to refound Glastonbury as a regular monastic house
946	Death of Edmund
954	The last king of York is deposed
959	Edgar becomes king
960	Dunstan becomes Archbishop of Canterbury
c.970	*Regularis Concordia* is compiled
973	Edgar is crowned and consecrated, and receives the submission of British princes
975	Death of Edgar; Edward 'the Martyr' becomes king
979	Murder of Edward; Æthelred 'the Unready' becomes king
991	The Danes defeat Alderman Byrhtnoth and the Essex levies at Maldon; treaty between England and Normandy
1002	Æthelred orders the massacre of all Danes in England
1003	Danish invasion led by King Swein
1013	Swein returns with a new army; the Danelaw accepts him as king
1014	Swein dies; the Danish army in England elect Cnut as their king
1016	(April) Æthelred dies; Edmund 'Ironside' becomes king
	(autumn) Cnut defeats Edmund at Ashingdon; Edmund dies and Cnut becomes king of all England
1017	Cnut divides England into four earldoms
1035	Death of Cnut
1037	Harold becomes king
1040	Death of Harold; Harthacnut becomes king
1042	Death of Harthacnut; Edward 'the Confessor' becomes king
1051–2	Conflict between King Edward and Godwin earl of Wessex
1053	Death of Godwin; his son Harold becomes earl of Wessex
1064–5	Earl Harold visits Duke William in Normandy
1066	(January) Death of King Edward; Earl Harold becomes king
	(September) King Harold of England defeats and kills King Harold of Norway at Stamford Bridge

1066	(October) Duke William of Normandy defeats and kills King Harold of England at Hastings
	(December) William is consecrated king
1067–70	English rebellions
1069–70	The harrying of the north
1086	Domesday Survey carried out
1087	Death of William I; accession of William II Rufus
1088	Rebellion in support of Robert Curthose
1093	Anselm appointed Archbishop of Canterbury
1096	Robert pawns Normandy to Rufus
1100	Death of William Rufus; accession of Henry I
1101	Invasion of Robert Curthose
1106	Battle of Tinchebray; Curthose imprisoned; Henry I takes Normandy
1107	Settlement of Investiture Dispute in England
1120	Wreck of the White Ship
1128	Marriage of Empress Matilda to Geoffrey of Anjou
1135	Death of Henry I; accession of Stephen
1139–53	Civil war in England
1141	Battle of Lincoln; Stephen captured; later exchanged for Robert of Gloucester
1141–5	Geoffrey of Anjou conquers Normandy
1149	Cession of Northumbria to David of Scotland
1152	Henry of Anjou (later Henry II) marries Eleanor of Aquitaine
1153	Henry invades England; he and Stephen come to terms
1154	Death of Stephen; accession of Henry II
1157	Henry regains Northumbria
1162	Becket appointed Archbishop of Canterbury
1164	Council and Constitutions of Clarendon; Becket goes into exile
1166	Assize of Clarendon
1169–72	English conquest of Ireland begins
1170	Coronation of the young king; murder of Becket
1173–4	Rebellion against Henry II; William 'the Lion' (king of Scotland) invades the north
1183	Death of the young king
1189	Death of Henry II; accession of Richard I
1190–92	Richard I on crusade
1193–4	Richard in prison in Germany
1193–1205	Hubert Walter, Archbishop of Canterbury (justiciar 1194–8; chancellor 1199–1205)
1197	Death of Rhys of Deheubarth
1199	Death of Richard I; accession of John; establishment of Chancery Rolls
1203–4	Philip Augustus conquers Anjou and Normandy
1208–14	Interdict in England
1214	Battle of Bouvines: French victory
1215	Magna Carta; civil war in England
1216	Louis (later Louis VIII) invades; death of John; accession of Henry III
1217	Battles of Lincoln and Dover; Louis withdraws
1221–4	Arrival of Dominican and Franciscan Friars in England
1224	Louis VIII completes conquest of Poitou
1232	Dismissal of Hubert de Burgh
1240	Death of Llywelyn the Great
1254	Henry III accepts papal offer of throne of Sicily

1258	Barons take over royal government; provisions of Oxford
1259	Treaty of Paris between England and France
1264	Battle of Lewes; Henry III captured; government of Simon de Montfort
1265	Battle of Evesham; killing of Simon de Montfort
1267	Henry recognizes Llywelyn ap Gruffydd as Prince of Wales
1272	Death of Henry III; accession of Edward I
1276–7	First Welsh War
1282–3	Edward's conquest of Wales
1286–9	Edward I in Gascony
1291	Edward I asserts his overlordship over Scotland
1294	War with France begins
1295	Franco-Scottish alliance
1296	Edward I invades Scotland; his conflict with the Church
1297	Edward I's conflict with his magnates; his expedition to Flanders
1306	Rebellion of Robert Bruce
1307	Death of Edward I; accession of Edward II
1314	Scottish victory at Bannockburn
1315–16	Great famine
1321–2	Civil war in England
1327	Deposition and death of Edward II; accession of Edward III
1330	Edward III takes the reins of government
1337	The Hundred Years War begins
1339–41	Political crisis in England
1346	English victories at Crécy and Neville's Cross
1347	English capture Calais
1348	First occurrence of plague in England
1356	English victory at Poitiers
1361	Second major occurrence of plague
1376	'Good Parliament' meets; death of Edward, the Black Prince
1377	Death of Edward III; accession of Richard II
1381	The Peasants' Revolt
1382	Condemnation of John Wycliffe's works
1388	'Merciless Parliament' meets; battle of Otterburn against the Scots
1389	Richard II declares himself of age
1394–5	Richard II's expedition to Ireland
1396	Anglo-French treaty
1397–9	Richard II's 'tyranny'
1399	Deposition of Richard II; accession of Henry IV
1400	Rebellion of Owain Glyndŵr begins (to 1410)
1403	Henry Hotspur defeated at Shrewsbury
1405	Execution of Archbishop Scrope of York
1408	Defeat of the earl of Northumberland at Bramham Moor
1413	Death of Henry IV; accession of Henry V
1415	English victory at Agincourt
1419–20	English conquest of Normandy
1420	Anglo-French treaty of Troyes
1422	Death of Henry V; accession of Henry VI
1435	Death of John, duke of Bedford; Franco-Burgundian treaty of Arras
1436–7	Henry VI comes of age
1445	Henry VI marries Margaret of Anjou
1449–50	French overrun Normandy
1450	Murder of the duke of Suffolk; John Cade's rebellion
1453	French overrun Gascony; Henry VI becomes ill

1455	Battle of St. Albans between Richard, duke of York and the royalist forces
1459	Defeat of the duke of York at Blore Heath and Ludford Bridge
1461	Deposition of Henry VI; accession of Edward IV
1465	Capture of Henry VI
1469	Rebellion of Richard, earl of Warwick and George, duke of Clarence
1470	Deposition of Edward IV; return of Henry VI
1471	Return of Edward IV; death of the earl of Warwick at Barnet; death of Henry VI
1475	Edward IV's expedition to France; Anglo-French treaty of Picquigny
1477	William Caxton's first printed book in England
1483	Death of Edward IV; accession, deposition, and death of Edward V; accession of Richard III; rebellion of Henry, duke of Buckingham
1485	Death of Richard III at Bosworth; accession of Henry VII

THE HOUSE OF WESSEX 802–1066

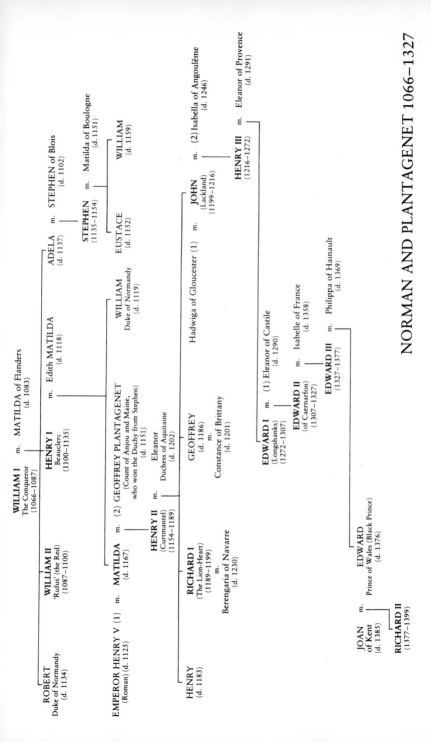

NORMAN AND PLANTAGENET 1066–1327

LANCASTER AND YORK 1327–1485

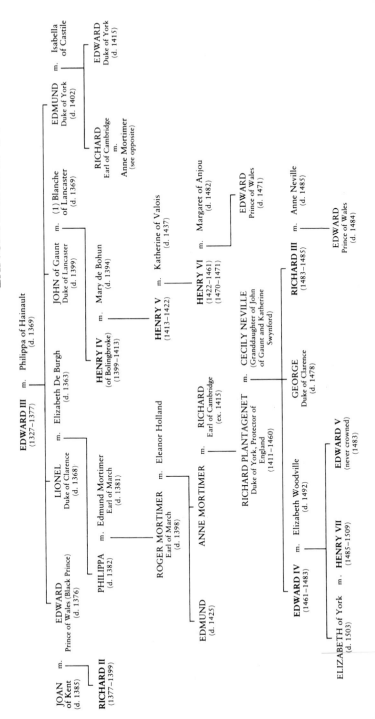

ACKNOWLEDGEMENTS

THE illustration on page 228 is reproduced by gracious permission of Her Majesty the Queen.

Photographs and illustrations were supplied by, or reproduced by kind permission of, the following: Ashmolean Library, Oxford, 92; Barnaby's Picture Library 33; British Library 71, 104, 139, 141, 178, 197, 199, 214; British Museum 4, 7, 9, 13, 21, 31, 40, 47, 62, 72, 233; P. J. Clayton 52, 84; Colchester and Essex Museums 15; Corpus Christi College, Cambridge 134, 146; Department of the Environment 20, 111; Dean and Chapter of Durham Cathedral 144; Michael Holford Library 113, 126, 155, 157; A. F. Kersting 88, 120, 124, 150, 170, 178, 188, 192, 209, 241, 247; His Grace the Archbishop of Canterbury and Trustees of Lambeth Palace Library 205; Mansell Collection 147; National Maritime Museum, London 148; National Monuments Record 17, 44; National Museum, Dublin 78; National Museum of Antiquaries of Scotland 29; National Museum of Wales 11; National Portrait Gallery, London 221; Public Record Office 128, 173, 176, 190; Rutland County Museum, Oakham 38; J. C. D. Smith 194; Society of Antiquaries 231; Suffolk County Council 20; Sussex Archaeological Society 19; Tyne & Wear County Council Museums 24; University of Cambridge Committee for Aerial Photography 26, 76, 117, 207; Dean and Chapter of Westminster Abbey 201, 217.

Maps: Those on pages 203 and 238 are based on two in *English Historical Documents*, vol iii, by H. Rothwell by kind permission of Methuen, London.

INDEX

Persons are indexed under the name or title used in the text, with cross references where necessary to alternative names. Page numbers in *italics* refer to illustrations or maps.

Perrers, Alice (d. 1400), 202
Perth, treaty of (1266), 154
Pevensey (Sussex), 114
Philip I, king of France (1052–1108), 122
Philip II Augustus, king of France (1165–1223), 140, 142, 144, 145, *146*, 164
Philip III, king of France (1245–85), 150
Philip VI, king of France (1293–1350), 194
Philippa of Hainault, queen of Edward III (1314?–1369?), *201*, 202
Picquigny, treaty of (1475), 231
place-names, 63, 68, 87, 94
plague, 210–11, 212
Plantagenet, George, *see* Clarence, duke of
Plantagenet, Richard, *see* York, duke of
Poitiers, battle of (1356), 194
Poitou, 145, 146, 148
Pole family of Hull, 206
Pole, William de la, duke of Suffolk (1396–1450), 227
Pontefract castle, 222
population, 67, 109, 179–80, 209, 211, 212
Portsmouth, 128
poverty, 183, 209–10
Powys, kingdom of, 66
Praemunire, statute of (1353), 239
Prasutagus, king of Iceni (d. 60), 21
prices, *see* wages
Probus, Marcus Aurelius, Emperor (232–82), 39
provinces of Roman Britain, *36*
Provisors, statute of (1351), 239

Radcot Bridge (Oxon.), skirmish at, 204
Raedwald, king of East Anglia (d. *c.*624), 69, 70, *72*, 75
Raegnald, Norwegian king of York (d. 921), 96
Raglan castle, 213
Ramsey Abbey (Cambs.), 210
Reading (Berks.), 91
Reculver (Kent), 37, 39
religion, 4, 29–31, 64, 78–9
  Christianity, 78–9
  see also Christian Church
Rheged, kingdom of, 66
Rheims, 195
Rhuddlan, statute of (1284), 189
Rhys of Deheubarth (1130?–1197), 136, 153
Ribchester (Lancs.), Roman helmet, *15*
Richard I (1157–99), 140–3; *also* 140,

159, 164
Richard II (1367–1400), 202–4, 215–19, *217*; *also* 220, 222, 234, 242, 245, 248
Richard III, formerly duke of Gloucester (1452–85), *231*, 232–3; *also* 218, 220
Richard I, duke of Normandy (d. 996), 103
Richard, duke of York, *see* York
Robert I (Bruce), king of Scotland (1274–1329), 191
Robert de Beaumont, count of Meulan (d. 1118), 128
Robert of Bellême (*fl.* 1098), 128
Robert Curthose, duke of Normandy (1054?–1134), 122–5, 127, 127–9
Robert, earl of Gloucester (1090?–1147), 133, 134, 135
Rochester, diocese of, 75
Rockingham (Northants), council at, 126
Roger, bishop of Salisbury (d. 1139), 131, 133
Roger of Montgomery, earl of Shrewsbury (d. 1094), 153
Rolle, Richard (1290?–1349), 239
Roman army, *13*, 14–16, *17*, 17–18, 26–7, *26*, 30–3, 41, 46–8, 57–8, 61, 62
Rotrou III, count of Perche (d. 1144), 130
Rouen, 196
  battle of (1450), 227
  siege of (1419), 236
Roxburgh castle, 218
Rudchester (Northumb.), 48
Ruthin (Clwyd), 211
Rye (Sussex), 196

St. Albans Abbey, *179*, 212, 239
Saladin (1137–93), 141
Salisbury, earl of, *see* Neville, Richard
Salisbury (Wilts.), Cathedral, *124*
Samson, abbot of Bury St. Edmunds (d. 1211), 184
Sandwich (Kent), 87
'Saxon Shore', 39
Scone, Stone of, *192*
Scotland, 154–5; *also* 248, 250
  England and, 125, 151, 189–91, *192*, 210, 216, 218
  Ireland and, 191–3
  Picts and Scots, 65–6, 96
  religion, 76–7
  Roman conquest, 27, 31, 35, 37, 42
Scrope, Richard, Archbishop of York (1346?–1405), 223, 235
scutage, 163
Seaford (Sussex), 211
Seneca, Lucius Annaeus (4 BC?–AD 65), 21, 22